ELLIOTT *and* ELEANOR

ROOSEVELT

The Story of a Father and His Daughter in the Gilded Age

Published by Black Dome Press Corp.
649 Delaware Ave., Delmar, N.Y. 12054
blackdomepress.com
(518) 439-6512

First Edition Paperback 2017
Copyright © 2013, 2016 by Geraldine Hawkins

ISBN: 978-1-883789-84-8

Library of Congress Control Number: 2016956750

Front cover: Elliott and Eleanor Roosevelt, July 1889. Reproduced from the holdings at The Franklin D. Roosevelt Presidential Library.

Back cover, left to right: Franklin Delano Roosevelt, 1933, Library of Congress; Elliott Roosevelt, circa 1884, Franklin D. Roosevelt Presidential Library; Eleanor Roosevelt, 1953, Franklin D. Roosevelt Presidential Library; Anna Hall Roosevelt, circa 1890, Franklin D. Roosevelt Presidential Library; Theodore Roosevelt, 1904, Library of Congress.

Design: Toelke Associates, www.toelkeassociates.com

Printed in the USA

10 9 8 7 6 5 4 3 2 1

ELLIOTT *and* ELEANOR
ROOSEVELT

The Story of a Father and
His Daughter in the Gilded Age

⇢ GERALDINE HAWKINS ⇠

BLACK · DOME

blackdomepress.com

Elliott and Eleanor Roosevelt, July 1889. Courtesy of The Franklin D. Roosevelt Presidential Library.

To the memory of

an extraordinary relationship,

that of

Maranda L. St. John-Nicolle

and her father,

the late Richard O. Loengard, Jr.

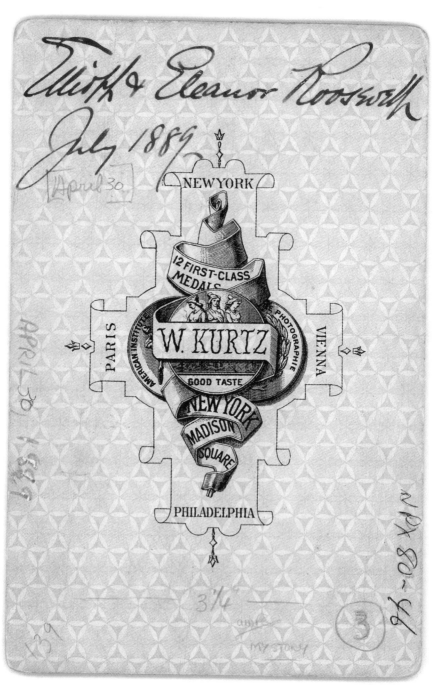

Back of July 1889 photograph (see p. iv), in Elliott's handwriting. Courtesy of the Franklin D. Roosevelt Presidential Library.

CONTENTS

FOREWORD

The nineteenth-century patrician father of a child destined to become famous, the poet and novelist Oliver Wendell Holmes, Sr., thought that he knew something about the range of possibilities that awaited the offspring of a given set of parents. Because a mother or father could detect within a child the subtle but irresistible forces of heredity, Holmes wrote, "To be a parent is almost to be a fatalist." Though he conceded that everyone has "a small fraction of individuality" that might make the difference between "a genius or a saint or a criminal," he argued that blood imposed stout limitations and that the destinies of children were, in large part, written in the "fatal oracles of Nature."

But if Holmes had been permitted to observe the extraordinary bloodline that began with Theodore Roosevelt, Sr., passed through Elliott Roosevelt and his illustrious brother Theodore, Jr., and flowed into the veins of Elliott's daughter, Eleanor, he might have marveled at the tremendous difference, both triumphal and tragic, that a fraction of individuality could make. The book that you are about to read tells the story of a powerful, almost saintly man who had two sons, the elder of whom is known to the world as the soldier, scholar and statesman who, as president of the United States, earned a Nobel Peace Prize and ushered his country into the modern era. The niece of that president married another future president, Franklin Delano Roosevelt, and became a woman uniquely connected with the word "first." She was not only First Lady of the United States but also the first chair of the United Nations Commission on Human Rights and the first chair of the Presidential Commission of the Status of Women. She became, in the words of her husband's successor, Harry Truman, "the First Lady of the World." Yet Elliott Roosevelt, who, as Theodore's brother and Eleanor's father, stood as the familial link between these two legends, was by many conventional measures a spectacular disaster.

Alcoholic, drug-dependent, and the father of an illegitimate child, Elliott was forever too susceptible to the call of pleasure. Just as fatally, he seemed incapable of confronting sorrow without some form of chemical buffer — and to be a Roosevelt of his generation meant having to endure sorrows aplenty. At seventeen, Elliott lost his beloved father. Six years later, on an unspeakable Valentine's Day, he witnessed the deaths of both his mother and sister-in-law. Other still more crushing losses were to follow. Broken by these reversals, Elliott would, during his final collapse, lose himself in a delusional fog, downing six or seven bottles of brandy and champagne each morning. When death freed him from the agonized ruins of his body and mind, he was only thirty-four. His soon-to-be famous brother deemed him a "man-swine" and a scandal, and Elliott mercilessly adjudged himself a failure.

Yet what matters about Geraldine Hawkins's book — and what makes it so very worthy of attention — is that it refuses to accept any simple judgment of Elliott Roosevelt as defining. Although she unflinchingly sets forth all the traits and deeds that would seem to damn him, Hawkins also understands the sympathetic side of Elliott: not merely the events that conspired against him and make him a fit object for our pity, but also the warmth of spirit, the charm and grace of his persona, and above all the kindness and gentleness of his character — all of which combine to make him, if not particularly admirable, a distinctly forgivable instance of well-meaning but flawed humanity.

Almost beyond question, the force most likely to redeem Elliott Roosevelt in the eyes of most was his patient, indulgent love of his daughter Eleanor. Emotionally abandoned by her cold judgmental mother, Eleanor turned to her father for forgiveness and reassurance. Ironically indeed, it was Elliott's shortcomings that made him so accepting of Eleanor's childhood failings; well acquainted with fault in his own right, he offered sympathy where his wife offered only scoldings, encouragement where she offered only insults. It is one of the paradoxes of human life that the vulnerabilities of two people can almost chemically combine to produce a shared strength. The strength that Eleanor gave her father was considerable but not enough to save him; the inspiration that he gave her bolstered and enabled her throughout her life.

Geraldine Hawkins's *Elliott and Eleanor Roosevelt* is a book about pain and about the crucial choices that we make when pain threatens to dominate our lives. To read it is to confront difficult, haunting questions: Why is love alone not sufficient to make a good person? Is the person who responds to loss by hardening himself and carrying on, like Theodore, Jr., really a better soul than the one whose sensitivity causes him to be overwhelmed? How can the same parents, the same formative influences, and the same tragic moments produce both a son who is evidently so invincible and another so desperately flawed? How does one deal with the inevitable loss of one's innocence without losing forever one's sense of confidence and well-being? Wisely, Hawkins does not seek to answer these questions. She chooses instead a subtler, smarter approach, planting her implied queries like seeds in the thoughtful reader's mind, where they are sure to bear extraordinary fruit.

A book about human weakness must also concern itself with human strength. Despite all the wealth and privilege to which she was an heiress, Eleanor Roosevelt endured a childhood of Dickensian horrors: rejection by her mother; the death of a sibling; the early loss of both her parents. Yet her life story is one that would send a behaviorist scrambling back to the drawing board. How is it possible, we may ask, that a child with such a tormented childhood grew up to become such a beacon of hope and compassion for millions across the world? The answer, quite possibly, is that Eleanor did not really consider herself strong — that she was instead a privately weakened person who simply taught herself to pay no further mind to her weaknesses. The woman who emerges at the end of Geraldine Hawkins's narrative is one whose early traumas left her not entirely whole, one who strove to manufacture wholeness by sharing charity and love with the rest of the world. The one thing that she could never recover, and without which she was forever incomplete, was the loving presence of her poor, departed father. As with the fictional Charles Foster Kane and his "Rosebud," Eleanor's many fullnesses could never wholly compensate for a single abiding emptiness. For that oracle of Nature, no triumph of individuality could furnish a rebuttal.

John Matteson
October 2016

John Matteson is a distinguished professor of English at John Jay College of Criminal Justice in the City University of New York. His first book, *Eden's Outcasts: The Story of Louisa May Alcott and Her Father*, was awarded the Pulitzer Prize for Biography in 2008. He is also the author of an Ann M. Sperber Prize–winning book, *The Lives of Margaret Fuller* and the editor of *The Annotated Little Women*.

Acknowledgments

The most important person involved in this project has been The Rev. Samuel B. Abbott, my once and future rector as well as loyal friend and faithful correspondent, without whose interest this would have remained a pipe dream. I am deeply grateful also for the enthusiasm of The Rev. Dr. Thomas F. Pike, who shares my appreciation for the Roosevelt family.

In my youth, two fine professors, Dr. James H. Belote (1922–1988) and Dr. Charles B. Hosmer, Jr. (1932–1993), took me seriously as a potential historian. I think of them every day and love them still.

Steve Hoare of Black Dome Press immediately recognized the potential of this project and was willing to guide a first-time author through the journey of publishing. I am indeed fortunate to have the benefit of his wise editorial judgment, his impeccable taste and, above all, his unfailing patience. He will always have my profound gratitude and respect.

I would like to extend my thanks to the distinguished biographers Sylvia Jukes Morris, the late John Patrick Diggins, and Peter Collier, all of whom were kind enough to read this manuscript in its various stages of development and to offer suggestions. Captain Walter E. Wilson, U.S. Navy (Ret.), not only was so magnanimous as to read the manuscript but to send eleven pages worth of corrections, thereby saving me much public embarrassment! Truly, he is a gentleman and a scholar.

John Matteson's Pulitzer Prize–winning volume *Eden's Outcasts: Louisa May Alcott and Her Father* is, quite simply, the most beautifully written biography I have ever read. To say that I am honored by the foreword he provided for *Elliott and Eleanor Roosevelt* hardly expresses my appreciation. His insights have taken my work and elevated it.

That my book could receive the approbation of Mary Ann Glendon, J. William T. Youngs, and Maurine Beasley, as well as the aforementioned

Walter Wilson and Peter Collier, is extremely gratifying. Their scholarship and talent is equaled only by their graciousness.

The cover design by Ron Toelke and Barbara Kempler-Toelke of Toelke Associates took my breath away with its beauty. I grew up hearing that "You can't judge a book by its cover," but if *this* book is judged by its cover, then we can look forward to glowing reviews!

I am grateful for the kindness of Wallace Finley Dailey, longtime curator of The Theodore Roosevelt Collection at Houghton Library, Harvard University; to his successor, Heather G. Cole, and to the friendly and helpful staff that made the many hours I spent there so enjoyable. I am equally thankful for the patience and good humor of Robert Clark, the late Karen Anson, Alycia Vivona, Virginia Lewick, Matthew Hanson, Patrick Fahy, Kendra Lightner, and all the crew at the Research Room at the Franklin D. Roosevelt Presidential Library in Hyde Park, New York.

The earliest editorial advice I received was from the late Barbara Reid, who tried (in vain?) to bring my literary style out of the nineteenth century. No one has ever had a gentler critic or better friend than Maranda St. John-Nicolle, or Dr. Sara Frear of Houston Baptist University, or the late Susan P. Browning; or Nancy Saunders, who has so often come to my rescue with all the grasp of practical things that I lack; or Karl Tiedemann, who made the gift of a brand-new, state-of-the-art laptop and has helped me more than once during periods of what Mr. Micawber called "temporary pecuniary embarrassment."

My sister LaDonne Duncan has been very supportive of this project; I am grateful for her insights and for the knowledge that I am always welcome with her family in California.

I do not know how I would have managed without the generosity and hospitality of my friends George and Stacy Lugo in New York. Their kindness goes above and beyond the call of friendship.

Many thanks also to Tim and Lynn Meyerson in Poughkeepsie and to my friends in Massachusetts, Frank and Kay Lhota and Ned and Leslie Crecelius, for providing a place to hang my hat. A pleasure to be their guest!

Barbara Thiel Johnson, J. Kelly Anderson, Guadalupe Ramirez, Alice Griffin, Karin Rosner, Richard Finegan, Susan A. Sage, Leslie Barrett Hobbs and her brother Christopher Barrett, have been extraordinarily encouraging, helpful and kind. The talented actress Noelle McGrath De Paula has helped by sharing her nuanced understanding of human behavior. Several of my coworkers in the National Park Service have honored *Elliott and Eleanor Roosevelt* with their enthusiasm, especially Franceska Macsali-Urbin, Kevin Thomas, Doris Mack, Pat Rolfe, and John Fox in Hyde Park, and Barry Moreno in New York City.

Between the time I began this project and the time I finished it, I spent several years as a journalist for the United States Navy Reserve. All of the officers and enlisted people with whom I worked were and are wonderful, but the most appreciative of whatever gifts I have as a writer were Elwood Berzins, Victor Beck. Michael Cody, Michael Dean, Scot Cregan, and Charles Evered, all officers at Navy Office of Information (NAVINFO), East. I won't forget them, or any other shipmates.

My friend Mark L. Johnson of King Features has kept me laughing; someday I will get him to like Eleanor Roosevelt. The same can be said for my stalwart friend Martha Danziger. Her brother Jeff Danziger, late of *The Christian Science Monitor*, kindly helped with the nuts and bolts of scanning illustrations.

My friend Julie Hedgepeth Williams, author of that fine book, *A Rare Titanic Family*, whom I first knew when we were both students of the aforementioned Drs. Belote and Hosmer, has been an indispensable font of literary and practical advice as well as delightful correspondence.

Years ago I might have ended up like Elliott Roosevelt had it not been for the supportive friendship of the late Julia L. Cole. I am glad to have the opportunity to say this, publicly, to her parents, Mr. and Mrs. Albert Cole of Las Cruces, New Mexico, and to her sisters Janis Lambert-Cole of Basking Ridge, New Jersey and Joanna Storrar of Princeton, New Jersey.

Thanks also to my old friends in Gramercy Park that showed an interest in this project in its early stages: Pamela Head, Kathleen Finneran, Karen Young, Alexandra Aronson, Diane Cress, Bernadette Gilliard, Margaret O'Connell, Deborah Rasberry, Sally Affanato, Eva McDowell, Tara Lang, Katherine Bobbitt, and the late Sharon Sutton, as well as Patricia Tobias, Melody Bunting, John Root, Jay Prignano and Richard Scalera.

Back in 1986, when I was a volunteer at Theodore Roosevelt Birthplace National Historic Site, I found in the book collection there an old volume by Lillian Rixey called *Bamie: Theodore Roosevelt's Remarkable Sister*. I told National Park Service Rangers (and friends) Kathryn Gross and John Lancos that I wanted to write a book called "Elliott: Theodore Roosevelt's Dissolute Brother." They laughed at my joke. I hope they like this book and that they enjoyed the hours we spent together at 28 East 20th Street as much as I did.

My parents, both of whom passed on many years ago, came of age during the World War II era; I came along late in their lives, and they, along with my maternal grandmother, shared stories that led me to think of Franklin and Eleanor Roosevelt almost as members of our family. They exposed me to so much that has brought me joy.

This author is overwhelmed to realize how blessed she has been

Geraldine Hawkins
January 2017

INTRODUCTION

When Eleanor Roosevelt was nearing the end of her life, she visited a young Episcopal priest and showed him a Bible she had carried with her since childhood. It had belonged to her father, she told him. The spine had split and the pages were falling out; she wondered if the minister knew where she might have it repaired. After giving her the information she needed, he sensed that she still had something she wanted to discuss. Her father had died under circumstances that might not be considered quite moral in a strict religious sense, she explained. Did the minister think that this could be a barrier to his being in Heaven? When her friend asked for details, Mrs. Roosevelt told him that her father had struggled with a drinking problem, that he was living with a woman who was not his wife, that in fact he had a few mistresses and one of them presented him with a child. The clergyman told her that he would not exclude her father on that basis; furthermore God must be more generous than any human, otherwise there was no hope for anyone. Mrs. Roosevelt told her friend that she was relieved and happy to hear that he thought so, that she had always loved her father and wanted very much to see him again.[1]

What sort of person was Elliott Roosevelt that sixty-seven years after his death, his daughter, at the conclusion of her own remarkable life, would be preoccupied with meeting him in the hereafter? What made his memory so compelling?

He was "the most lovable of all the Roosevelts,"[2] and in a mysterious way, one of the most influential. Elliott Roosevelt was the brother of the twenty-sixth president of the United States, the godfather of the thirty-second president, and the father of the only woman ever to be known as "First Lady of the World."

He was also an alcoholic.

Elliott suffered all the torments of this condition long before it came to be thought of as a "disease," and he died, aged thirty-four, a couple of generations before a reformed alcoholic and a compassionate clergyman hammered out the Twelve Steps of Alcoholics Anonymous in the same church in which Elliott had married his bride, Anna Rebecca Hall, so many years before.

"Death ends a life, but not a relationship."[3] So begins a play that had a successful Broadway run a few years after Eleanor Roosevelt died. No one understood this better than she. "He dominated my life while he lived, and he was the love of my life for many years after he died,"[4] Eleanor wrote of her father. He was "the person who loved [her] best in the world."[5] "He was the one great love of my life as a child, and in fact like many children I lived a dream life with him; so his memory is still a vivid, living thing to me."[6] "He lived in my dreams and does so to this day."[7]

Most historians of the Roosevelt family have taken a view of Elliott's situation similar to that of Eleanor's cousin Alice Longworth.

"Poor Eleanor!" Mrs. Longworth (Theodore Roosevelt's daughter) remembered.

> She took everything — most of all herself — so tremendously seriously. If only she had allowed a little levity into her life. She had a miserable childhood, which I don't think she ever got over. There was her exquisite, empty-headed mother, Anna Hall, who was one of the most beautiful women of her time. She was rather mean to Eleanor. She called her "Granny" and made her feel unwanted and unattractive.
>
> Eleanor also had two [in fact, three] very pretty Hall aunts and a hateful grandmother.
>
> Then there was her father, my Uncle Ellie, who was the black sheep of the family.

Someone should write something on Uncle Ellie and call it "The Rake's Progress." There was this attractive and intelligent young man who ruined himself with drink.

He was considered far more promising than my father when young but once he started hitting the bottle the slide downhill was spectacular. My father was always having to save him from some predicament.

Conversation about Uncle Ellie and his problems was frequent when I was young. I could tell because it would stop when I entered the room. So I started listening at keyholes instead. That's how I learned of my father's departure for Europe to take Uncle Ellie out of the dives of Paris and the arms of a series of rather nice mistresses, who apparently were frightfully responsible about him.

Apparently he had a vague form of epilepsy which wasn't helped by the drinking. I have only vague recollections of him, mostly fast-moving ones. He would take one out for walks as a child and set off at such a pace that one's feet hardly touched the ground. He died when I was about ten and there was a lot of grief-making in the family. Auntie Corinne was particularly devoted to him. I am told there is a picture somewhere of Uncle Ellie laid out on his deathbed with Auntie Corinne grieving a good deal at the foot. Oh, how the Victorians relished that sort of thing! The black sheep who finally succumbed. I was always intrigued by the strange contrast between the louche Uncle Ellie and that pillar of rectitude, my father.

Uncle Ellie's death must have had a dreadful effect on Eleanor. She had always doted on him and been kept away from him. Much of her shyness and insecurity stemmed from her forced separation from him and the unhappiness it created.

She always made a tremendous effort to do everything she thought was expected of her. She was always so good and so nice about everybody that it became quite intolerable.

... Franklin had to sneak the occasional martini even when he was in the White House. But I suppose the riproaring example of Uncle Ellie would have been enough to put anyone off drink for life.[8]

Alice Longworth and others may have seen Elliott as "the black sheep of the family," but what sort of "black sheep" would write, "My precious little Nell: I thought of you all day long and blessed you and prayed often for your happiness and that of your precious small brothers,"[9] and urge his daughter to cultivate "unselfishness, generosity, loving tenderness and cheerfulness"?[10]

"Dear little daughter," he wrote, "you are your father's love and joy."[11]

Eleanor was almost ten when her father died; she was twenty when she married his godson, Franklin Delano Roosevelt. Elliott was a handsome, beguiling man who broke most of the promises he made to his daughter. Franklin was a handsome, beguiling man who would break a few of the promises he made to his wife. She believed that both — in their very different ways — were great men. Throughout her life, when speaking of her father, Mrs. Roosevelt would suggest that perhaps an individual need not be strong and successful in the eyes of the world in order to be great. Perhaps lightheartedness, kindness, an understanding heart, and "the ability to fire a child's imagination" could make a difference in the world, too.

"He never accomplished anything which could make him of any importance in the world at large, unless a personality which left a vivid mark on friends and associates may be counted important. ... No less important in our daily lives are the things and the people which only touch us personally."[12] "He never could learn to control his heart by his head. With him the heart always dominated."[13] "Always with him a great love and tenderness was the predominating note." "He loved people for the fineness that was in them and his friends might be newsboys or millionaires. Their occupations, their possessions meant nothing to him, only they themselves counted."[14] "He loved his children dearly and was very thoughtful of us always. He always called me 'Little Nell' after the girl in Dickens's *Old Curiosity Shop*."[15]

Eleanor Roosevelt may well have considered Ernest Hemingway's observation that the world destroys "the very good and the very gentle"[16] a fitting epitaph for her father. Just as he consistently supported Eleanor and seemed to be the only one who discerned in her qualities that, in her old age, would cause her to be thought of as a symbol of human kindness, so she would always defend her father and remain loyal to his memory. "Through the power of her love and the strength of her will, Eleanor transformed this wreck of a man into a noble figure," one historian has written. It was all part of "their secret transaction to validate each other."[17]

Elliott's influence on his brother was profound as well. As children, the asthmatic Theodore, although older, was by far the weaker of the two, and it was Elliott's ability and willingness to protect his brother from bullies, as well as his dexterity as a sportsman, that were in large measure responsible for Theodore's determination to build up his strength and to become such a vocal and enthusiastic champion of "the strenuous life." As they entered their teens, however, the roles were reversed as Elliott began to suffer mysterious seizures and blinding headaches that debilitated him and kept him from following his brother to Harvard.

Elliott admitted that he lacked "that foolish grit of Theodore's," but what he lacked in "grit," his family maintained, he compensated for in different, supposedly less "masculine" characteristics such as tenderness, sensitivity, and friendliness. Theodore had an abundance of these traits as well, but in the older brother they were balanced by a force of intellect and character and a fierce competitiveness and combativeness that Elliott was never able to summon. He never was able to validate *himself* in his own estimation.

It was as a memory — in the continuing "relationship" — that Elliott Roosevelt's contribution to history was made; in his influence, throughout their lives, on his brother, his daughter, and even his godson and son-in-law, "whose perfect reincarnation he was supposed to be."[18] And this, perhaps, is the compensation of history — that the tragedy of one life is woven into a design requiring the discernment of posterity.

⚔ 1 ⚔

"RIGHTEOUS ENTHUSIASM"
ON GRAMERCY PARK

Elliott Roosevelt's boyhood home in Manhattan's serene Gramercy Park district was reconstructed many years after he died as a monument to the triumphant life of his brother. The National Historic Site at number 28 East 20th Street sits amidst furniture stores, delicatessens, restaurants, and the rough-and-tumble of New York life; but when Elliott was born there, on February 28, 1860, the street consisted of a row of brownstones looking exactly like the one in which the Roosevelt family lived.

On the southwest corner of Broadway and East 20th Street, one can still see the mansard roof of a crumbling structure that once was the original Lord and Taylor department store. Elliott and his family watched the construction of this building, which was regarded as a novelty because of its steam-powered elevators. One has to proceed east on 20th, crossing Park Avenue to Gramercy Park itself, with its soft glow of streetlamps and slightly overgrown foliage, in order to glimpse the genteel privilege and sense of well-being enjoyed by wealthy New Yorkers in the days before the Civil War.

The room in which Elliott Bulloch Roosevelt was born consisted of a bedroom set made of rosewood and satinwood and constructed

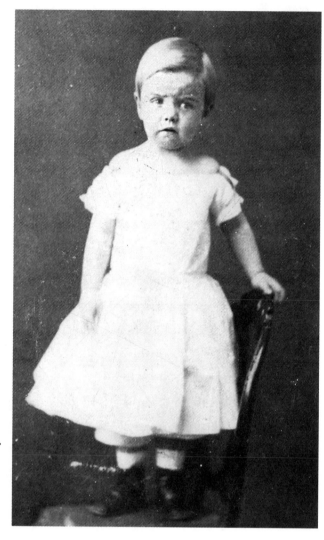

*"Precious Boy
Ellie," 1860.
Courtesy of
The Houghton
Library, Harvard
University.*

by a carpenter named Leon Marcotte, who was well known in his day. The Victorian furnishings provided the backdrop for the lively Roosevelt family, which at that time consisted of Theodore Sr.; his wife Martha (known as Mittie); her sister Anna Bulloch; a daughter, also named Anna but called "Bamie" (shortened from "Bambina") or "Bye"; Theodore Jr., nicknamed Teedie; and Elliott. Two years later another daughter, called Corinne, would complete the family.

Like most well-to-do Victorian families, the Roosevelts had a parlor facing the street in which their guests were entertained, a library where the family spent their evenings together, a nursery in which their governess-aunt Anna Louise Bulloch slept with the children, a spacious, ornate dining room in which food was brought up from the basement using a dumbwaiter, and a tiny, closet-like apartment that served as a guest room. On the top floor were the quarters wherein resided the Roosevelts' five full-time servants.

It is difficult to imagine how any child could have had more loving parents than Elliott Roosevelt. By all accounts they were models of moral correctness, civic responsibility, and parental affection. Theodore Roosevelt, Senior, is invariably described by his contemporaries as possessing a boundless capacity for enjoyment of life as well as unflagging devotion to what he perceived to be his duty. The Rev. Henry Codman Potter, Rector of Grace Church in New York, said from his pulpit that "No man who ever saw Theodore Roosevelt in his saddle in the park, or in his seat at a dinner, would have been guilty of the silly impertinence of calling him a bloodless ascetic or a dyspeptic saint."[1] His eldest son wrote of him years later:

I was fortunate enough in having a father whom I have always been able to regard as an ideal man. It sounds a little like cant to say what I am going to say, but he really did combine the strength and courage and will and energy of the strongest man with the tenderness, cleanness, and purity of a woman. ... He certainly gave me the feeling that I was to be both decent and manly, and that if I were manly nobody would laugh at my being decent. In all my childhood he never laid hand on me but once, and I always knew perfectly well that in case it became necessary he would not have the slightest hesitation in doing so again, and alike from my love and respect, and in a certain sense, my fear of him, I would have hated and dreaded beyond measure to have him know that I had been guilty of a lie, or of cruelty, or of bullying, or of uncleanness, or of cowardice.[2]

The influence of the first Theodore Roosevelt determined the character of the second, and provided a standard by which he measured his conduct and accomplishments.

Gradually I came to have the feeling on my own account, and not merely on his. There were many things I tried to do because he did them, which I found afterwards were not in my line. For instance, I taught Sunday School all through college, and afterwards gave it up. … In doing my Sunday School work I was very much struck by the fact that the other men who did it only possessed one side of his character. My ordinary companions in college would, I think, have had a tendency to look down upon me for doing Sunday School work if I had not also been a corking boxer, a good runner, and a genial member of the Porcellian Club. I went in for boxing and wrestling a good deal, and I really think that this was partly because I liked them as sports, it was even more so because I intended to be a middling decent fellow, and I did not intend that anyone should laugh at me with impunity because I was decent.[3]

When this father, who represented a chivalric ideal for his sons, was dying from intestinal cancer at the age of forty-six, his namesake son was attempting to follow his example at college, and it was Elliott who witnessed their father's suffering. This was, as David McCullough has written, "the blow from which Elliott would never quite recover."[4]

Both boys were taught by their father to be "decent." Theodore Sr. had no use for the double standard by which men and women of his day were expected to behave. He was revered in equal measure by his daughters. Reflecting on her father's life, his youngest daughter wrote, "Nothing is as difficult as to achieve success in this world if one is full of great tolerance and the milk of human kindness."[5] His son Elliott had "great tolerance" and "the milk of human kindness" in abundance; alcoholism prevented him from living a life as industrious and joyful as that of his father.

Theodore Sr. had a tender respect for the feelings of women that he passed along to his sons. As an adolescent, his daughter Corinne suffered from the same asthmatic condition that afflicted Teedie. Their father was as solicitous of his daughter as he was of his son. "I was delicate at one period and could not dance as I had always done, and I remember when I was going to a little entertainment, just as I was leaving the house I received an exquisite bunch of violets with a card from my father, asking me to wear the flowers, and to think of his wish that I should not overtire myself, but also of his sympathy that I could not do what I had always done. Comparatively few little girls of fourteen have had so lover-like an attention from a father, and just such thought and tender, loving comprehension made our relationship to our father one of perfect companionship, and yet of respectful adoration."[6]

This was a family in which Elliott was not embarrassed to open a letter with the salutation, "Oh my Darling Sweetest of Fathers,"[7] and to address his mother as "Dear Little Motherling." Theodore and Elliott would regularly refer to each other, respectively, as "Dear Old Beloved Brother" and "Dear Old Nellie Boy." A recent Roosevelt biographer complained of "the sentimentality that afflicted the family,"[8] but the love between them was hardly an affliction. The family's affectionate nature stemmed from the warmth of Theodore and Mittie.

The first Theodore Roosevelt was born September 22, 1831, to Cornelius Van Schaak Roosevelt and Margaret Barnhill Roosevelt. Theodore was the youngest of five brothers, one of whom, the eccentric Robert Barnhill Roosevelt, would live in the house adjoining Theodore's on East 20th Street. (He would change his name to "Barnwell" because he thought it had a more genteel sound.) Cornelius was the sixth generation descended from Claes Martensen Van Rosenvelt, and all of Claes's descendants to this point, excepting those who migrated up the Hudson River, were born in Manhattan. Cornelius was a banker whose house on Union Square was known for the Sunday dinners during which only Dutch was spoken. This 14th Street house figures prominently in a photograph of President Lincoln's funeral procession, in which top-hatted men line the streets and stand on rooftops to hear the muffled drums and the clatter of horses' hooves as they pay their respects to the war leader in the flag-draped casket. The sadness is dispelled slightly by the presence of two little heads in the window of the Dutch merchant's house, and legend has it that these two tiny heads are those of Theodore and Elliott Roosevelt.

Cornelius was an affluent man of business; among his many ventures was a partnership in the founding of Chemical Bank in New York. He was one of the five original directors of this institution, the only national bank that paid its obligations in gold, even at the height of the Civil War. He could afford to bestow lavish gifts upon his children, and the house on East 20th Street was a wedding present to Theodore Sr. and Mittie. As late as 1920, his great-granddaughter Eleanor received an income in excess of $1,600 from his estate.[9]

Cornelius was descended from a Knickerbocker family that from its American beginnings built a reputation for involved citizenship and uncompromising rectitude in both personal and financial matters. Historians have been confident in asserting that all of Cornelius's Manhattan progenitors were upstanding, respected citizens who included bankers, engineers, and state senators. Cornelius's brother, one of many Roosevelts called James, was a congressman, served on the New York Board of Aldermen, as a member of the state legislature from Manhattan, Justice of the New York State Supreme Court, and as United States District Attorney for Southern New York.

Then there was Clinton Roosevelt. "He lived to be a hundred," remembered Elliott's cousin John Ellis (Jack) Roosevelt. "Got into trouble and a lawsuit over the changing of the name of the Burghers of New York to the Aldermen. He had been a Burgher but he wouldn't have his name put up for 'Alderman.' The lawsuit and trouble seemed to stimulate him and revivify him." (One Roosevelt genealogy records Clinton's age as ninety-four when he died.)[10]

Theodore Sr. took a position in one of his father's inherited businesses, Roosevelt & Sons on Maiden Lane in Lower Manhattan, in partnership with his brother — yet another James. Roosevelt & Sons began as a hardware business, later trading in building supplies; by the time Theodore took over the reins, the firm dealt primarily in the importation of plate glass from France and England. "In an age when circumstances made it easy to sink in commercial quicksands, it rested upon rank, reflecting in each phase a persistent integrity of management,"[11] wrote one of Theodore Roosevelt's early biographers.

Theodore Sr. inherited a strong Christian commitment from the example of his parents. Cornelius worshipped in the Dutch Reformed Church, but his wife Margaret was a Quaker who worked at her religion. She was much beloved of her grandchildren. "My grandmother was quite demanding," recalled John Ellis Roosevelt. "We all loved her. She was very hospitable. Well, she was very good to us grandchildren. Wanted to feed us all up. Fed us too well. Stuffed us."[12] The gentleness intrinsic to the Quaker faith would seem to have been passed along to her son Theodore and to her grandson Elliott. Whereas Theodore Jr. throughout his life would seek fights in which he could take part, Elliott would make the avoidance of any sort of confrontation a way of life.

Another trait that Elliott inherited from his father was what his daughter called his "attractive social personality";[13] a contemporary of Theodore Sr.'s referred to his "perennial capacity for enjoyment, a gay zest in the companionship of others."[14] He belonged to the Union League Club, the Century Association, and the St. Nicholas Society, among others. In a typical letter to Mittie, written after having served as best man at the wedding of her brother James. D. Bulloch, he reported that "The wedding has passed off delightfully and I have enjoyed everything to the full limit."[15] In a characteristic instance during a train ride to Philadelphia, he met a fellow who "took his seat next to me and I amused myself by drawing the little there was in him out during the twilight."[16] Like Theodore Jr. and especially Elliott, the first Theodore was able to bring out the best in people, or at least to make them feel that they were interesting and attractive.

Mary Todd Lincoln was impressed with Mr. Roosevelt and asked him to ride in her carriage with her and to help her pick out hats on one of her many shopping excursions. He was invited to sit in the Lincoln pew at New York Avenue Presbyterian Church in Washington. Both women and men found him captivating, as they later would both aggressive Theodore Jr. and gentle Elliott.

Theodore Sr.'s passionate sense of *noblesse oblige* was sustained by genuine spiritual conviction. "His was no gloomy religion, or canting profession of any one faith; but his daily life was in sympathy with all who truly love God and their fellow men, and his example a precious heritage to the city of his birth," wrote a lifelong friend. "In his father's elegant mansion on the corner of Fourteenth Street and Broadway I knew him first as a gay, lighthearted lad. ... It was beyond the power of fortune to spoil the pure quality of his nature."[17]

One month before Elliott was born, his father wrote this letter to Mittie in Philadelphia: "This morning I went to Sunday School and the day was so bright that it brought out a very large attendance. George Peet [one of the boys in the class] told with a very smiling face that his sister had the scarlet fever. When I told him I was afraid of the other boys catching it and would not be able to let him stay, he cried almost piteously."[18] At the 11:00 service "the sermon of the season" was taken from Luke 12:47–48, which could be described as the creed of the Roosevelt family: "… To whom men have committed much, of him truly they will ask the more." Theodore Sr. received no financial remuneration for any public services, ever.[19]

Theodore told his wife that he wanted to spend "all the time and much more than I was now doing to God's service and I would still fall far short of any hope of salvation except through His divine mercy."[20] Later in the day Theodore found a child wandering aimlessly: "I gave him a tract, on condition that he would go home and read it, which I found an hour or two afterwards that he had done by dropping in and examining him on the contents. I laid myself out to see how many [children] I could persuade to meet me at the Mission Church in the evening who would not have come otherwise. About ten came in the evening which I thought a pretty good afternoon's work. One was a very peculiar case: Mrs. Owens, the mother of the humpback whose husband died a short time since, seemed sinking into a kind of melancholy and never left her room — to use her own expression, was 'kinder' upset. I used every argument of religion in vain: her husband's desire expressed in my presence on his dying bed was of no more use, only bringing tears, at last I asked it in consideration of the kindness I had shown her she would grant me a personal request. This gained my point, and she told me after the service that she was very glad she had come."[21]

Theodore Sr. was ardent, convincing, and good. He was one of the most respected citizens in New York City, as evidenced after his death by this undemocratic but appreciative *New York Times* editorial: "The practical exclusion in this City of the rich from politics, no doubt tends to separate them from public enterprises. Such men as Mr. Roosevelt and his dozen or more compeers, ought to, and in most other communities would, have been our political administrators and leaders. The Government of this City by an ignorant mass of poor people and their chosen representatives, in effect shuts out the other class. Even when a man of cultivated class ... is chosen by the democracy, he does not appoint to places of honor even the best of his own party. The rum-shop democracy compel him to put at the head of departments and elsewhere utterly unknown and incompetent persons. But this exclusion should not shut out our cultivated and wealthy citizens. There are great works of a public nature needed to be done in New York, and where the workers are few."[22]

It is impossible to overestimate Theodore Sr.'s influence on his family, in particular on his sons. "Americanism" for his son President Theodore Roosevelt would always be "self-respecting, duty-performing, life-enjoying"[23]; in his talks at the Newsboys Lodging Houses, Theodore Sr. made it a practice to speak of "patriotism, good citizenship, and manly morality."[24] The first Theodore, like the second Theodore, was remarkable for his "zest for life, cheerfulness, and righteous enthusiasms."[25]

The Roosevelts' Gramercy Park house was a "twin building," meaning two identical floor plans adjacent to each other — but the residents could not have been less alike. Robert Roosevelt was a counterweight to the rectitude of his brother, with two sets of children, one with his wife and the other with his longtime mistress. He was eschewed by most of his family, although his nephew Teedie would one day "read law" in his office, and one can only speculate as to the influence of this philanderer on Elliott.

Where Theodore Sr. "laughed at the absurd politics that oppose a rogue to a rascal,"[26] Robert's resume would include Minister to Holland, acting Mayor of New York City, President of the Board of Aldermen, and member of the Brooklyn Bridge Commission. He is the only man on record who, when asked to be Chief of Tammany Hall, refused. To add insult to injury, this libertine was also a Democrat.

Ten years before Elliott was born, his father, then aged nineteen, attended a dinner party at the home of his eldest brother, Silas Weir Roosevelt. Another of Silas's guests that evening was Dr. Hilborne West. Hilborne had recently married Susan Elliott, one of the children of Mrs. James Stephens Bulloch by her first marriage. Susan Elliott West was from Roswell, Georgia, and Hilborne had just returned from a visit to his wife's plantation-owning family. Hilborne's vivid, Walter Scott–like descriptions of the feudal South appealed to Theodore's adventurous nature, and he asked Hilborne to give him a letter of introduction to the Bullochs. It was during this first visit south that Theodore Roosevelt, Sr. met Martha Bulloch, called Mittie, aged fifteen.

Some accounts have it that Theodore was met at the door of the Bulloch home by a little girl called "Toy," a slave who slept at the foot of Mittie's bed. Mittie later told her daughter Bamie that the letter announcing the date of Theodore's visit had been overlooked or misplaced. "The whole household was aroused by the ringing of the front doorbell, ... All the Negroes were off at a corn shucking at a neighbor's plantation," with the exception of the little girl, "who having answered the doorbell, appeared before the startled group upstairs with a formal visiting card. All was immediately hospitable bustle, and he was made to feel more than welcome, and passed a most enchanting two weeks."[27]

Theodore and Mittie did not see each other again until three years later, when the young woman made the journey north to Philadelphia to visit her half-sister, Susan Elliott West. The fact that Theodore Roosevelt happened to stop by en route to New York after a trip to Europe may have influenced Mittie's decision to visit the Manhattan home of Theodore's brother, Silas

Weir Roosevelt. By the time Mittie left New York, she and Theodore were engaged. For the next few months it was necessary for them to conduct their courtship through the mail, but this only strengthened the attachment. "I only live in your being,"[28] Mittie wrote Theodore. The surviving letters are remarkable for their ardent nature and for the eloquence that characterizes so much of nineteenth-century correspondence:

> Thee, Dearest Thee,
>
> I promised to tell you if I cried when you left me. I had determined not to do so if possible, but when the dreadful feeling came over me that you were, indeed, gone, I could not help my tears from springing and had to rush away to be alone with myself. Everything now seems associated with you. Even when I run up the stairs going to my own room, I feel as if you were near, and turn involuntarily to kiss my hand to you. I feel, dear Thee, as though you were part of my existence, and that I only live in your being, for now I am confident of my own deep love. ….

Theodore responded to this letter at once:

> I felt, as you recalled so vividly to mind the last morning of our parting, the blood rush to my temples and I had to lay it, your letter, down for a few moments to regain command over myself. I had been hoping against hope to receive a letter from you. …[29]

Three days before Christmas, 1853, the wedding of Martha Bulloch to the first Theodore Roosevelt took place at the Roswell plantation amid all the trappings of the Old South; it has been speculated that Mittie's white-columned home was one of the models for Tara in Margaret Mitchell's *Gone With the Wind*.[30]

Mittie and Theodore were both unusually vivacious people. They both enjoyed life; Theodore, for all his earnestness, had "a redeeming love of dancing"[31] and, as Rev. Potter noted, cut quite a figure riding his horse along the bridle path in Central Park. Her son Theodore remembered Mittie as "a sweet, gracious, beautiful Southern woman, a delightful companion, and beloved by everybody."[32]

Mittie was an accomplished raconteur; she would entertain her children for hours with southern tales they never forgot, in which she would assume the identities of all the characters with performances that involved her extraordinarily flexible face, voice, and body. (Mittie transmitted her social ease and elegance to Elliott, as well as her vivid way with a story; at the age of twenty, Elliott wrote letters home from exotic lands with descriptive prose so compelling that many years after he died his daughter had them published under the title *Hunting Big Game in the 'Eighties*.)

And yet, for all their shared good cheer and liveliness, there were some striking differences between Mittie and Theodore. Where Theodore Sr. was robust and hearty, with friendly eyes and a bushy beard (Teedie described his father as "a very handsome and good-natured lion"[33]), Mittie was fragile and emotional, with the air of sweet distraction that is often associated with the archetypal southern belle. Her daughter Corinne remembered that her brothers often carried their mother "upstairs as if she had been a baby, and they always said she was like a lovely Dresden china object of art. My brother Theodore delighted in the combination of wit, grace, and gentleness, which she possessed to an unusual degree."[34]

The fact that, throughout the Civil War and afterward, Mittie stuck by her convictions and remained an unreconstructed Georgia Confederate, despite the opposing sentiments of her husband, could indicate that she was a woman of unyielding principle; it is perhaps more likely that she was inclined to be influenced by feeling rather than by reason.

Mittie Bulloch's family were among the "Colony People," consisting of five or six families who owned the cotton factory established in Roswell, named for Roswell King, who bought the property in 1838 and persuaded many of his relatives and friends to move inland from the coast. (When Franklin Roosevelt came to Georgia seeking a cure for the effects of polio in the 1920s, the dilapidated resort town he found was called "Bullochville." A few years later he bought the facility and changed the name of the town to "Warm Springs.")

Mittie's mother, Martha Stewart Bulloch, was the second wife of Mittie's father, James Stephens Bulloch. His first wife had been Hester Elliott, daughter of John Elliott, U.S. Senator from Georgia. There were three children from this second marriage: Anna Louise, who would figure prominently in the lives of the Roosevelts, especially Elliott and Eleanor; Mittie; and Irvine.

Major Bulloch, as James was called, gave Mittie one of the first great sorrows of her life when he fainted while teaching Sunday School in his Presbyterian church and died the same day. "I was quite a kid at the time," wrote Robert Rodgers, a childhood friend and relative of Mittie's, "but I shall never forget the scene."[35] Mittie's half-brother Stuart Elliott, for whom Elliott Roosevelt was named, was, like his namesake, a remarkably caring person for whom "the heart always dominated." Ironically, in a highly uncharacteristic incident, his impulsive heart led him to kill a man in a duel, which he regretted instantly and constantly for the rest of his life.

Mittie Roosevelt had a tender, gentle heart. Her children doted on her; to Elliott she was his "Sweet Little Dresden China Mother."[36] She had her eccentricities; she took several baths a day and invariably wore white muslin. Visitors to the brownstone on East 20th Street were enchanted by the lady of the house — "Such loveliness of line and tinting," in the words of one of her guests, "such sweet courtesy of manner!"[37] "She had the sort of silky black hair that takes a russet tinge under the glow of candles … her skin was the purest white … with a coral rather than a rose tint in her cheeks."[38] If Mittie was vague and sentimental, she was also sensitive and tactful. She loved flowers and surrounded herself with bunches of violets. She enjoyed painting and sculpture and is said to have had cultivated tastes. She was easily moved by character as well as by beauty, which is in all likelihood what attracted her to her husband.

When Mittie married Theodore, she realized that not only was she moving to a new state, but taking on an entirely different way of life from that which she had known. "I am sure that Mrs. Roosevelt was never in Roswell but once after the war," remembered Rodgers. "I have heard that she went to her old home, then owned by Mr. Ward and went over the whole house from garret to cellar, and on leaving asked Mrs. Ward for something as a memento of her old home. Mrs. Ward told her to take anything she wished, and she took the doorknob from the door of the room that was her bedroom as a maiden. The women of the Bulloch family were very beautiful. You know that childhood impressions are the most vivid and lasting. Today, [after] more than forty years, I remember 'Mittie Bulloch,' Mrs. Roosevelt, and I think I could recognize a picture of her among a thousand."[39]

While Martha Bulloch Roosevelt could claim some French forebears, her ancestry was more Scottish than anything else. One of her ancestors, The Rev. Alexander Stobo, was an adventurous Scottish missionary who set out originally for Panama, was forced to leave there by the Spanish, attempted to return to Scotland but was shipwrecked on the coast of Charleston, South Carolina. James Bulloch, another transplanted Scotsman, married Stobo's daughter, and this was the beginning of Mittie's American family. This family would be nearly as prominent in the South as Theodore Roosevelt's was in Manhattan, the most noteworthy member being Archibald Bulloch, the first president of Georgia during the Revolutionary era.

When these two families were joined on that December day in 1853, the young couple could not have imagined how much of the next century would be shaped by their children, in particular by the relationship between their two sons — the elder of whom would become an American icon, as well as the younger, "whom everyone agreed was the sweetest one in the family and who would move through life with his brother in an odd and tragic *pas de deux* that defined them both."[40]

⚜2⚜

SKINNY AND SWELLY

The household in which Elliott Roosevelt grew up was at once unusually loving and noticeably troubled. Much of Elliott's childhood was spent watching his siblings struggle with ill health. His eldest sister was born with an unstable back and wore a brace that was both conspicuous and painful. The little girl's plight was a constant weight on the sympathetic hearts of her parents, in particular her father, to whom she was especially close. Both Teedie and Corinne were asthmatic, the boy to an extent that caused the family to fear for his life. No one knew when these attacks might occur. Elliott watched helplessly as his brother fought for every breath, as their father walked the floor with Teedie for hours on end, and as their mother spun her swashbuckling tales to calm the child after his seizures and take his mind off his suffering.

As children Teedie was frail and scholarly, while Elliott was gregarious and vigorous. Elliott's robust constitution offset a highly emotional nature, much like that of his mother. Elliott was easily affected by incidents such as his brother's frequent seizures. He seems to have had, for a boy, an unusually tender heart. He was frequently called upon to protect his older brother from rough boys only too willing to take advantage of the thin child with glasses. For a young man who was known and loved

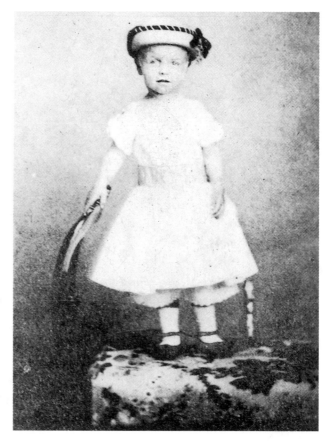

*Three-year-old
Elliott, circa
1863. Courtesy
of The Houghton
Library, Harvard
University.*

for having a mild disposition and a general unwillingness to display any-thing other than an even temper, Elliott's readiness to use his fists to come to the aid of Teedie testifies to the bond between the boys.

Elliott was more comfortable with other children in a setting in which he could act on his father's concern for the less fortunate. His family enjoyed telling the story of the time when, at the age of seven, Elliott went out to play wearing a brand-new overcoat and promptly gave it away when he saw a shivering child in rags.[1]

Ragged children were not an uncommon sight in the Manhattan of Elliott's boyhood. His family lived in a prosperous area where what is still called "gracious living" was the standard, comfortably dominated by the spire of Grace Church at 10th Street and Broadway; but not at all far from this haven, one could find another New York entirely. In these poorer neighborhoods cholera and malaria were a fact of everyday life. The clash of poverty-stricken Irish immigrants with those who had no tolerance for their alien ways led to violence and to the notorious Draft Riots when Elliott was in his fourth year. "I do not wonder that the poor mechanics oppose conscription," commented Mittie. "It certainly favors the rich at the expense of the poor."[2] She referred to the wealthy man's option of buying a substitute, a course her husband would choose.

"These narrow ways, diverging to the right and left, and reeking everywhere with dirt and filth," wrote Charles Dickens after a tour of the infamous Five Points section in 1841. "Debauchery has made the very houses prematurely old. ... Here are lanes and alleys paved with mud knee-deep; underground chambers where they dance and game; ruined houses opened to the street, where through wide gaps in the walls other ruins loom upon the eye; ... hideous tenements which take their name from robbery and murder; all that is loathesome, drooping and decayed is here."[3]

Yet, for many, the city was the place to be. The finest libraries, theaters, and museums were in New York. Elliott's father was one of the founders of the Metropolitan Museum, and the charter for the Museum of Natural History was signed in the front parlor at 28 East 20th Street.[4] "During this period New York was very much in the condition described in Edith Wharton's novel *The Age of Innocence*," Bamie wrote many years later, "though naturally I did not recognize it at the time."[5]

Elliott was the favorite of the women in the family, especially of his aunt and governess Anna Bulloch, and of his sister Corinne. Aunt Annie was unmarried for many years and devoted to the Roosevelt children. She seems to have had a special attachment to Elliott, but then so did everyone.[6] A typical letter to her from Elliott begins with the salutation, "My

Darling, Darling, Darlingest Aunt Annie," and is signed "Chub alias Ellie." Elsewhere he writes, "You must not forget your little Chub."[7] There was a strong affinity between Elliott and Corinne; in later life, when the family's patience with Elliott was exhausted, Corinne would stand by him.

The women in Elliott's early life were exceptionally sweet. There was his Quaker paternal grandmother, Margaret Barnhill Roosevelt. The devotion she inspired in Elliott's father is evident in this letter Theodore Sr. wrote to Mittie when he was in Philadelphia: "The clergyman in his sermon today spoke of those mothers whom we should strive to prepare ourselves to meet in Heaven, and I felt how much I owed to mine."[8]

"She had settled notions," Elliott's cousin John Ellis Roosevelt recalled of their grandmother. "If a child wasn't eating it was ill. There was always cake in the pantry and the butler had orders that the children were always to have it when they wanted."[9]

There was also Mittie's mother, Martha Stewart Elliott Bulloch, a southern lady in a lace cap who was loved by her grandchildren for her frequent and conspicuous displays of warmth and tenderness to them, called her "melts." "Years after her death," David McCullough writes, "the mere mention of Grandmamma's name was enough to make the youngest three burst into tears."[10]

Not much is known about the Roosevelt servants, with the exception of an Irish girl called Dora Watkins, who was so indulgent with the children that she came near to being considered a bad influence. The women in the family were matched in their sweetness by Elliott's father, who doted on Mittie. McCullough writes that "an employee at one of his charities remarked that he had never understood the meaning of the word 'gentleman' until the evening he watched Theodore Roosevelt escort his wife around the premises."[11]

A source of deep sadness to Theodore and Mittie Roosevelt that undoubtedly affected Elliott, by all accounts the most sensitive of their

Martha Stewart Elliott Bulloch, circa 1860. "Years after her death," David McCullough writes, "the mere mention of Grandmamma's name was enough to make the youngest three burst into tears." Courtesy of The Houghton Library, Harvard University.

children,[12] was the great tragedy of American history — the Civil War. The fact that the deep, emotional loyalties of the parents lay on opposite sides of this conflict caused them both profound heartache, but it seems not to have in the least diminished their love for each other. "We often speak of you, dear Mother, and I feel deeply for you," Lucy Sorrell Elliott, wife of Mittie's half-brother Stuart, wrote her mother-in-law (Mittie's mother) from Georgia, "for you occupy a trying position, with your heart at the South, you have those so dear to you at the North."[13]

Confederate naval history owes a great deal to Mittie's brothers: Commander James Dunwoody Bulloch (called "Admiral Bulloch" by both Theodore Roosevelt, in his *Autobiography*, and Margaret Mitchell in *Gone with the Wind*) commissioned the indispensable commerce raiders

CSS Florida, CSS Shenandoah, and *CSS Alabama*; the last shots from *Alabama* were fired by their brother, midshipman Irvine Bulloch. Their contributions to the Confederacy proved so deadly to the Union that, after the war, they were not included in the general amnesty. James Bulloch's tombstone reads, "American by birth, Englishman by choice."[14]

Irvine Stephens Bulloch, circa 1861. Courtesy of The Houghton Library, Harvard University.

Theodore Sr. was a staunch Lincoln Republican and an opponent of slavery, but rather than shoot at his wife's fellow southerners (including her two brothers), he chose to serve his country in a civilian capacity. He was tireless in these endeavors. Theodore Sr. joined the Loyal Publication Society, an association which sought to persuade the public that there were good reasons for the war; he became a member of the Union League Club's executive committee, which recruited and trained the first black soldiers; and he persuaded Congress to create an allotment commission, the purpose of which was to encourage enlisted men to send a portion of their pay to their families.

After the Allotment Commission became policy, Theodore was appointed as one of three commissioners for New York. He traveled on horseback from outpost to outpost and convinced the men to make sure that their families had enough to make ends meet; he was one of those who set up the Protective War Claim Association, which looked after the needs of the soldiers by collecting back pay and pensions; and he founded the Soldiers' Employment Bureau, an employment agency for disabled veterans.

Theodore Roosevelt, Sr. served his country as devotedly as any man. And yet, according to his daughter, for the rest of his life he would regret not having worn a uniform.[15]

From his father, Elliott inherited physical vitality (at least as a youngster), a genuine appreciation of and concern for people, and a tenderness that was perhaps his most noticed characteristic. His taste for a colorful, adventurous life was a legacy of his mother's family. He inherited from her, perhaps, "a hint of white columns and wisteria bowers,"[16] his love for beautiful things, his vividness of expression, his loquaciousness and his refinement. "The large, kindly spirit of Theodore Sr. hovered always over his son,"[17] T.R.'s biographer Edmund Morris has written, just as, throughout her life, the gentle spirit of Elliott Roosevelt would be his daughter's chief source of strength and comfort.

From earliest childhood, Elliott's most important relationship was with his brother. The boys were, always, each other's best friend, although even as toddlers Teedie was determined to have the upper hand with Ellie.[18] Mittie provides a glimpse of this in an early letter:

Elliott came into my bed and fell asleep while I was stroking his ears. Teedie was miserably jealous about his sleeping by me ...

After Teedie is allowed to climb into bed with them, his mother writes:

Teedie was in the most lambent frame of mind. He would say, "Ellie, shall I stroke your little ears?" Ellie would assent and be perfectly quiet, then Teedie would say to me in the most hysterical manner, "Oh, do look, Mamma, how he do obey me."

The Roosevelt children led a wonderful life at their house on East 20th Street. Every Sunday, weather permitting, there would be a brisk afternoon drive in one of their father's carriages. Each day there were Bible readings and family prayers, with the children scrambling for the prize seat, the one next to their father.

The children's birthdays were magical occasions because their father would spend the day exclusively with the child whose special day it was, doing whatever the youngster wanted. Eccentric Uncle Robert Roosevelt and Aunt Lizzie, along with Aunt Lizzie's animals (including a truly obnoxious monkey that she dressed as a little boy) provided a constant source of amusement. In the summertime the family went to the Hudson Valley where their father rented a succession of summer houses, and later to Oyster Bay, Long Island, where he settled on a house that the family called Tranquility. Here the children explored the woods and had endless

Elliott, at about six, circa 1866. Courtesy of The Houghton Library, Harvard University.

fun with a pony they called General Grant. Above all, they were infinitely secure in the love of their parents.

In 1869 their father decided that the time had come for them to spend a year abroad, making the "grand tour" of Europe. They left in May aboard the *Scotia*, a paddle-wheel ship the children found delightful to explore.

From Teedie's diaries of the trip, there emerges a picture of two boys for whom all experiences were enhanced by having been shared with each other. (Punctuation and spelling are Teedie's.)[19]

When I put 'we 3' I mean Conie [Corinne] Ellie and I. When I put 'big people' I mean Papa Mama and Bamie. — Journal entry

Elliott, circa 1866. Courtesy of The Houghton Library, Harvard University.

from May 12 to Sept. 9, 1869

We go to Europe today. We sail in the English steamship, Scotia. ... We have nice staterooms and a gentelman showed us all round the ship. We started at 5. We 3 jumped around the deck and played. When we went to bed I was a little seasick. — May 12, 1869

Clear, cold and calm. I was sick at breakfast. It is rather monotonous. I read and played with Ellie and Conie most of the day. — May 13

As it was a little rough and I a little sick and being down I could not go to service. While being in bed with nothing to do I got so homesick. In the evening I and Ellie went up on deck for a while. — May 16th

Our cousins came to visit us [Mittie's brothers were in Liverpool] and we had a fine play with them. We jumped and romped. When they went away we three had a great play together. Read, wrote, or drew. — May 26th, Liverpool

We went to Chatsworth in the cars today. ... We saw several deer and then went running across the grounds to the Edensor Hotel. We had a splendid supper and Ellie and I had a room to ourselves. In bed Conie would get frightened and come from her room into ours. Then Ellie would put her to bed but back she would come. — May 31st

We went to church in the morning. I had a headache and Conie and Ellie made a tremendous noise playing to my expense and rather laughed when I remonstrated, but I called Bamie and she made them as they could not play quietly sit quietly. — June 20th

Papa took we two boys out for a drive in a 'handsome' (kind of cab). — June 21st

In the morning we walked in hide park and as we walked by the lake Conie and I hauled in 70 dead fish about 2 inches long. Ellie and I went to a riding school in the afternoon. We saw a most queer and amusing punch and Judy. It was so funny. — June 24th

We 3 children went to the Christal [sic] palace again. We saw some new things and Ellie bought a new book. — London, July 8th

We 3 children went to richmond. At first we did not have a nice time for Ellie hurt Conie and they quarreled but after dinner we played robber in a park and rushed down hills and through very narrow paths through a large tract of houses and had some delicious rasberrys. — July 9th, London

... Stayed at home and read the Bible and learnt 2 verses. We went to the Kensington Garden with Ellie and ordered the cab to come home with. — June 11th, London

We went to Antwerp. ... We all played round the decks at sea hide and go seek and Ellie lost his watch. Bamie was the 1st Ellie 2nd Mama was 3rd and Papa and Conie not at all seasick. — July 13th I was awake at three o'clock and got up before 7. I was the first one that got on the continent. We then saw a pretty church and the town hall. We had such nice fruit. In the afternoon we went to a park and Ellie promised me to go up to the sky in ten years. [?] — Antwerp, July 14th

We went to church. Did nothing. ... Ellie had sugar and water and I milk and the rest coffee. — Amsterdam, July 18th

We explored the hotel (Conie, Ellie and I) and met with several cross chambermaids. — August 6th, Chanmonix

I was very sick on the sofa and lay in bed all day and had to take arrowroot. Mama told me stories and Papa did the same. I think Ellie and Conie the kindest kind of brother and sister. — August 29th

Ellie was sick and it rained. Conie and I explored the house all but a place where a terrible gurgle, gurgle drove us away. — Sept. 1st

An excursion to a Dutch farmhouse. ... We bought a lot of cherries, rasberrys, strawberrys. After Ellie had eaten as much as he could stuff took a run outside the carriage to help him dighest. — Holland, [undated]

... We saw a palace of the Doges. It looks like a palace you could be comfortable and snug in (which is not usual). ...

Ellie and I had a little run outside for 5 minutes in the morning we then stayed in until before dinner when we went out and built a castle of dirt and knocked it down with stones. ... — Dec. 6th, Niece [sic]

... For dinner 'we three' children went to the English restaurant. Ellie stayed playing there with some boys and Conie and I came back to the hotel with our umbrella's raised for it was raining. There I played with my coins and Conie read aloud to me. Then Ellie came and we went into the hall and we played and romped. We tossed balls about walked up the hall with our eyes shut and tossed bread on the heads of waiters, and ran about generally.

Ellie and I went and changed some common centimes for rare ones. Then — but before i go on I must tell you what a play we had in bed early this morning. It was dark as pitch when Ellie and i began to jump. This woke Conie. She came in. we got noisy. We jumped and pulled the covering off the bed and kicked and made an awful noise. Then Father came and made us quiet. — Genoa dec. 10th

Ellie and I had splendid fun. If the caraige walked for a minute we would jump out of the windows and as the caraige went on we would scramble in (as we could not open the door) any way and every way. ... — Dec. 18

Conie Ellie and I played in bed and in the morning and then all except Bamie and we 3 went out. Tomorrow is Christmas !!!! hip! hip! hurrah !!!! ... Ellie and I stuffed our pockets with pieces of bread. We went through the house throwing bread at each and letting it drop down stairs and laughing at everry thing anything and nothing and then we came in to one of the rooms and found a lemon and went to the lardor where we got some sugar and made some lemonade. We 2 boys drunk it with relish. We then had lunch and then we 3 went out in the hall and threw some bread on another floor and then a man picked them up and looked fierce at us. — Rome, Dec 24th

We all go to Mt. Vesuvius. Perhaps we 3 will not go up it. we do not think we will. Finely we galloped up a gully (short cut) with snow. We arrived at a large ungainly house where we dismounted. Here Ellie and I exchanged snow balls. — dec. 31, Naples

We had a splendid day today. Ellie went out to get a sword and gun and I went to Mrs. Dickeys for Charlie. Going back I bought Bamie's present and we met Ellie with gun and sword. he lent the gun to Charlie and I picked up some stones. I was a little rebellious soldier. Ellie struck me with his sword. ... I revenged the blows of the sword by runing away. I ran to a small hillock of dust and canes and took my stand. Up they came and Charlie made at me with the gun and cut my hand with it. I struck him in the chest and he fell on his back. But Ellie was on me with his sword and had me on my knees but I hurled him on Charlie. ... — Jan. 15, Rome

... I bought Ellie's gun from him. ... — Jan. 19

... Ellie and I made war on each other. ... — Jan. 23, 1870, Albano

Ellie and I played bull with cloaks and had great fun. ... — Feb. 4th, Rome

Ellie and I went to church all alone and heard a most interesting sermon. ... After dinner Ellie and I went up on the Pincien walk and did nothing and saw a dog fight the cat. — Feb. 5th, Rome

We went out on the Pincien but I forgot to say that we went to buy Conie a ball and Ellie got into a tremendous rage because I would not buy a ball with him and Conie would walk with him and ran away (for an hour). — Feb. 7th, Rome

Ellie and I played in the garden at fighting each other and taking forts and then we read and played. ... — Feb. 19th, Florence

The second most important relationship in Elliott's life was with his father, "just my ideal," as Elliott would describe him, "made to govern and doing it so lightly and affectionately."[20] Theodore Sr. was, perhaps, an ideal for which Elliott wished to strive but despaired of ever approaching. He was called "Ellie" within the family, and took to calling himself "Nell," as if he felt feminine in comparison with stronger men who were more focused than he.[21] Elliott loved music, loved to sing and, in a family not known for musical talent, seems to have had what was considered a pleasant voice. He took care with his appearance and made sure that he was always impeccably groomed. In this, he was the opposite of his brother. Elliott liked to write limericks and came up with one about his brother:[22]

There was an old fellow named Teedie,
Whose clothes at best looked so seedy
That his friends in dismay
Hollered out, "Oh! I say!"
At the dirty old fellow named Teedie.

When Corinne was away on a brief visit, she can only have groaned and laughed at this message from her devoted Elliott:

When our sister said good-bye ...
We our best did not to cry ...

We have done our best to joke
But it has ended all in smoke.

But a letter came from her
Asking us out to dinner
Then was our cup o'er filled with joys
And we yelled "Hurrah"! for the
"Sister of the Boys"[23]

Elliott appears to have realized from an early age that his most noticeable gift, as well as his principal defense in a frighteningly competitive and demanding masculine world, was his charm. When Teedie began to build up his strength in the small gymnasium their father installed on the second floor "piazza" at East 20th Street, Ellie was his partner in wrestling and boxing. The brothers kept journals of their athletic competitions in which Teedie was referred to as "Skinny" and Elliott was given the cognomen "Swelly" thanks to his unfailing affability.[24]

At first, Skinny was unable to give Swelly much competition. However, as time went on, he began to contribute his share. "Boxing is one of Teedie's and my favorite amusements," Elliott wrote, "it is such a novelty to see the stars when it is not night."[25]

On October 6, 1873, Elliott wrote from Dresden to his Aunt Anna this account of adventures in boxing:[26]

Last night we had another boxing fight. … I will give you the true and startling account with all the particulars under our boxing ring names. The 'mighty men of valor' numbered three: Skinny — Tedie. Swelly — Ellie. Brussels — Johnnie.

1st Round Skinny — Swelly.

Results. Skinny lips swelled and bleeding, Swelly sound in every limb if nose and lips can be classed as such.

2nd Round results. Skinny nose bleeding and cheeks of a carmine hue. Swelly's one cheek looking as if it had a mustard plaster on it. …

A few days ago I had a round with a fellow named Edward Jacobs who is taller than Tedie and certainly not a rail. Indeed I would call him a decent sized barrel, but any way we are just matched because he never had the gloves on but twice or 3 times before or boxed in any way or if he had he would have made short

Elliott, "the sweetest one in the family," circa 1869. Courtesy of The Houghton Library, Harvard University.

work of me. He hammered down on my left arm until he broke my guard and then disregarding himself he tried to hit my face so you see I could very well keep him about even by keeping out of his way and making sudden dashes.

I am going to ask Father if I can have boxing lessons when I get home.

As Theodore grew in strength and confidence, his brother steadily lost ground in these areas until, by a strange twist, the roles of the brothers were reversed.

❊3❊

"YOUR LOVINGEST
OF LOVING SONS"

Elliott Roosevelt was fourteen years old when something started to go wrong inside his brain.

His intelligence was far above average, but he was hardly a genius like his brother. By the time he reached his teens, he was undoubtedly feeling outdistanced intellectually. "I do try to study and I get along quite well but I declare it takes me such a long time to do what Tedie does in so short a time."[1] He was always unsure of himself and his place in the scheme of things. Always, he doted on his father. "… Father if you were only here. … I wish I could kiss you."[2]

"What will I become when I am a man?" he wrote to his father. "Are there not a very large number of partners in the store? … I think Teedie would be the boy to put in the store if you wanted to be very sure of it, because he is a much quicker and more sure kind of boy, though I will try my best to be as good as you if it is in me, but it is hard. But I can tell you that better when I get home and it does not look nice to read."[3]

During the summer of Elliott's fourteenth year, it was decided that Theodore, and not Elliott, would go on to Harvard. This decision had to do primarily with the mysterious illness that had befallen Elliott. He began to have periods of delirium, fainting spells, blackouts, "rushes of blood to the head," and a sudden, appalling pain in his head that made him "scream out."[4] Suddenly, he was afraid to sleep by himself.

"It is so funny, my illness; it comes from the nerves and therefore is not at all serious, but my body is getting so thin I can get a handful of skin right off my stomach, and my arms as well as legs look like I have the strength of a baby," he wrote to his brother. "I jump involuntarily at the smallest sound and have a perpetual headache. ..."[5]

No one was ever able to diagnose Elliott's condition accurately. The family doctor called it "congestion of the brain."[6] In later years, family members would say that he suffered from epilepsy. In this case, "epilepsy" seems to have been a catch-all phrase; the nature of his illness never has been clear. Was it in fact "a nervous breakdown" as one historian has asserted?[7]

Theodore Sr. was a firm believer that travel was the most effective form of therapy for every sort of ailment, a conviction shared by many of his contemporaries. In the autumn of 1874, he took Elliott with him on a business trip to England, but while Theodore Sr. was in Paris and Elliott was in Liverpool visiting Mittie's relatives, Irvine and Ella Bulloch and their children, Elliott became seriously ill. His father conveyed his distress in his letters home:[8]

The attack has been decidedly the worst he has had and very difficult in character. It came from overexcitement but of so natural a kind that I foresee it will be very difficult to guard him from it. A pillow fight was perhaps the principal exciting cause; ... It produced congestion of the brain with all its attendant horrors of delirium, etc. The doctor says that there is no cause for anxiety as it is only necessary to avoid all excitements for two or three years and he will entirely outgrow it. He is perfectly well again now, but of course weak and confined to his bed. ... Ellie's sweetness entirely won the heart of the doctor as it has that of all the servants here. The doctor says ... Ella's [compassion] is invaluable, and her nursing has been most judicious. He says that the boy should lead a quiet life in the country and I have vainly puzzled my brain to think how this can be accomplished ... "Thy will be done." Irvine and Ella are as kind to me as they can be and Ellie is perfectly happy with them. ... I write by Ellie's bedside he sleeps with me tonight.

Some historians have suggested that at this point Elliott retreated into illness as a way of avoiding competition with his brother. This conclusion presupposes that all illness is psychosomatic, and it seems an unfair assumption. Nevertheless, there is little doubt that even as a small boy Elliott felt that he was in the shadow of his brother's formidable intelligence. During the Grand Tour, when there was some doubt as to whether he was well enough to join his family on a journey, he protested, "I want to learn about these things too, like Teedie."[9]

It seems strange that something as normal and innocuous as a pillow fight would knock the wind out of an adolescent boy, but Elliott was not protected by the shell that most people have by his age developed, and perhaps his mental turmoil indeed manifested itself in physical distress. Everything was upsetting him at this point. "He evidently still has a fear of being left alone at night (i.e., is nervous) although he stoutly denies it," wrote his father. "He sleeps in my bed. I think it would be very wise for Theodore and himself to occupy the large bed in [the] back third-story room for awhile together. I should be afraid to leave him alone."[10]

Elliott's chief pleasure at this time was letters from home. He was especially anxious for any word from his brother.[11]

It is a pleasure to receive your letters and gives Ellie so much enjoyment to hear them read. His first inquiry is if there is anything from Teedie when a bundle of letters is brought in. You will have to assume more of the responsibilities of elder brother when we return.

Ellie is anticipating all sorts of pleasures with you that he will not be able to realize, and it will require much tact on your part not to let him feel his deprivations too much. ... His sickness at night, although worse, often reminds me of your old asthma, both of you showed so much patience and seemed more sorry on account of those about you than for yourselves. Aunt Ella is singing to him upstairs now; music often seems to soothe him when he is nervous.

The doctor in England said that Elliott's problem was "hysteria"[12] (another nineteenth-century catch-all phrase). Once again Theodore Sr. prescribed an excursion as soon as they got back to America, this time to the South in the company of John Metcalfe, the family doctor. They would visit Mittie's family in Georgia. Just as Theodore Sr. had written his namesake son and told him to look after Elliott, now he instructed Elliott always to stand by Theodore, whom he called a "noble boy."[13] Perhaps in entrusting the boys to each other, their father was acting on an intuition that his own life was drawing to a close.

Elliott was easily hurt, and when no letter arrived on his birthday, he felt overlooked. "Lately I have been feeling rather hurt for I always answer a letter as quickly as received and if you all did this I would get a letter nearly every day. ... I have received no birthday letter from 6 West 57th Street [where the family had relocated] so I think they must have forgotten me."[14] But the post must have been delayed, for a short time later Elliott's cup of happiness was full.

My own dear Father.

I got your kind "Father" like letter ... to day oh! It was so nice to feel you had thought of me on my birthday. ... Dear old Governor — for

I <u>will</u> call you that not in publick but in private for it does seem to suit you, you splendid Man just my ideal, made to govern & doing it so lightly & affectionately that I can call you by the name as a pet one. — its not such a long time since you were fifteen & any way as I was saying to Mrs. Metcalfe today you are one of the few men who seem to remember they were boy's once them selves & therefore can excuse pieces of boyish folly committed by their boy's.

Do you think it would be a good plan to send <u>me</u> to school again perhaps as I am not going to college I could make more friends there. I will do just as you think best, mon pere. I gave you my plan of study in my last letter but I would just as leif study at a school as at home for Thee is way behind or rather before me & perhaps although I don't now I may in future years see it was best for me.

I feel rich too in the prospect of my allowance, next first of January, it seems a long way off.

Are we going to Oyster Bay next summer don't you think Thee & I could sponge on all of our uncles & you & have a sail boat. I <u>know</u> we could manage her & would not be likly to drown.

My darling Father you have made me a companion & a very happy one. I don't believe there is any boy that has had as happy and free of care a life as I have had.

Oh. Father will you ever think <u>me</u> a "noble boy," you are right Thee is one & no mistake a boy I would give a good deal to be like in many respects. If you ever see me not stand by Thee you may know I am entirely changed, no Father I am not likly to desert a fellow I love as I do my Brother even you dont know what a good noble boy he is & what a splendid man he is going to be as I do. No, I love him, love him very <u>very</u> dearly & will never desert him & if I know him he will <u>never</u> desert me.

Father my own dear Father God bless you & help me to be a good boy & worthy of you, good by.

Your Son

This sounds foolish on looking over it but you touched me when you said always to stand by Thee in your letter.[15]

As Theodore prepared for college, Elliott did not like being left behind and he pleaded with his father to let him go to St. Paul's School in New Hampshire, where he could be with his cousin Archibald Gracie, son of his beloved Aunt Annie and his closest friend outside of his immediate family. Theodore Sr. agreed to send him, and Elliott began his prep school experience with his usual enthusiasm. Elliott's first evening at the school, he wrote his father:

After you left today I went out and watched the boys playing when I suddenly saw Archie walking over the grounds. I never saw a boy so astonished as he was when I slapped him on the back. He took me all over the school. ... I and Archie walked all the afternoon. At six o'clock we took tea, before that Dr. Coit assembled us all in the school room and gave out the order of study, and called the roll. After tea during which I made the acquaintance of several fellows — we had prayers and now quarter past seven I am in the big school room writing you. I have no regular desk and am very uncomfortable as to room, but as the Doctor said, "patience and all will be well." All the boys got at me for their respective clubs ... We came down to breakfast at eight, ham, sweet potatoes and mush. Chapel for morning prayers. ... Study. Collect and gospel for an hour church until half Past twelve. And now we have half an hour to write Letters. There goes it's up.

Love to all from Ellie

Elliott asked his father for "shaving brush, stamps," and "any small nick nack I may have for my alcove."[16] Elliott was chosen to be a member of both the cricket and boating club and enjoyed school, although his alcove was "cold as Greenland" and his roommates were "chatterboxes" who kept him awake and were "neither bad or good fellows."[17]

His letters are a window into the preoccupations of the privileged: "Tomorrow there will be a hare and hounds the first of the season it will be only a five mile run, but the big one coming in October will be fifteen miles. ... I and the coxswain of our crew I guess will run together. I will wear only my brown trousers and the old blue Oyster Bay shirt. ... The fellow or hound first in gets a prize."[18] He made sure his brother was kept apprised of his physical exploits: "Today Kayser and I walked for about two hours doing our last two miles in twenty minutes! Tell Thee."[19] Early on, he made a point of rooting for his brother's future alma mater: "Are you not sorry Harvard did not beat," he asked his mother. "I am but I am glad Columbia won instead and that Harvard beat Yale any way."[20] Elliott tried to do his best. "I think I am getting over my intense bashfulness or rather lack of presence of mind when called up to answer before the whole class."[21] "I am studying as hard as I can," he reported to his father, "and I think all my teachers are satisfied with me."[22] But in the same letter, dated as early in the term as October 1, he added:

Yesterday during my Latin lesson without the slightest warning I had a bad rush of blood to the head, it hurt me so that I can't remember what happened. I believe I screamed out, anyway the Doctor brought me over to his house and I lay down for a couple of hours; I had by that time recovered and after laying down all the afternoon I was able to go on with my afternoon studies. I lost nothing but one Greek lesson by it. It had left me rather nervous and therefore homesick and unhappy. But I am well now so don't worry about me. I took some of my anti-nervous medicine, and I would like the receipt of more. You told me to write you everything and I would not bother you with this, but you want to know all about me don't you?

P.S. II Don't forget me please and write often.

Love from Ellie

Elliott's abortive prep school career distressed his relatives and friends. "Poor Ellie Roosevelt has had to leave on account of his health. He has 'ever been subject to a rush of blood to his head' and while up here exerted too much both physically and mentally," Archie Gracie wrote his mother. "He studied hard and late. One day he fainted just after leaving the table and fell down. ... His brother came up to take him home. ..."[23]

Apparently Theodore Sr. decided at this point that what his sensitive son needed was some toughening up.

Perhaps life on an army post in Texas would do him good — he would once again be in the company of Dr. Metcalfe, as well as his cousin John Roosevelt. And so Elliott was sent to Fort McKavitt for a taste of life in the Wild West. Several of the officers there were friends of his father from the war years, in particular a General Clitz. Theodore and Mittie Roosevelt knew that they would take care of Elliott who, despite his frailty, was an adventurous soul who wanted very much to be considered a man among men, like his father. ("Oh dear splendid old pater ..." began some of his letters.)[24] He relished the thought (and later the experience) of "roughing it" with soldiers and cowboys.

Elliott was remarkably well-traveled for a sixteen-year-old boy of his time, having sailed down the Nile with his family on a houseboat during one of their excursions abroad, and spent his thirteenth birthday in Jerusalem, where he visited "the mosque of Omar." "We had to put on slippers as no Christian is allowed in side of a mosque without them the mohometans take their shoes off but we are afraid of cold so we put on slippers which answer the same purpose [keeping] outside dust from touching the sacred inside of a mosque," he wrote his uncle Jimmie Bulloch in England. "It is made inside of beautiful marbels, they are repairing the roof now because in the war here the arab boys took off the tiles and sold them to strangers. … We were also shown the place where mahomed put his foot when he jumped up to heaven and left the print of it."[25]

Elliott lived with a family in Germany shortly after, in the company of Teedie, Corinne, and his cousin Johnnie Elliott during yet another sojourn to Europe while the family's new house on West 57th Street was being completed. "My Dearest Darling Father," he wrote, "We are getting on

The houseboat, called a dahabeah, *in which the Roosevelts sailed down the Nile in 1869. Reproduced from the holdings at The Franklin D. Roosevelt Presidential Library.*

quite nicely with our German we understand it a little and have begun to speak it a little to each other. We have holiday tomorrow ... but for the day after we have our drawing lessons. I have a scene in Saxon, Switzerland, Teddie has some heads. Then we have our German, half of the ninth lesson in 'Otto,' a page of writing and twelve lines of the 'Lieder' with a review of two verses more and I have my music after dinner. Then they have given us leave to have Johnnie, Conie and Maud here next Wednesday to spend the afternoon and take tea and we will have a dance."[26]

They spent their time in Dresden rowing, boxing, swimming, drawing, walking in a park or in the country, and studying German with Miss Anna Minkwitz. Elliott frequently wrote to his parents in German, adding English postscripts. "Dear Father ... I just put these few lines to tell you that I have written this letter all alone except one word and the formation of one of the smallest sentences. I know I have many faults but I wrote it because I thought it would please you 'you darling.'"[27] After another attempt "all alone" two days later, he added, "Miss Minkwitz says that I have learned as much German as I could, because Languages come very hard to me."[28] He faithfully corresponded with his Aunt Annie, at one point writing graphically about his sore toe and including an illustration.[29]

At this time the children formed a club that met on Sunday evening and included their cousins John and Matilda Elliott, whom Mittie had arranged to be in Dresden while her children stayed with families there. They read stories and poems to each other that they had worked on during the week. One of Elliott's offerings was called "Bloody Hand," which may have been inspired by this incident: "Yesterday afternoon Johnnie came here and we had some fun boxing. The only effects were Tedie has a black eye and had a bloody nose, but we all gave several good blows ... since yesterday my hand has been trembling so you must excuse my hand-writing."[30] "Yesterday Johnnie came and we played soldiers and forgot all about speaking French or German." This letter is signed "Your lovingest of loving Sons."[31]

Elliott wrote an essay while in Dresden titled "Just My Luck" that reveals his self-deprecating sense of humor:

1. I was walking down-town in winter. I saw a lady, was taking off my hat to her when a shovel full of snow came down from a house and smashed my nice new beaver. Just my luck.

2. I was walking one night to a ball at 11 o'clock in my dress suit. The cats were meowing frightfully when suddenly a window opened and a pitcher of cold water was dumped down on my head and I heard a voice say "I'll stop those cats anyway." Just my luck.

3. I went to propose to a young lady. The room being dark I slipped and ripped my pantaloons in the seat. I sat down on a chair trying to hide it & after a little while the young lady said "I have dropped my handkerchief," and I stooped over to look for it when she said oh! You are sitting on it and seized a hold of my shirt and pulled violently I had to tell her and she screamed and ran away so I saw there was no response in that quarter.[32]

They kept up their churchgoing habit while in Germany, although the language barrier made much of the service incomprehensible to Elliott. He wrote his mother that his teacher translated the first hymn for them before church, "so I understood that and some of the sermon but the difficulty was I would understand two words then I would not understand any more for quite a long time. The text I heard it was from first Corin. XII chap and 3rd verse. But I do not remember the words. ... I think I will write to father also to day so you must not expect a long letter from me besides as you left me yesterday there is not much to say."[33]

By the time of his next visit to "the German church," Elliott's understanding of German had improved. Perhaps the fact that the text dealt with two brothers caused him to listen intently.

Today I went alone with Fraulein Emma to the German church. It is the third time this time I understood almost every thing and remembered as much as I would at home for Miss Emma asked me all about it. The reading was the Parable of the lost son the text was Mat. 21 chap. 28 to the 31st verses, about the man who told his sons to go and work in the viniard and one said "no" and went and the other said "yes" but went not. He asked which was the best the one that went or the one that did not go and then he said the one that went and he went on saying that all men were like one of these brothers, the real thing of his sermon was that if you repented you would go to heaven. It was a very long sermon all the sermons are long in those churches it must have [been] an hour long. Will it not be jolly when we get home?[34]

Miss Minkwitz was fond of the Roosevelt children and gave them gifts on Corinne's birthday, including Elliott, despite his professed lack of facility with languages. "... Mine was a beautiful picture Bible. I have never gotten so handsome a book as a present before. ... We ought to give Mrs. M. some thing before we leave. But I have no chink at least not enough to give her anything worth keeping." The boys maintained their violent exercise routine: "In the afternoon we boy's boxed and I was cock of the path (or room). I gave Tedie a bloody nose and lip and Johnnie a flat nose and what is funniest escaped scot free my self."[35]

The Roosevelt brothers were a peculiarly nineteenth-century upper-class combination of fisticuffs and refinement, of which the following account is illustrative: "My Darling, Dear Father. ... We took tea with [mother] last night ... Between the dinner and the ice cream Tedie and Johnnie and I went in to her bed room and had a box with the gloves. First Tedie and I had a round both of us got blown before we gave each other any good blows, but the next round was much more effective. Tedie got a bloody nose and a blow on the mouth which made it bleed but they all said I beat even Tedie because he got a little excited and I gave him one on the forehead and then a quick right-hander on his ear then the finishing one on his nose. Then came ice cream. After that we went at it again but this time Johnnie and Tedie but when they came out of their two rounds they were about matched in red faces and that was all. ... I got another blow in my mouth which gives it is now swelled appearance but I gave Johnnie a red eye which Tedie said turned black. I am glad of one thing that tho' Tedie can beat me in running and wrestling and Johnnie in running that I can beat them in boxing."[36]

The Roosevelts were surprised to find that not all of their countrymen shared their standards of courtesy and sportsmanship. "There are a bad set of Americans here, just two days ago an American set to work and pummeled a lot of Germans standing peacefully by and when the police came he boxed them. And to judge from the language I hear from the English and American boy's here I think they are what we boy's would call hard eggs but really the English are the hardest."[37]

Teedie was the focus of the family's concern in Dresden. "My darling Mother," wrote Corinne, "you ask me to tell you about Tedie. I really do not think he is at all well he has just had another attack of Asthma. I don't believe Dresden is that right place for Tedie. I think Ellie and I are very well. ..."

Certainly Teedie and Elliott were not too delicate at this point to do some roughhousing, as Elliott wrote his mother on the back page of Corinne's letter: "I can not write well because I am on the edge of the table in very unpleasant position. Yesterday Tedie and I were playing together he trying to put a pea down my back he pushed me against the wall and then in the struggle I fell in to a pane of glass and broke it and have a little cut on my arm. Please excuse my not writing to you sooner but I have not time."[38]

Travel was prescribed in the winter of 1875, in the company of Dr. and Mrs. Metcalfe, to the temperate South. The doctor was very fond of Elliott and called him "Buddy."[39] Elliott wrote to his "Dear little Muz" from her home state, devastated still from the Civil War but upholding a vestige of the atmosphere Mittie remembered:

> I have just come in from the city, what a beautiful one it is, it made me feel quite sad to see such magnificent old houses look so very deserted, but there are some beautiful ones left yet. I think this city is perfectly lovly [sic]. I walked up Bull St. to the Park & in the squares and gardens I saw orange trees with fruit & magnolia trees & Palm trees & flowers of all sorts in the open air, just think in February & most likely as the Doctor said you are being frozen up in N.Y. I see lots of pretty little white babys with huge big black 'Mamas'(?) parading the streets. ... I have used up nine handkerchiefs since I left home. I could rather wish to have a better nose. ... Mrs. M. sends the enclosed violets picked in the open air and says she will take good care of me. ... I am enjoying myself very much and the doctor is very funny and jolly. Your loving Son, in haste for supper.[40]

Then, hunting in Florida with the doctor ("three of us brought home a bag of 36 birds"), which was apparently exhilarating judging from Elliott's spirits as he composed the following:

> This flowery epistle is composed & flows from my steel pen on this the twenty fifth day of the second month of the eighteenth hundred & seventy fifth year A.D. It leaves me & the learned Doctor & his much-to-be-honored spouse in all desirable health & happiness but for the thorns two of which grow

mightily on that rose called Florida firstly the wicked flea & secondly the Blasted heat, it being now by that present invention called a Thermometer 84 [degrees] above that small point called zero. I hope it finds you also in the best of nature's many gifts, good health & spirits. ... M.D. and his wife have just gone out for a perambulation in the chariot. ... But as the fair heavens looked overcast and frowning I did not grace the company with my presence for which they are no doubt thanking a kind providence.[41]

In Gainesville Elliott went to church and heard a sermon from the text "'Repent, for the kingdom of heaven is at hand,' which the speaker held forth a good deal on drinking which was very nessary [sic] as most of the population get drunk every night." His brother Theodore has had a mishap of some sort: "I received your letter telling me about Thee day before yesterday ... what a pity it was. I hope the dear old boy is well by this time. I suspect he was shewing off some fancy figure and 'pride must have a fall' you know, but realy. I am sorry for 'Brudy.'" The Florida birds managed to elude the hunters, but Elliott enjoyed the experience nevertheless: "... We waited till after dark but none came till we could not see them but only hear the whi<u>rrrr</u>, whi<u>rrrr</u> through the air then I came home. I had Milton [a servant] with me to shew me the way!!! He is so funny in the morning about 7:30 or 8:00 he comes into my room & wakes me but I pretend to be asleep & he sets to work & makes my fire or black's my boots or something & commences talking to himself or to me as the case may be & keeps it up until I can stand it no longer & burst out laughing when he laughs too & then I <u>have</u> to talk to him."[42]

From the early 1870s until the early 1930s, vaudeville was, if not the national pastime, certainly the most popular avenue of show business. Elliott provides a glimpse of it in its infancy:

I had heard from our negro servant a good deal about a show as he called it that is a traveling magic entertainment and as the Doctor said I would most likely have a chance to see all the fashion of Gainesville I went and it was very amusing. You get a ticket for 75 cents and a small envelope containing a card or a blank if you get a card you get at the end of the performance a prize of some kinde [sic]. I bought two of these cards what I got I will tell you afterwards. At eight o'clock I walked into town to the hall where Signore Silvano's show came off. It (the hall) was about as big as our library. I entered into the room immediately at the entrance on an empty box sits the ticket seller but as I had my ticket I passed by, up the hall through the lines of wooden benches, avoiding the lakes of tobacco juice (for every one, both men and black women smoke & chew here) to my seat in the 2nd row. The band (two fiddles) struck up for one minute & then at the ringing of a bell stopped and the usher who is Sig. S. mounts on an old trunk and then on the stage. Then comes a series of tricks pretty good but during which I look around. The room is lighted by a few dirty oil lamps by the light of which I see the fasion [sic] in the reserved seats (75 cents) around me & the nig's & co., in the unreserved seats back. All the country Belles dressed in their best attended by devoted Swains in their best. I will give you a description of one of these belles. A brown dark dress with a huge red bow in front & a red sash with a red worsted cloak trimmed with white feathers, a small straw hat set on the top of a head of hair banged, crimped and curled & hands with rings whether real or not I do not know covering her fingers, add to this all the airs and graces & affectations of a New York flirt and you have I believe <u>the</u> belle of Gainesville.[43]

Elliott, May 24, 1875, around the time he was sent to Texas. Courtesy of The Houghton Library, Harvard University.

Elliott concludes by telling his father that in the distribution of prizes he received "a <u>pink</u> <u>undershirt</u> and fine gloves. ... I wish you could have seen Dr. and Mrs. M.'s faces when I came home last night with my prizes."[44]

⚜

The adventure in Texas would be completely different, however, from the genteel outings to which Elliott was accustomed. He was excited, but he had been terribly homesick at St. Paul's and must have wondered why no one seemed to think he could function at home.

Elliott thrived in Texas. His friendliness and love of fun more than compensated for the fact that he was a wealthy (and sickly) Easterner — and a city dweller at that. He had a remarkable ability to turn nearly everyone he met into a friend, including people with whom he would seem to have had little in common. His father warned him about the sort of company he should keep: "Be careful always in chance acquaintances, I hope your new found friends may prove an exception to a general rule but feel quite anxious to hear."[45]

Elliott's father wrote to him as a confidante and nearly as an equal. They were trusted friends as well as father and son.

33 Pine Street
New York, NY
Jan. 6, 1876

Dear Old Nell:

I took Theodore around the park this morning and then said good-bye to him, and he went off most cheerfully to Cambridge again. He has had a glorious time although he missed you as well as I suspect envying you a little notwithstanding the young ladies. I went out last night to dinner at Mr. Morton's to meet Chief Justice Waite and the night before to Mr. Evarts for the same purpose. I enjoy the old gentlemen of sixty as much as I do the young girls of sixteen, so had a delightful time at both places. The sleighing remains perfect and bids fair to do so for the next month or so and the horses improve on plenty of exercise; I never miss a day. ...

6 West 57th Street
Uncle Jim insisted on my walking up with him when I had reached this point and I have just said good-night to the family who have retired, and sit down to finish this page; if I have time, after thinking up something to tell the newsboys tomorrow, I will write another. Bamie went out to dinner and brought Conie,

who dined with Maud [Matilda Elliott], home with her, both have had lovely times. A wet sleet is falling making the pavements one sheet of ice so that everyone walks in the heavy snow in the middle of the streets, a bad prospect for church tomorrow.

Your loving,
FATHER

Sunday Jan. 7th, 11:00 P.M.
(All have gone to bed)

My boys at the Lodging House were very interesting tonight. One little fellow eight years old was particularly so, he had neither father nor mother and felt perfectly able to care for himself. He described how a policeman had 'bringed' him to the Station House once but seemed really not quite sure which particular crime it was for. All the boys were intensely bright and wide awake. I stayed there late and afterwards could not refuse to stop with Dr. Schaffer [one of the founders, along with Theodore Sr., of the Orthopedic Hospital], and read over his report about the Orthopedic Dispensary which is to be presented at our annual tomorrow night. These two causes have made me very late and already "Thee" has been called over the banisters by your mother. I wonder if anyone has told you that our main course at the New Year's dinner was a saddle of venison from Mose Sawyer, I was really touched at his remembering me after not seeing him for so long. ... We had a remarkably good sermon from Dr. Ludlow, he has been called upon to exercise many Christian virtues lately. The consistory which is composed principally of representatives from the other churches desire him to resign; the members of our church however will probably have their own way.

Remember me to Johnnie and tell him we all enjoy his letters.

Your loving

FATHER

P.S. Hope you are both setting a good example to one another and taking care of each other morally and physically including smoking.[46]

Elliott's first letter home was to his mother. "Dear little Muz," he called her, and conveyed a sense of how much pleasure he was taking in his Western travels.

We left Palestine yesterday morning and for the first time traveled as we ought to do to enjoy Railroad traveling. ... We arrived here last night after dark and I have not been out this morning so I can form no opinion of the town [Houston] except that the dogs howl longer and louder than any other city dogs but those of Constantinople, and the mosquitoes are more persisting little brutes than any I have before met with in this part of the world. Of course the doctor has met with any number of acquaintances and had innumerable invitations to go out shooting at their respective plantations. I ought to be making cartridges for him now but I have all afternoon to do it in so there is no hurry. I am feeling very well. Sleeping soundly and eating like a little Pig, I am afraid.

He then thanks his mother for her New Year's card: "You dear little thing; it was such a sweet little remembrance."[47]

Elliott's next railroad trip was to Galveston, the frontier town on the Gulf of Mexico.

The Railroad from here to that place passes through one vast prairie, well watered; at least in this season — a little too much so, — and with now and then a small forest, this timber always running along the bank of some stream. We arrived at Galveston at one o'clock and after dinner we took a walk around the town. ... Galveston itself seems to be a very enterprising little city of thirty-five thousand or so inhabitants. Its stores are fine looking buildings, some of them very large and its private residences are, generally speaking, very pretty looking little houses, with a few very large handsome ones. ...[48]

At this point Elliott feels guilty about having to be treated so well for being ill and attempts to convince his father that he is a healthy and brave lad. "Do you know, Father, it strikes me as just a sell my being down here, it's a very pleasant one but a sell nevertheless, for I feel well enough to study and instead here am I spending all your money down here as if I was ill. I don't believe I will ever be 'weller' than I am; it's rather late to think of this but the doctor evidently don't think I'm sick and I am not, and altogether I feel like a general fraud, who ought to be studying."

He is deeply appreciative: "The doctor and Mrs. M. are just as jolly and kind to me as can be. Oh! I'm having a lovely time, there is no doubt at all on that score and I am ever so much obliged to you, Darling Parent, for giving it to

Your loving son
ELLIOTT[49]

⧉4⧉

"VOX BUFFALORUM"

Perhaps because they lived such sheltered lives, the Roosevelt boys often slipped into an alternate, daydream world of rugged adventure. The life's blood for this world was the writing of Captain Mayne Reid, whose specialty was "Juvenile tales of adventure, known as Boys' Books."

Captain Reid produced volume after volume, with titles such as *The Scalp Hunters, The Rifle Rangers, The Boy Slaves, The Death Shot, The Desert Home, The Naturalist in Siberia, Free Lances, The Forest Exiles, The Bush Boys,* etc. A typical entry, *The Rifle Rangers,* described on the title page as "A thrilling story of daring adventure and hairbreadth escapes during the Mexican War,"[1] includes among its illustrations a drawing of an alligator biting off a man's leg. The prose consists primarily of dialogue, punctuated by descriptions and classifications of different types of animals, and narrative like the following, from *The Young Yagers*:

> Hendrik breathed freely, though he puffed and panted a long time after getting upon his perch. His mind was at ease, however, for he saw at once that the rhinoceros could not reach him. The most it could do was to get its ugly snout over the edge of the rock, and that only by raising itself upon its hind-legs. This

it actually did, blowing with rage and projecting its broad muzzle as close as it could to the feet of the hunter, as if to seize him with its elongated and prehensile lips. It did so only once. Hendrik was as angry as the rhinoceros, and with juster cause; and now, feeling confident of the security of his position, he bent forward, and with all his might repeatedly kicked the thick lips of the brute with the heels of his heavy boots. The rhinoceros danced about, uttering cries of rage and pain; but, despite the brutal impetuosity of its nature, it no longer attempted to scale the cliff, but contented itself with rushing to and fro at its base, evidently determined to lay siege to the hunter.[2]

Like the Roosevelt boys, the heroes of Mayne Reid's stories have Dutch names—Hendrik, Groot Willem, Diedrik, Hans, Jan, etc. It is no wonder that Theodore and Elliott were captivated.

Elliott took pleasure in his sojourn in the frontier country of Texas the way only a frail city boy whose imagination had been nourished by Mayne Reid's stories could. He was abnormally vulnerable to homesickness. "I have been so homesick this week I did not know what to do," he had written his father from St. Paul's School. "Oh, how I love you, my own dear Father ... I am getting on pretty well, so very homesick but I fight against it. Everyone is very kind to me. ..."[3]

Elliott was an exceptionally appreciative and affectionate young man, assuring his mother that "Both the doctor and Mrs. [Metcalfe] are very, very good to me and I love them both very much indeed," and signing his letters "Your tenderly loving son."[4]

Elliott looked to his father for love and guidance, but he was equally devoted to his mother, addressing her as "Darling Little Muz."

I received your letter of Jan. 9th today. It was so nice and chatty I thank you little mother ever so much for it. ... You can't think Mother sweetest how welcome letters home are, today more so even than ordinarily for it seems a very long time since I had heard from you all. ... Yesterday nothing much happened except that it rained all day, starting to do so just when I was about seven inches from the hotel on a hunting trip, you could not call it shooting for I saw but two birds the whole time. I had to ride home in the open wagon and got nicely wet while doing it too ... This morning I went to the Episcopal Church, a very damp little affair but with a very fair congregation where there was a good service and really an excellent sermon of the right length, being about fifteen minutes.[5]

Hunting and churchgoing were to be lifelong enthusiasms for Elliott. The first seems, perhaps, puzzling in light of his gentleness; perhaps this pastime was actuated by his admiration for his brother and his desire (at this period) to keep up with him.

His conscientiousness about churchgoing is troubling, for in later years Elliott would seem not to have found the solace he needed in religion. However, even at his most confused and dissolute, he would periodically immerse himself in Christianity and urge his daughter not to neglect this dimension of life.

While Elliott loved all of his siblings, his letters to his sister Corinne at this time are particularly affectionate. "Dear Little Young'Un," Elliott wrote fourteen-year-old Corinne from Houston:

You gay little Baby belle, to have forty calls on New Years', pray how many of your swains called twice to make up that goodly number? ... You sweet little girl, it is very nice to be missed I can tell you, but I would give a good deal to see 'little feller' and all the family again. I have nothing new to tell you except that next week I go with Capt. Hayes on a surveying trip he makes on one of his own roads. ... Now sweet little baby sister good-bye from

Your loving
BROTHER[6]

Elliott seems never to have met anyone he did not like. After a hunting trip, he described to his mother "the five people who composed the people going on the hunt, namely Col. N. Prime who knows both you and Father and who takes a fatherly interest in me and is very kind, pleasant and jolly, Lieut. Barratt, the quarter-master, Lieut. Gibson the adjutant and as nice a little man as ever lived, Mr. Wallick the post trader, and myself."[7] The men had to stay close together on account of the possibility of an attack by Indians.

For all the fun Elliott was having, once again he became "a little unwell," and disparaged himself by saying he had "done nothing but be lazy."

Our life during the days in camp was of course but one continual hunt and I am sorry to say very little shoot. In the evening we would station ourselves at different turkey roosts and shoot them as they came in from the hills where they feed during the day. We were what they call very unlucky down here for we only got ten turkeys all told. I did my fair share of the shooting, also I am bound to say of the eating. We began our hunting early and ended late. Getting up at five and getting home from the turkey roosts late at night. But didn't we sleep, oh no! I had no idea such a sound nap could be had on a buffalo robe with a blanket to cover you. Of course the gentlemen took great care of me as being an effeminate civilian, and I had a perfectly glorious time.[8]

Elliott spent the remainder of his time in Texas worrying about his family, enjoying the company of the military officers at Fort McKavitt, joining wagon trains, and savoring the natural beauty of Texas. "Everything is in an advanced state in Texas, by everything I mean fruits, flowers, and vegetables and by Texas I mean the civilized parts thereof," he wrote. "The peaches in San Antonio are already as large as walnuts and all the fields are green."[9]

Elliott did not entirely lose his sickliness in Texas, although his references to his health are fleeting. Dr. Metcalfe did not want him riding in a stagecoach for they "upset me so."[10] Nevertheless, he took pains to reassure his parents.

> My life here is a very jolly one as you have most likely decided by my previous letters. I have been free from all trouble with my head except on my return from the turkey hunt ... I am all well now. Altho' enjoying myself as much as anybody ever did in their lives down here, still I can look forward with more pleasure to the time when I will see all your dear home faces again, it is nearly two months since we had that little chat on the steps in the coupe. Oh! dear splendid old Pater, I wish I could tell you how much I love you but I can't you know, so there's no use wishing.[11]

One habit Elliott picked up at this time was smoking cigars, but he resisted at first, so that he could write to his father:

> I have not taken a drink or a smoke, but I do want to do the latter very much, I don't care how much you laugh and I can see you do it just as plainly as you did that night in the study. It seemed rather hard at first to say 'I never drink' or 'I never smoke,' when asked about every five minutes during the day, for the young offi-

cers have unfortunately no way of spending their time but in one of the two of those employments, but it was not a very difficult thing to do.[12]

In an observation that eerily foreshadows the way in which people would one day speak of him, Elliott writes: "It seems a pity to see a young fellow, who has so much time, for a lieutenant's duties are not very hard, for his own use, spend it in such an unprofitable way as they seem to do, just merely from the fact that 'everybody' does it." In the same letter he longs to be his father's little boy: "P.S. Why so formal in your last note Father? Calling me Elliott instead of Nell."[13]

When Elliott was almost sixteen, his father sent him a new gun, which Elliott pronounced "a great success." "I never saw anything like it," he wrote his father from Palestine, Texas. "It kills the birds of its own accord unless I point it in another direction, which I am sorry to say sometimes happens."[14] At this time Elliott considered settling down on the frontier. His Texas friends informed him, "if you do own a farm there of one league you own a very nice little fortune for the soil is very fine not only for grain, fruit & cotton but also pasturage is splendid for raising horses. Can't you see me in future years driving a drag up & down drawn by six little Texan mustangs?"[15] One wishes he had followed through on this desire, as his best days all of his life were spent away from New York. Several years later his brother bought a ranch in the "Badlands" of North Dakota and sought solace there during the most difficult period of his life.

Elliott ventured deeper into some remote outposts of Texas, this time in the company of his friend Patrick Jameson. He wrote to his father from "a little beastly hive of an office" in Weatherford, "way out on the very frontier. After we leave this town revolvers are the order of the day for safety. ... We have enjoyed our weeks camping out hugely and have brought ourselves down to the proper amount of dirt and jollity. ... It is glorious fun and we are both of us enjoying ourselves very much. Our fellows are a very jolly crowd and improve very much on acquaintance. ... After a glorious 'fill' of game and biscuits ... we all lie down around the big camp fire & tell stories & crack jokes. ... Men of an entirely different kind, all out of Tx are sitting around here, talking of how buffalo herds are selling and how good 'the clipper whiskey' & other topics of an equally interesting nature."[16]

A few days later, Elliott and Patrick were joined by a friend named Ed Malcolmson. They managed to get separated from the rest of their party.

> ... We waited & watched & no wagons so at last we concluded that they had gone on to Graham not having seen the fork we turned up in, it being so dark. We were camped by a house so as we had no blankets & it was most fearfully cold we tied our horses to the gate post & left the saddles on to keep them warm & as Ed said I had 'a persuasive air with me' I went up to the little log hut & knocked. The door was opened & the master appeared. I talked with him for awhile & then a friend of his appearing on the scene he offered to take Ed with him & the first fellow took me in. The hut was crowded & a huge fire burning so although there were chinks on all sides & a cold wind blowing still we kept fairly warm. There were three girls too quite good-looking so I made the rest of the evening pass quite pleasantly only I was a little worried about the other chaps not having turned up. At about ten o'clock the landlord or rather ranchman came in with "Gentlemen your beds are ready" whereat, as I had been riding since seven o'clock & not had a mouthful to eat either I got up & making my good night to the ladies, the elder of which being the mistress sat pipe in mouth in the chimney corner; I rose followed

by some six others all pretty rough-looking chaps & followed mine host into an adjoining room no roof but logs and the merest framework of walls. Three rolls of blankets on the floor, three men took one, two another and a cow boy, from way out west, and I took the third. I used Tar, who had stuck to my heels all the evening in mortal terror of two other dogs belonging to the house; for a pillow partly for warmth & partly to drown the smell of my bed fellow. In this manner I shivered through the night up to five when "breakfast gentlemen" brought us all to our feet and without more adoe [sic] we ran for the fire in the next room & were served by the old lady still pipe in mouth with bacon & bread a frugal meal but if you laugh at it think I had not had a mouthful since six a.m. the day before. Roughing it; eh? At about eight Ed & I got on our nags & rode into Graham here, where we found the fellows put up at the hotel & what chaffing & jokeing as we had. The chap on whose paper I am writing asked us to come over to his office & write our letters which we did.[17]

In Austin, Elliott encountered an unscrupulous horse trader: "Yesterday I took a ride on a 'splendid' horse a man wanted to sell me as a bargain at eighty-seven dollars. I rode it for a mile and then it went and leant up against a fence. I suppose it thought the fence was going to fall down. After that I walked said horse home & declined the bargain."

Elliott liked Austin, declaring it "the nicest town we have met with in Texas and well taken care of and with a good police force. The Capitol, jail — now in process of construction — Land Office and Governors house all being very fine buildings & there are also several nice stores in the City. We will not leave here unless the roads to San Antonio are much better. There is not much good shooting around here which is a great pity, but shooting good & dirt seem to go hand in hand in Texas."[18]

He regaled his mother with his rustic adventures:

Muz I think you would have been amused at my efforts to get a bath yesterday. I put my washing things & clean clothes in my hand bag & sallied out after walking up town & came upon the sign "International Bath House." This sounded very grand but the little bit of a wood house did not look as if it was capable of a bath 'between nations.' never the less I felt dirty enough even to bathe with a Kiowa Indian so I walked in. It was realy quite nice and by dint of choosing a clean tub & a good many towels I managed to get a very nice bath. Privately I don't think the Dr knew me when he met me afterwards with the — as Thee would say — outer layer removed. I thought at one time during the bath I had found a shirt I lost last week but it proved only a night garment of the month before.[19]

Elliott followed through with the Roosevelt social conscience while in Texas. He wrote his mother from San Antonio that one day in order to pay a visit to the "deaf & dumb asylum" he took a carriage, rode horseback, and finally "ferried in a queer old-fashioned ferry across the Colorado." He told Mittie that "the cleanliness of the place … would take [her] heart by storm. … I felt, as you would have said, like rolling on the floor."[20]

The girls all of them inhabit one room & spend their time in good useful amusements, such as sewing — they make all there own bedding & clothes — and other things you would know better than I. The boys after study hours are formed into detachments and go & work either in the garden or the grounds cutting wood, or in the printing office etc. We were there after work hours were over & they were all playing it seemed so sad & at the same time so queer to see a lot of fine healthy chaps playing ball & not saying a word.[21]

The Western experience did wonders for Elliott, so much so that he was sent back to Fort McKavitt the next year, this time with his cousin John Roosevelt along. Years later Elliott wrote to his daughter that he had joined in a stakeout of some hostile Indians. She maintained that he "saw their cruel savage side but he also saw the pathos of a people being driven from their land and he admired the fine things in the race, and when I was eight he made me learn the whole of Hiawatha! ... These early camping and shooting experiences added to the love of all sport which seems to have been inborn in my father. Years later a friend of mine who had lived with her husband on a ranch near Uncle Ted's in the Badlands of the Dakotas told me she remembered my father well and the surprise he occasioned among the cowboys for all his shooting and riding. It seemed to be natural to him, whereas Uncle Ted acquired his skill through persistence and against great odds, for he was delicate as a boy and shortsighted all his life."[22]

The letters from this second trip are once again filled with reassurances to his parents that "Your son loves you so dearly." Elliott had not changed much from the time he wrote at age thirteen: "Father I am trying to be a good boy and I hope you will not be disappointed in me in one way, but for my smartness in study. I do not know what it is but I realy think I study as hard as I can but it does not go like Tedie or Conie."[23]

February 28, 1876, Elliott wrote from Fort McKavitt:[24]

The first letter of my birthday Must be written to my parents
So,
My own dear Father & little Muz,
Here am I sixteen years old, how very grown up I do feel. This

is my second birthday away from all you dear ones at home. …
Besides Lawrence the only other servant the General has is Aunt
Emily. For the first time I know what real southern cooking is.
She is a regular old "Mama" & very proud of her cooking & the
good things she has made for me would take your breath away.
Father I would write more to you but this letter is realy in answer
to Mother's. I am very well & still trying — you know what for.
… Remember, I don't say the use of tobacco is not a perfectly
lawful enjoyment. Now good by my two dear parents, the band is
playing & I want to hear it. I wish you could too. Love to all from
your devoted sixteen year old son

Elliott

Three weeks later Elliott was in New Orleans, and his letter to his
mother ran a curious gamut of emotions:

I am sitting in my room, it is just about eight o'clock. Harry Metcalfe and I were going to the theater but poor little Anna Clafflin
is so very ill that she is not expected to live & therefore we have
given it up. She is still at the house but it made me feel so very
sadly and nervous that as I could be of no use I left. There are
five doctors there so if there is a chance, she will have the benefit of it. … They took me down to the levee where I spent a very
interesting hour, looking at the steam boats and the toute ensem-
ble of the busy scene, from here we walked up Canal Street to see
the youth & beauty of New Orleans & by George there are some
A.1's of the latter class to be seen … there to a semitary [sic] —
you know they can not bury under ground so, it was a veritable
city of vaults. … Little Rose Clafflin having found out that I have
both read the Arabian Nights & seen "real, live" Sultanas and

Sultans, when ever she sees me keeps me employed in telling her of them. She is a dear funny little child & very amusing.[25]

In New Orleans, Dr. Metcalfe gave Elliott "a beautiful hunting knife" as a farewell present, and then he was on his way back to Fort McKavitt and General Clitz. "I wish I had a revolver or a small fire arm of some kind," he wrote his parents. "I never will come to an out of the way place like western Texas again without one."[26] Elliott traveled with his cousin Jack, also in the West for his health, riding trains from New Orleans to St. Louis to Dallas, "chess, cards & conversation served to pass the time as quickly as it can be passed on the cars."[27]

How glad I will be to see the dear old General again. I know he will like Jack he is such a nice fellow. Six weeks will bring us well to May and then Jack & your son will be thinking of their respective homes with much pleasure. The former of the two is so well you would not know him as the same man who left N.Y. so sick on the fifteenth of Dec. Imagine Jack the invalid sleeping all day & every day for the last two months in the open air. Rain, snow, cold, have all had no effect on him & both of us have come back as strong & hearty as any two fellows I know. McKavitt will just finish us up. Jack has gained twenty-two pounds & I sixteen on this little excursion.[28]

Elliott shared his father's interest in politics and followed the tumultuous 1876 presidential election.

So Hays [sic] is really counted in. I wish you could hear the dismal forbodings that the democratic members of our party (I was the only Republican) have for the "Old Union." We have had some glorious battles. ...[29]

Two days before his seventeenth birthday, Elliott longed for the company of his father, but he had no outlet other than correspondence.

Still another letter from me. You will think I am desirous of making myself … a newspaper correspondent from the length & number of my Epistles. But I have been so long deprived of talking to you & I have so much to say that it seems as if I never could stop. … Capt. Lee gave us an escort of two men & also two fine mounts to take us into Fort Worth. Yesterday we left at ten a.m. after breakfasting at the Capt's mess. We rode steadily all day, halting for lunch half an hour. We rode some three hours into the night, by the light of a most glorious moon, before we found a ranch. There we put up for the night, the men camping near by. It was a queer place of which I will write you another time.[30]

Elliott prepared his father for the contents of a package due to arrive in New York. "There will be a very fine big buffalo bull head which I shot for you. If you will have it mounted for me and consider it a Christmas present for Mother and yourself."[31]

With his friends Patrick Jameson and Ed Malcolmson, Elliott took the train to San Antonio and then the boys rode their horses back to Fort McKavitt and General Clitz, "to stay as long as the General wants us and we enjoy it."[32]

It will be rough work riding, you know. Mason Co. has the worst reputation of any of the frontier countys but Jack & I are now quite accustomed to taking care of our selves & your little Smith & Wesson is a prime little weapon. Any way there is no danger for us, it is only our horses. If we enjoy McK. as much as we anticipate we will not leave for a month or six weeks when it will be time to think of returning to the hearts of our dearly loved familys. Did I tell you I found Tar a very fine dog with a superb nose & all but entirely untrained so that he was of no earthly use to me? ... Our trip west is nearly over and we have had our fair share of good & bad luck. Bad in that we lost our horses & had to sell our wagon on trust until April & no one knows how much longer — good in sport & in having with a few exceptions very jolly & pleasant society. The only trouble was that all the fellows not having the same amount of "filthy lucre" those who would have liked not to have roughed it quite to such an extent were forced pro.tem. to the same level as the common buffalo hunter & skinner. I & Pat threw ourselves into the life & skinned with the rest but old Jack as he said did not come down here for that & would not & realy it was such dirty work that Pat & yours truly had to give up eventually too. It has taught me a great many things Sir, among others that a fellow seventeen can walk from fifteen to thirty miles a day for eight days on a pint of cold beans & plenty of fresh meat & in the evening roll himself up in his blanket & sleep as soundly as on a feather bed. This much I know for I tried it.[33]

Elliott sent home a buffalo calf skin "which I shot & skinned myself. ... The big head I told you of, it has the finest pair of horns that were shot by any of us fellows." He included a pair of antlers in his package as well.[34] Elliott was very proud of the buffalo head he sent home to West 57th Street; his description of obtaining it is worthy of Mayne Reid.

When the buffalo head gets home I want it stuffed; Thee can tell you the best man to do it; & it will be my present to you & Father for next Christmas. It is a very fine old bulls head the best pair of horns that were shot by the party. How would it look for that bare place in the hall. I never shall forget shooting him. I saw the herd he was in some two miles off in the middle of a prairie, grazing. Fortunately I was to leeward of them so that I walked up to within half a mile of them & then crept, the last quarter flat on the ground wriggling along until I had wormed myself within fair shooting distance a hundred odd yards I suppose. This old chap was standing in deep meditation & I picked him out from among the herd as the King of Buffalo. Not daring to creep closer for one or two were already looking at me, I took aim & fired. All the herd were off like a flash & one must be there to appreciate how the Earth trembles & rumbles when four or five hundred buffalo stampeed [sic]. My old bull fell on his knees with blood streaming from behind his shoulder but as I arose from my recumbent position he did likewise & with tail erect & eyes bloodshot to that extent they looked as if they were bleeding prepared to charge. There was nothing for it but shooting for a mad buffalo charging you on an open prairie is not to be sneezed at; so down I squatted again & taking the best shot I could I broke his shoulder blade. He charged just the same but round in a circle, pawing & goring the ground & rolling over & over again, affording the grandest specimen of brute rage you can imagine. At last he wore himself out; though still I had to keep behind his head out of sight; & I finished him with one other shot. That is the history of the head.[35]

Arriving in Dallas, "Jack & I were much amused at the various personages we were taken for and the sensation we made. I was taken first for a buffalo hunter & skinner, then last but by no means least for an English lord."[36]

During his Texas sojourn Elliott began an account of his adventures in the form of a mock newspaper called "Vox Buffalorum," the first issue of which is dated January 14, 1877, "terms of subscription one pipe full of tobacco, per diem (strictly in advance)." It is remarkable for the light-hearted and inconsequential nature of its entries, in which Elliott refers to his friends as The Great Mogul, The Great Kangaroo, and The Great Dirty Face, and to himself as The Great Grub Stower.

This paper contains many sporting, artistic, scientific, classic, physic, and sick interests and no decent hunter with any pretensions to literary taste or to one grain of sense could possibly be without it.

Salutatory

We have just assumed the immense responsibility of editing this paper so justly popular and so strictly moral.

We are duly impressed with the importance of our mission and with the great influence it must have on the human race at large but we have full confidence in our own power and feel perfectly able to edit this or any other paper. Our Staff consists of the Great High Buf-falo Editor, The Great Fighting Kangaroo Editor and the Devil. Should any one feel offended at any editorial remark we will imme-diately refer him to the two last named members of the Staff.[37]

One odd feature of Elliott's writing at this time is his occasional reference to himself in the third person as "she" and "her." Whether this reveals, in Blanche Cook's phrase, "a remarkable gender confusion"[38] or if Elliott saw himself as a weakling and as girlish in comparison with his more aggressive brother is unclear, but it is curious nevertheless.

Wanted

Somebody to help Nell keep her attire in order. A Respectable colored person can make good wages and will be paid by the camp at large.

Local item

Our distinguished friend Jack appeared at the breakfast post with a clean face. We are proud to take notice and applaud such energy and go aheadiveness especially when we take into consideration its previous nasty appearance and the amount of labor it must have taken to arrive at the happy result.

Apprehensions having been entertained that Nell was sick on account of her only having eaten one quail and a prairie chicken at breakfast one day. We beg to inform her many friends that she has since recovered and is now able to tackle four rabbits. She was last seen chasing Tar to recapture a side of bacon.[39]

We would delicately suggest to Pat that the camp water bucket is not the proper place for the tail of his coat.

Conundrums

Why is Nell the politest of the hunters?

Because she misses all the game. — Editor

The above is a calumny. — Nell

… Tar ran after a rabbit today — needless to say he did not catch it.

A great disturbance occurred last night amongst the canine fraternity. We expect from the peculiar nature of the sounds heard that Curly and some common cur such as Jim fell out and she went for him. Pat is respectfully requested to tune his snore or stop it altogether as it sounds at present like the rasping of a file on a cross cut saw with bovine accompaniment. The Editorial person was stepped on by some disrespectful fellow going out of the tent this morning. A repetition of the occurrence will call forth a stern rebuke.

Wanted

An antidote for bad puns.[40]

To know the exact amount Nell can eat at one sitting.

Nell has killed her first buffalo. We are afraid that she will fall over backwards she holds her head so high up.[41]

Dress Yourselves

We are very much grieved to notice that some of the Buffs are very negligent in their dress. Why can they not take pattern from us? It is as easy to be nice in camp as in town.[42]

Vox Populi

We all like perfume; it is healthy, refreshing, tickles the nasal organs, makes music up one's nose, paints flowers on one's mind, engraves sweet recollections on one's memory. But Oh Ye Gods: a perverted smeller is of all things hideous the most frightful. The Great Dirty Face delights in a skunk. Oh ye Stars: fall on him obliterate him grind him into a pole cat turn his nose into a carrot (it is now a turnip), put his head in a wash tub, make a pumpkin of him but save us from all his sort.[43]

Foreign Intelligence

Two buffalo hunters came into camp and told a lot of lies. Quite refreshing to hear something from abroad.[44]

At Last

We see the Great Dirty Face looking very solemn of late, we see deep thought in his eye (we cannot see his face). When he takes off his belt he does it with a great deliberation, looks uneasy and we presume from these and other symptoms that he is going to wash himself.[45]

In some ways Elliott was wise in advance of his years. In "Vox Buffalorum" he made the perceptive observation that "a satirical portraiture is always over drawn, never charitable and seldom veritable."[46]

We are proud to be able to commend the Buffs on their continued good spirits and have no particular fault to find, for with a few exceptions the high moral Buff character has been sustained and stern discipline has been the order of the day. We have been compelled to administer sundry chastisements to Pat, Nell and Jack the Great Mogul but in all instances Justice has been tempered with mercy and by dint of a little judicious rubbing the offenders have been restored to their sorrowing friends as well as ever. We think however that a little more respect shown to our editorial selves would redound to the credit of the camp at large, with this remark we close our summary.[47]

Our subscriptions come in slowly; where is that Tobacco?

Item

One pair of Nell's specks gone up salt creek.

Found

By Nell the appetite of a half-famished cur. The White Grub Stower smoked his first pipe of Tobacco on Wednesday night. Old Grub emptied his pipe in two shakes of a deer's tail and retired from view (we suppose to say his evening prayers which were longer and more feverish than usual). Never mind Old Grubby, Rome was not built in one day. So pull away and Nil desparandum [sic].

Weather Items

Lots of water above beneath around. We would suggest to the brother Buffs to keep their old wet duds from about our bunk. Give unto Caesar only that which belongs unto Caesar.[48]

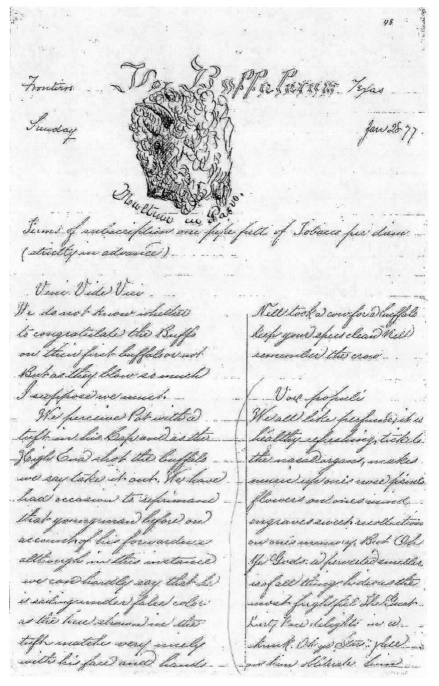

"Vox Buffalorum," Elliott's newsletter sent to his family. Courtesy of The Franklin D. Roosevelt Presidential Library.

From "Vox Buffalorum." Elliott's drawings illustrated his misadventures in Texas. Courtesy of The Franklin D. Roosevelt Presidential Library.

From "Vox Buffalorum." Courtesy of The Franklin D. Roosevelt Presidential Library.

From "Vox Buffalorum." Courtesy of The Franklin D. Roosevelt Presidential Library.

From "Vox Buffalorum." Courtesy of The Franklin D. Roosevelt Presidential Library.

From "Vox Buffalorum." Courtesy of The Franklin D. Roosevelt Presidential Library.

⚜5⚜

"Thoroughly and Strangely Unselfish"

Theodore Roosevelt, Sr. had never made a serious foray into the world of politics, preferring to spend his energy in private philanthropy; but this changed in 1876. For several years both the New York Republican Party and the United States Senate had been dominated by the charismatic and arrogant Senator Roscoe Conkling. A politician to the core — attractive, proud, brilliant, loose in his morals ("too good-looking to be pure," some said).[1] Conkling could not help but be offensive to Theodore Sr. and his idealistic friends, who abhorred his "business as usual" attitude and his tolerance of corrupt practices. Conkling, in turn, had nothing but contempt for men who related well to the particularly needy and who demanded honesty in government, dismissing them as "old maids," "men-milliners"[2] with nothing else to do. Conkling was a "Stalwart," an intimate of President Grant and very much at ease with the scandal-ridden Grant administration.

Theodore Sr. was appalled by the excesses of Grant's second term and became involved in an insurgency to wrest control of the Republican Party from sly politicians like Conkling and not a few of Grant's other associates. This movement was headed by *Harper's Weekly* editor George

William Curtis and Senator Carl Schurz — "Lincoln Republicans," as was Theodore himself. Curtis had built his life, and his newspaper, around the idea that it was the prerogative of educated, conscientious men to take charge of public affairs. He saw in Theodore Sr. the embodiment of his hope for the country, a man who "walked these streets the image and figure of the citizen which every American should hope to be."[3] They knew each other socially, since each frequented the Century Association and the Union League Club, which organized a Republican Reform Club.

Their deepest fear was that Roscoe Conkling would succeed Grant to the presidency. "From the moment he let his presidential aspirations be known," David McCullough writes, "there seemed to be a smell of brimstone in the air."

The notion that was most offensive to Roosevelt, Schurz, Curtis, and their supporters was that the party, and partisan politics, were to be given more consideration than the best interests of the country as a whole. This was a system based on patronage, on "spoils," on everything except merit and disinterestedness. Conkling did nothing for which he could be indicted; he simply controlled the system in New York and thrived on the way in which things were done.

The Republican Reform Club attended the G.O.P. convention in Cincinnati, where they hoped to nominate a man with a stainless record, Benjamin H. Bristow of Kentucky. Although Bristow was Secretary of the Treasury in the Grant administration, he uncovered one of the many scandals therein, and the reformers trusted him. Theodore Sr. made many new friends at the convention, including literary men James Russell Lowell and Richard Henry Dana.

Theodore Sr.'s great moment came when he made a speech from the balcony of the inn where he was staying. Although no text has been preserved of this address, apparently it was so trenchant an indictment of

Conkling and Conkling's system that it was enough to turn that master politician into a vindictive enemy.

The Republican Reform Club succeeded in thwarting Roscoe Conkling's presidential ambitions, and the nomination went to Governor Rutherford B. Hayes of Ohio, who had a sturdy enough reputation for probity to satisfy the reformers, but was not so strident in his rectitude as to offend the "bosses."

When Hayes won the election, he sent Conkling's circle into a tailspin by floating the idea of freshening the air at the New York Customhouse by replacing Conkling's man Chester Alan Arthur with a man above reproach — Theodore Roosevelt.

The chief officer of the customhouse, known as the Collector of the Port of New York, made more money than the president of the United States; the revenues collected at the Port of New York were greater than those of all the other ports of entry in the country; the responsibility of the position was enormous. The collector presided over more than a thousand customs brokers, collectors, and clerks who carried on their business in a gigantic building that foreshadowed Grand Central Station, with its conspicuous clock in the center of the ground floor and the constant flow of human traffic within its walls.

Chester Arthur emerged from the genteel poverty into which he was born to this position of power and influence. The son of an Irish immigrant Baptist minister, Arthur was born, not in a log cabin, but in a tiny frame house in Vermont. He was a respected public servant, his reputation tainted only by his association with Conkling. The movement to replace Arthur was a direct affront to Conkling.

Early in his tenure, President Hayes issued an order forbidding assessments of civil service workers based on party affiliation or favors owed to any political party, and preventing civil service employees at the federal level from any role in the conduct of party business — another attempt to strike a blow at Roscoe Conkling's empire. Hayes offered Chester Arthur the post of U.S. Consul in Paris, which Arthur refused; he loved being Collector of the Port of New York.

Despite Arthur's refusal, Hayes stood firm in his attempt to replace Arthur with Theodore Roosevelt, whose name was synonymous with integrity and who would make of the customhouse something more than an opportunity for political hacks to pursue their own financial interests through transactions that stretched the law to its limit.

Conkling was enraged that his crony was about to be removed, and as head of the Senate Committee on Commerce, he was in a position to do something about it. He denounced Roosevelt, Hayes, and those who comprised the Republican Reform Club as men "who believe themselves to occupy the solar walk and the milky way, and even up there, they lift their skirts very carefully for fear even the heavens might stain them. ... They would have people fill the offices by nothing less than divine selection." In an executive session of the Commerce Committee, Conkling took over an hour to denounce Theodore Roosevelt, Sr. in bitter personal terms, calling Theodore his "enemy." The senators on the committee owed it to the voters they represented, Conkling said, to reject Theodore Roosevelt.

Conkling got his way. Roosevelt's nomination was defeated by a vote of thirty-one to twenty-five. "A great weight was taken off my shoulders when Elliott read the other morning that the Senate had decided not to confirm me,"[4] Theodore wrote to his eldest son at Harvard.

No one can imagine the relief. To purify our Customhouse was a terrible undertaking which I felt it was my duty to undertake but I realized all the difficulties I would encounter and the abuse I must expect to receive. I feel now so glad I did not refuse it. The machine politicians have shown their colors and not one person has been able to make an accusation of any kind against me.

Theodore Roosevelt, Senior, who "went about doing good." Circa 1875. Courtesy of The Houghton Library, Harvard University.

Indeed, they have all done me more than justice. I never told your mother but it would have practically kept me in the city most all the time in summer and that would be no joke. I feel sorry for the country, however, as it shows the power of the partisan politicians who think of nothing higher than their own interests. I fear for your future. We cannot stand so corrupt a government for any great length of time.

Shortly afterward, when events took an unexpected turn, the editorial in *The New York World* read as though it could have been written by Henry Adams:

Men in like positions of business and society [to that of Theodore Roosevelt] are as a rule incapable of taking a genuine or sustained interest in anything beyond their own business. ... It is also a fact worth reflecting upon that in New York, at least, the proper arena of a solid, intelligent and public-spirited citizen is closed to such a citizen. Clearly the natural place for such a man as Mr. Roosevelt is in the councils of the city he wished to serve. In New York such a man could not be chosen to the city council, would not serve if he could be chosen, and if he could be chosen and would serve, would be perfectly impotent and feel entirely out of place. A century ago the list of the Aldermen of New York was the likeliest place to look for its most esteemed inhabitants. A comparison of those lists with the lists of recent Boards of Aldermen may be partly the effect and partly the cause of the decay of public spirit among the respectable citizens of New York, to whom we commend the comparison as instructive and suggestive.[5]

Elliott Roosevelt received the first crushing blow of his life less than two months later. His father, whom he loved "so dearly" and who had set him such a beautiful example, died after much suffering, all of which was witnessed by Elliott. A malignant tumor had developed in Theodore's bowel and was crushing his intestines; it would take a breathtakingly brief amount of time for him to die.

The poignant, anomalous sight of this good man on the rack of pain dislodged something inside of Elliott. It is impossible to say exactly what happened to Elliott's sense of himself and of his place in the world. Perhaps he came to believe that all good men, like his father, were destroyed by lesser men; perhaps his faith collapsed like a house of cards that he never was able to reconstruct. Perhaps he was unable to face the pain and grief connected with his father's death, and at the same time was unable to get past it — so that the image of his suffering father floated in and out of his dreams and distracted him during his waking hours.

Like his father, Elliott loved to entertain; he thrived on making people laugh and cheering them with loving gestures. Perhaps Elliott's cultivation of his charm, his love of sport and (in the opinion of some) his nearly frivolous ability to concentrate on hunting and riding and sailing, his absorption in the social scene, his pursuit of pleasure — perhaps these were his way of avoiding the implications of his father's premature, painful death. "Thoroughly and strangely unselfish, with untiring energy and bright cheerfulness, he literally 'went about doing good,'" wrote Theodore Sr.'s friend William Dodge in a letter to Joseph Choate of the Union League Club.[6] Indeed, what meaning could be found in the frustration of the hopes of Theodore Sr. by a man like Roscoe Conkling?

The younger Theodore Roosevelt would spend the rest of his life preaching righteousness, exhorting men and women to good deeds, using the presidency itself as a "bully pulpit." It would seem as though Theodore Jr. sought out evil in order to have an enemy to fight. Theodore's character was patterned consciously after that of his father. It may be that Elliott felt unfit for such an inheritance — that he lacked the moral fiber, the strength, the concentration. Knowing that he could never live up to his father's example, he may have decided that it was futile even to try.

As time went on, the more Elliott failed, the more disgusted with himself he became. Possibly he found it difficult to believe that there was any redemption for him, coming to believe that he was a weakling and a reprobate and not worth saving, his gifts of humility and diffidence souring into self-pity.

At seventeen Elliott nursed his father through his last hours and served as "the midwife of his death."

It happened quickly.

On December 11, Theodore Sr. found that he had been rejected for the post of Collector of the Port of New York. December 16, he wrote the letter to Theodore Jr. in which he expressed his fear for the future of his country and of his son. December 18, Aunt Annie Gracie wrote in her diary: "Ellie stopped on his way downtown, said his father was taken very ill around 4 o'clock this morning. Bamie's party tonight. I saw Thee before I went into drawing rm., very ill. Conie sat with him until two o'clock." On Christmas Day she wrote: "Saw dear Thee a short time before we went to church. Afternoon sat with him while Bamie rested. He made us all but Mittie go in to Xmas dinner. ..."

Elliott's father's hair turned gray overnight. He frightened Elliott by saying, "Nellie when I am gone you must take my place in tenderness and care of your mother." Theodore Sr. spoke to Elliott about the importance of prayer and told him to continue the ritual of prayers in the evening with his family. "Tho' I don't talk of these things much Nell I think of them all the time." He "was in fearful agony," Corinne wrote to her friend Edith Carow. "Oh, Edith, it is the most frightful thing to see the person you love best in the world in terrible pain ..."[7]

His pain came and went. A couple of mornings, he felt well enough to be taken for rides in his sleigh with Bamie. But when they came back, the pain returned, worse than ever.

When news of the severity of Theodore Sr.'s illness reached his friends, the Roosevelts were visited by a stream of callers asking if they could be of any assistance. Gathered outside his home were the once-homeless children who owed their safety and their shelter to Mr. Roosevelt.[8]

Elliott, who was unable to eat or sleep, never left his father's side; he nursed his father, said Corinne, "with a devotion so tender it was more like that of a woman."[9] Elliott expressed his torment in this composition on his father's last hours:

Feb. 9, 1878

This morning at ten while I was sitting in my room smoking, Corinne ran in and said, "Ellie, Father wants to be moved, will you come upstairs?" I went immediately and found Father still under the influences of sedatives, sitting on the rocking chair in the morning room. As I came he beckoned to me. I ran to him and ... my arms about him, he got up and with my help tottered to the mantel. Here suddenly his face became distorted with pain and he called out loud for ether. I left him, got the bottle and taking him in my arms put him on the sofa and drenching the handkerchief I held it on his face. Mother, Bamie, and Mary Ann [a servant] came up and we sent for the doctor. This was 10:15. From then until 11:30 all the strength I had could barely keep him on the sofa. He never said anything but "Oh! My!" but the agony in his face was awful. Ether and sedatives were of no avail. Little Mother stood by with a glass of water which I drank at intervals, being deathly sick. Pretty soon Father began to vomit after which he would be quiet a minute, then with face fearful with pain [he] would clasp me tight in his arms. ... The power with which he could hug me was terrific and then in a second he would be lying, white, panting, and weak as a baby in my arms with sweat in huge drops rolling down his face and neck. ... At 11:30, thank God, the doctor came. I ran up to the Ellises, found Dr. Thomas and returned to find the doctor about to give Father chloroform. On its application Father became quiet instantly but the two doctors despaired of his life and from then until 1:30 Mother sat at his head and I by him with the chloro[form] and handkerchief. We put him from one chloro[form] sleep into another ... Dr. Polk relieved Mother and I at 1:30 when we tried to take a bit of lunch. The afternoon Dr. Polk, Mother, Uncle Jim, [Dr.] Thomas, and I were by his side all the time. ... At 6:30 Mother and I went down and tried to eat dinner. I felt so sick I stayed to smoke a cigar and after felt well and more myself. I stayed in the little room with Uncle Corneil and Jim and Aunts Laura and Lizzie ... Going upstairs at 7:30 I found the servants in the hall waiting with scared faces in Corinne's room, Aunt A[nna], B[amie], and C[onie] all in tears. Mother, Dr.'s Polk and Goldthwait and Uncle Jimmie by the bedside. Father seemed the same but his pulse much feebler. Dr. P[olk], Bamie, and C[onie] went to bed. Uncle Jim came up and Mother and the two uncles and Dr. G[oldthwait] and watched. Oh, my God, my Father what agonies you suffered. ... So it went on. At eleven fifteen he opened his eyes. I motioned to the Dr. who applied the tube and brandy to his mouth. He did not make an effort to suck even. We put the glass up and dropped it [the brandy] down. He turned sharp to the left and throwing up his arms around, he gave one mighty clasp and then with a groan of pain turned over and with his right hand under his head and left out over the side of the sofa began the gurgling breathing of death. ... And then Dr. Polk sitting by his side. Mother kneeling by him. Bamie by her. The little Baby [Corinne] trembling and crying, kneeling by me on his left side and all the rest standing near. His eyelids fluttered, he gave three long breaths. It is finished. No, my God, it cannot be. "Darling, darling, darling, I am here," cried my little widowed mother. I knelt down and prayed, "Our Father which art in heaven, hallowed be Thy name, Thy will be done, Thy will be done." As the last breath left his body the little clock on the table struck one — one half past eleven. Thirteen and a quarter hours of agony it took to kill a man broken down by three months sickness.

We got the girls and Mother to bed. The uncles watched the dead. I lay down on the sofa in Father's dressing room but not to sleep;[10] if only I didn't have to meet Theodore tomorrow and tell him all, and I promised if there was danger to have him there, may God forgive me.[11]

Elliott could not believe what had just happened. "I went in three times during the night to see Father but it was all over."[12] "... He had been prostrated by some insidious disease, the character of which the physicians were unable to positively ascertain,"[13] reported *The New York Herald,* but *The New York World* declared that Theodore died "by strangulation of the intestines."[14] "Mr. Roosevelt's disease was a malignant fibrous tumor which was imbedded in the convolutions of the anterior portion of the peritoneum,"[15] Joseph Pulitzer's journal explained helpfully.

Theodore Roosevelt, Sr. was laid out in the parlor of his home at 6 West 57th Street in a plain rosewood coffin with a plate reading:

Theodore Roosevelt
born September 22, 1831
died February 9, 1878

Theodore's brothers Robert, James, Alfred, Cornelius, Hiram, and Clinton were present to help the immediate family receive guests. The Rev. Dr. John Hall of Fifth Avenue Presbyterian Church prayed briefly over the casket before it was closed and covered with a black velvet pall. Dr. Hall and his colleague, The Rev. Dr. William Adams, President of Union Theological Seminary,[16] led a funeral procession two blocks down Fifth Avenue from Fifty-seventh Street to the church at Fifty-fifth Street. The pallbearers, who included Theodore's friends William Dodge and Joseph Choate, carried the casket up the main aisle to the chancel while the organist played a dirge. As Elliott looked around at those who came to pay their respects to his father, he saw among them Morris Jessup, J. Pierpont Morgan, Hugh Auchincloss, and the mayor of New York. A quartet, which included one of Elliott's uncles, sang the hymn "Art Thou Weary, Art Thou Languid?" Dr. Hall then read from Psalms, "Lord, thou hast been our dwelling place in all generations,"[17] "having reference to the righteous man's hope in God and his trust in life beyond the grave."[18] The quartet then sang "Safe in the Arms of Jesus." Dr. Adams told the mourners:

It is no perfunctory service which we are called to render on this occasion. This large assemblage of sorrowful men testifies to unfeigned grief. The death of this friend is a public loss. How intimately he was associated with art and public affairs; how many there are who have been recipients of his kindness — occupants of tenement-houses, the newsboy on his cheerless round, the cripple in the hospital. All these will speak tenderly of him who was so much to them. He never would have applied the words of the patriarch to himself, but we may fitly apply them to him: "He was eyes to the blind, feet was he to the lame, and a father was he to the poor." More than twenty years ago, when he was a young man, it was my privilege to introduce him to the communion of the Christian church. And from that time till the close of my pastorate, I sustained intimate relations with him. At the very outset of his Christian career he formed a purpose which has been developed in all forms of Christian philanthropy. He gave his time, his sympathy and his help, summer and winter, year after year. It was not by proxy, it was not by the giving of money, that he was able to do so much, but it was by personal sympathy and a genial manner that he was able to diffuse so much light in so many homes. He was in personal connection with as many philanthropic interests as any one who could be named. The end of his work is not yet. ... It is the lesson of the hour. There is a charity based upon educated Christian principles, as there is one based upon charitable instinct, a mere impulse. That impulse may be strong; it may be weak. It is like giving a cup of water to the thirsty, but this charity of principle and Christian purpose is like digging a well which shall quench the thirst of thousands after its water has passed away. It is a great mystery to which we bow, that one in his ripeness should be so cut off. This is an unfinished state of things in which we are now. We are moving toward that place where all these things shall find their consummation in another and better life.[19]

"The venerable Dr. Adams," reported *The New York World*, was "listened to with the deepest attention, and the voice of the speaker oft broken with the feelings that nearly at times overmastered him, was only interrupted by tokens of grief from the congregation. ... He could see the expression of grief reflected on the faces of the large assemblage before him."[20] The family then followed the sixteen carriages in the funeral train and a hearse drawn by two horses "unplumed and plainly caparisoned" that took Theodore Sr. to the family plot at Green-Wood Cemetery in Brooklyn.

All who knew Theodore Sr. gathered strength from his kindness. "He took life with great seriousness, but he took it laughing, which meant that to him all activity, however difficult, was a source of enjoyment; to him there was no such thing as a chore."[21]

Upon hearing of the death of Theodore, William A. Booth, president of the Children's Aid Society, called a meeting in which to compose this message:

There is given to some men such a rare combination of thought and action that the two processes become almost identical; and when these are associated with a high moral purpose, the results are of a character which exceed estimation. Of such was Mr. Roosevelt. But the qualities which will always most endear his memory to those for whom he performed his cheerful service were the warmth and sincerity with which he maintained his personal relations with the poor and unbefriended. The power of conferring an obligation without its being felt, and the personal sympathy which made every newsboy in the institution, which he had adopted as his peculiar charge, feel that he was his own individual friend, and would continue so through life, ... The trustees of the Children's Aid Society, on behalf of themselves and those associated with them as teachers, and of the many thousands of young children who have known his voice as that of their best friend, desire to make this record of their affection and esteem for their associate, friend and benefactor Theodore Roosevelt, now taken from them by death.[22]

Theodore Sr. set the standard for the Roosevelt tradition of service; perhaps his chief legacy to his children was his teaching that goodness and joy were synonymous. "Remember that almost everyone will be kind to you and love you if you only are willing to receive their love and are unselfish," he had written to Corinne on her birthday. "This, you know, is the virtue that I put above all others and, while it increases so much the enjoyment of those about you, it adds infinitely to your own pleasure ..."[23]

A few minutes after his father died, Elliott heard Mittie, who had never been as vocal about her faith as her husband, say to her daughters, "I expect he is safe in the arms of Jesus now." "Yes my little bereaved Mother. He is,"[24] Elliott wrote in his diary; still, he could not help being nearly as nonplussed as the obituary writer for *The Nation*: "[Theodore] was … physically so vigorous and manly a man that there was every reason for believing as well as for wishing that he would reach old age; and his untimely end, in the midst of everything that could make life attractive, is perhaps as striking a reminder as his friends could receive what shadows we are and what shadows we pursue."[25]

⊰❦6❦⊱

"I Enjoy Being with the Old Boy So Much"

"**W**e have been fortunate," wrote Theodore Roosevelt, Jr., "in having a father whom we can love and respect more than any other man in the world." It is impossible to overestimate the effect of the loss of his father upon Elliott Roosevelt. Theodore Sr.'s death had been neither quick enough for his family to be grateful that he had not suffered nor lingering enough for them to be relieved that his ordeal had ended. Instead, the Roosevelts had been tortured by the worst of both scenarios intrinsic to a death in the family: Theodore was heartbreakingly young — only forty-six; and as his youngest daughter had written, there is no torture like that of watching the person one loves the most in great pain and feeling powerless to help. "Oh my God my Father," wrote Elliott, "what agonies you suffered. ... So ended the life of a man who walked with God." Even the newspaper headlines agreed with Elliott.[1] *The New York World* (Feb. 15, 1878) told of "... The Manly and Christian Life That So Suddenly Ended." This article quoted Theodore Sr.'s friend Joseph Choate, who considered "Mr. Roosevelt as the most unselfish citizen of all the unselfish citizens in this great city, and that although Mr. Roosevelt was only in the forty-eighth [sic] year of his age, he had accomplished

more good than men who had led active lives for many more years than
Mr. Roosevelt had been spared in which to do his good work among men."

Elliott pasted all of the obituaries for his father in his scrapbook. He
found that his father was even the subject of a sermon.

The Rev. Dr. Henry C. Potter, of Grace Church, took for his subject yesterday the spiritual difficulties attending the possession
of great wealth. His text was the illustration of the camel and
the needle's eye. This, he said, presented a discouraging prospect
to men of wealth and was meant to do so. "Wealth is, or seems
to be," Dr. Potter said, "such a considerable power in the world
that the Church has tried in many ages to acquire and wield it
— the Pope dying worth $22,000,000. The progress of all good
enterprises seems to be so largely dependent upon it that there
is a natural temptation, in speaking to men of wealth, to soften
the language of the text. But wealth has its place and office in
the constitution of our moral society and in the Church of God.
Distribution of the riches of the wealthy in indiscriminate lar-
gesses to the poor would be no boon, but an evil. There were rich
men in the early Church, also, but they held their riches subject
to their loyalty to Christ. Money has a singular power to brutal-
ize men, and the lust of it can transform a noble nature into an
unscrupulous, reckless one. It can make men utterly insensible to
life and to heavenly aspirations. In these hard times such admo-
nitions, some of us think, have about as much appropriateness as
temperance to a man whose diet is bread and water. But the question whether people are unduly influenced by love of riches is best
answered by the way in which such persons bear hard times. It
is the temper with which a man parts with a thing which shows
how much he values it."

Theodore Roosevelt's life, Dr. Potter continued, was "at once a poem and a benediction." He was "a man thoroughly alive to his finger-ends … conspicuously exposed to the dangers of the possessors of great wealth," and yet no one, Dr. Potter asserted, ever thought of Theodore's money, or thought to ask "so beggarly a question as, 'What did he leave?'" He left "the fragrance of a good name … His visage stamped in the hearts of thousands of men and women and children, whose lives [he] had brightened and ennobled and blessed … Above all, [he] left a lesson to you and me, to say to wealth, You are my servant and not my master."

One wonders how well Dr. Potter's affluent congregation took to this "lesson," but the Rector realized that "Theodore Roosevelt, in the Newsboys' Lodging-house, in the Cripples' Home, in the heart of the little Italian flower girl, who brought her offering of grateful love to his door the day he died, … left behind [him] monuments, the like of which mere wealth could never rear, and the proudest achievements of human genius never hope to win."[2]

This was indeed the crippling blow of Elliott's life, but from what, specifically, did he never recover? The premature death of one's father was hardly a novelty in the late nineteenth century. Was it simply that he found himself suddenly bereft of guidance from the man who had been his wisest and most understanding friend? Was it his faith that was shaken — faith in a benevolent God who rewards the righteous; faith in himself and in his own talents and abilities (he was never sure of these); faith that events work to some good purpose? His father's goodness was extraordinary. His description in the newspapers can only be called Christ-like: "It might truly be said of him that eyes was he to the blind, feet was he to the lame and a father was he to the poor. … The qualities that most endeared his memory were the warmth and sincerity with which he maintained his personal relations with the poor and unfriended."

The death of Theodore Sr. cut the ground out from under Elliott. He was left without an anchor or a confidante. From Harvard, his brother Theodore wrote, "When I fully realize the extent of my loss, I think I shall go mad." But Theodore did not have it in him to go mad. Theodore's lifelong approach to tragedy was to avoid dealing with it by burying himself in his work and in his interests. He considered it morbid to focus on anything other than getting on with life, forcing his pain under until it was "too dead to throb." A few years later, when his first wife died, Theodore ripped all references to her out of his diary, never spoke of her again (not even to their daughter), and made no mention of her in his memoirs. Elliott did not have that kind of emotional discipline, and he was of a different temperament entirely.

Theodore continued to flourish at Harvard, despite the intensity of his grief. A few months previously he had written that he could say truly that he had never spent an unhappy day that was not his own fault, a remarkable statement considering his struggles with both asthma and the bullying of more robust boys. With his father's encouragement and direction he overcame these challenges, but his father's death was Theodore's first experience with a vicissitude over which he had no control.

In their loneliness the brothers turned to each other. It became important to them to pursue solitary pastimes in remote areas where they would not be distracted by others — and this often meant hunting. In December of 1879, Theodore and Elliott sailed a twenty-one-foot sloop off Long Island Sound in search of ducks. With Elliott at the helm, they broke through the ice close to the shore, and as the boat glided through the open water, the boys spied a flock of ducks and shot furiously. Feathers covered the sloop, reminding the boys of a pillow fight. They were enjoying themselves to such an extent that they failed to take note of the increasingly inclement weather until the sky grew too dark to ignore. Tiny icicles dripped from Elliott's beard as he peered into the freezing wind, keeping a resolute hold on the tiller as he led the boat to shore.

Suddenly a much larger vessel appeared through the mist and threatened to collide with the sloop, but Elliott managed to hold to his course and pilot his boat back to shore, by which time he and Theodore were so exhausted and frozen that it was all they could do to let down the sails. Theodore still greatly admired Elliott. "He kept his eyes steadily ahead," Theodore wrote, "not flinching for an instant although the cold was terribly bitter."[3]

Theodore was saved from prolonged grief by the entrance of his first love. Alice Lee was a Boston debutante courted by Theodore with all the determination he could muster, which was of course considerable. When at long last she accepted him, Elliott, in a characteristically gracious gesture, organized a luncheon and a dance at Boston's Jerome Park in Alice's honor. On a clear winter day three large sleighs carted the guests over the powdery snow in what must have been one of Theodore's happiest days as Alice was welcomed into the Roosevelt family.

Elliott paid frequent visits to his brother at Harvard, where their athletic competitions continued. "As athletes we are about equal," Theodore wrote. "He runs best, I row best. He can beat me sailing or swimming; I can beat him wrestling and boxing. I am best with the rifle, he with the shotgun, etc., etc."[4]

Elliott went to work in the office of his uncle James Gracie at a bank in Lower Manhattan. During the summer months he lived with his mother at Tranquility, the Roosevelt home in Oyster Bay, and commuted into the city. Each of Theodore Sr.'s four children inherited roughly $125,000, which translated into a yearly income of around $8,000, so that Elliott was under no financial obligation to work. This, too, was disastrous.

Without his father to guide and encourage him in more serious pursuits, it was inevitable that Elliott would spend more and more time exercising his charm in the social world and on the playing field, two areas where he knew that he could shine. His inheritance created a situation in which all he had to worry about was choosing the manner of entertaining himself.

With Theodore's marriage imminent, the brothers spent as much time as they could together, as though they knew that they were about to be engulfed by the adult world and its mysterious responsibilities.

Theodore had a bout with illness during the summer of 1880 while on a visit to Bar Harbor, Maine, with Alice Lee and their friends Dick and Rose Saltonstall. Turning to the family's all-purpose remedy — travel — the brothers took one last adventure together. They would go hunting in the Wild West — or rather, the Wild Middle West: Illinois, Iowa, and Minnesota. While still in Chestnut Hill, Alice's home in Massachusetts, Theodore wrote to Nannie, wife of their friend John Ellis Roosevelt, "… Just think of my feelings tomorrow as I leave Alice for six weeks! Really, Nannie, you don't know how blue I feel over the prospect. I am going off to Minnesota, with Nell, for some prarie [sic] chicken shooting; I love hunting, but I hate to leave Alice. …" This is the only known time Theodore ever signed himself "Teddy Roosevelt."[5]

Before they set off they posed together in a photographer's studio. With a fake rural scene behind them, the young men have almost exaggeratedly serious looks on their faces; Elliott appears convincingly to be leaning against a tree. They are wearing tall hunting boots and small white hats with the brims turned up. We see Theodore's face before he covered it with a moustache, framed by mutton chop whiskers; he looks resolute as he stares straight ahead, cradling his gun. Elliott, leaning his chin on his hand, looks at Theodore; he is at his most handsome, sporting a beard, pocket watch, and pipe.

Although the boys did not make it as far as the territory Theodore called "the Far West … the real West," they did well enough in the Middle West, at least as far as hunting was concerned. They managed to shoot over four hundred birds! Ducks, geese, grouse — it was open season.

But letters from both brothers show that the real fun was in just being together. "I am so glad … we two brothers have been able at last to be together … All the happier we are solely dependent on each other for companionship," wrote Elliott to Bamie. This was echoed by Theodore, who wrote simply, "I enjoy being with the old boy so much."[6]

Even so, the sojourn was shadowed by a reminder of Theodore's old torment and a foreshadowing of Elliott's nightmare.

From time to time, the young men ventured into Chicago to get supplies and decide where they wanted to go next. "I think [Theodore] misses Alice, poor dear old beloved brother. But I try to keep him at something all the time and certainly he looks a hundred percent better than when he came out,"[7] Elliott wrote to their older sister, adding that their brother was "as brown and well as can be." But a few days later, in Minnesota, Theodore had a devastating attack of asthma that kept him awake all night, having to sit up in order to take what breaths he could.

On their return to Chicago after a week in Iowa, Theodore wrote to Corinne that Elliott reveled in "the change to civilization," but for an alarming reason:

As soon as we got here he took some ale to get the dust out of his throat; then a milk punch because he was thirsty; a mint julep because it was hot; a brandy smash 'to keep the cold out of his stomach'; and then sherry and bitters to give him an appetite. He took a very simple dinner — soup, fish, salmi de grouse, sweetbread, mutton, venison, corn, macaroni, various vegetables and some puddings and pies, together with beer, later claret and in the evening shandygaff. Elliott says these remarks are incorrect and malevolent; but I say they pay him off for his last letter about my eating manners.[8]

Whether Theodore was attempting to make Corinne laugh by describing their brother's mammoth appetites, warning her of impending trouble, or confirming a suspicion the two of them had already, we cannot say; but using the slightest excuse for a drink is a clear sign of alcoholic behavior.

The time Elliott spent among the rough characters in Texas had given him ease and confidence among people whose backgrounds were different

Alice Lee (center); Teddy Roosevelt (right) looks at her. Below them, left to right, are Elliott, Corinne, Bamie, and an unidentified friend. Photograph taken circa 1879 during Teddy's Harvard days. Courtesy of The Houghton Library, Harvard University.

from his; by contrast, as far as we know, this was Theodore's first journey west of Fifth Avenue. In the late summer the boys were befriended by some Illinois farmers. In a letter to his mother dated August 25th, Theodore wrote: "Last Sunday night we got this motley crew together to sing hymns. ... Thanks to Elliott it was a great success. It was all I could do to keep a sober face when I saw him singing from the same book with the much-flattered Mrs. Rudolf and Miss Costigan."[9]

When the brothers returned, they could look back on their haphazard trip as a time when their friendship was deepened and their admiration for each other was at its peak. Theodore made their mother happy by telling her that he wanted Elliott, and Elliott only, to be his best man at his wedding and that if Elliott were in India instead, then he would have no best man. In a prophetic letter to Bamie, written while out West, Elliott restated what he felt years before when he had told his father that Theodore was "a more sure kind of boy":

Thee is well able and no mistake — shrewd and clever, by no means behind his age. What I have often smiled at in the old boy are I am now sure some of his best points — a practical carrying out in action of what I, for example, am convinced of in theory, but fail to put in practice.[10]

Elliott was brilliant at what his niece Alice Longworth would call "elbow-in-the-soup treatment," meaning the ability to make anyone with whom he spoke feel that they were the most interesting person he had ever met. He was different from his brother in that he lacked what he called "that foolish grit of Theodore's."

"Perhaps there is no more important component of character than steadfast resolution," wrote President Theodore Roosevelt. "The boy who is going to make a great man, or who is going to count in any way in life, must make up his mind not merely to overcome a thousand obstacles, but to win in spite of a thousand repulses and defeats."[11]

There was another crucial difference, summed up by their sister Corinne: "If I were to do something he thought very weak or wrong, Theodore would never forgive me, whereas Elliott no matter how much he might despise the sin would forgive the sinner."[12]

⊰**7**⊱

"A Sluggard's Paradise"

O ver a century after it was commissioned, a flagon depicting a bespectacled hunter shooting a tiger while riding an elephant surfaced at York Town Auction, Inc., in Pennsylvania. The flagon was a gift to President Theodore Roosevelt from the Gould and Whitney families, but in 1958 a Roosevelt descendant in financial straits sold the flagon, with a note stating that the carved scene on the "loving cup" was of the president hunting with Mr. Gould and Mr. Whitney. All that was known for certain was that the design was ordered from Tiffany and Co. on December 16, 1896.

It soon became clear to researchers at York Town that, while Theodore Roosevelt never hunted in India and did not visit Africa until after he left the White House, Elliott Roosevelt traveled to India as a young man of twenty, and that he — not Theodore — was the figure whose image was carved on the flagon.[1]

Eleanor Roosevelt was proud of her father's prowess as a hunter and of the adventurous spirit that fueled his journey at such a young age. Always looking for some way in which to honor her father's memory, the year she became First Lady she edited his collected letters and published them in a volume called *Hunting Big Game in the 'Eighties*.

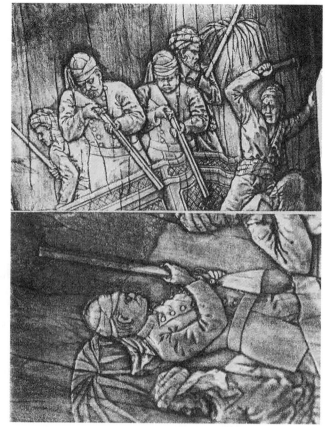

Elliott's image on a "loving cup" discovered in 1958. Courtesy of Wallace Dailey, Harvard University.

"The trip to India was made at a time when probably few young Americans had taken trips of that kind, and the opportunities which my father had, through the letters which were given him, made it a very unique experience," wrote Eleanor. "One cannot help but feel throughout these letters that he had a gift with people which made them gladly send him on to their friends, and they always seemed to do for him everything which could possibly be done. His illness, which he makes so light of in India, was really a very serious illness and I think explains the undermining of his constitution and probably was a factor in his early death."[2]

Always anxious to present her father in the best possible light, Eleanor subtitled her volume: *The Letters of Elliott Roosevelt, Sportsman,* "sportsman" being a more flattering noun, perhaps, than "playboy." Shooting and riding "seemed to be natural to him, whereas Uncle Ted acquired his skill through persistence and against great odds, for he was delicate as a boy and short-sighted all his life," wrote Eleanor. "No one could wonder therefore that after my grandfather's death when each child inherited his share of money [$125,000] my father then about twenty years old decided on a trip around the world instead of college, and planned to hunt the elephant and the tiger, a lure to every sportsman."[3]

Elliott's namesake grandson wrote that "… He paved the way for Uncle Ted, who became identified as a great African safari man. So Elliott, largely overlooked by history, emerged as a major influence on one President and, had an indirect role in the making of another."[4]

While Eleanor looked for every opportunity to compare Elliott favorably with Theodore, Elliott was not a competitive type and had no desire or inclination to outdo his brother in academic life. It was perhaps with a great sense of relief as well as excitement that he boarded the ship that

Loving cup, engraved with one of Elliott's adventures in India. Courtesy of Wallace Dailey, Harvard University.

would take him to Liverpool as the first stop on a sixteen-month tour.

This may have been the happiest time of Elliott's life, an idyll in which he could practice his charm and pursue his enthusiasms in exotic places. His talent for making friends ensured that the voyage to England was a joy.

One of these shipboard friends was Thomas Hughes, author of *Tom Brown's School Days*. "The pleasantest times have been the long talks and walks with dear old 'Tom Brown'," wrote Elliott. "He has been glorious to me. I dine with him next Sunday in London. He and I generally have a grand talk at dinner after which with our cigars we adjourn to 'The Captain's Cabin,' and continue the argument until I am called away by other evening engagements," including visiting a couple who "are kind enough to wish me to go to Cannes and play whist with them all winter! That's what it is to belong to the whist club."[5]

One wonders about Elliott's "long talks and walks" with Thomas Hughes, who must have reminded him of his brother Theodore. *Tom Brown's School Days* is a hymn to the sort of "muscular Christianity" that the Roosevelt sons were taught by their father and that Theodore Roosevelt exemplified. "Tom Brown" records that while listening to the school's headmaster:

We listened ... to a man we felt to be, with all his heart and soul and strength, striving against whatever was mean and unmanly and unrighteous in our little world. It was not the cold clear voice of one giving advice and warning from serene heights to those who were struggling and sinning below, but the warm, living voice of one who was fighting for us and by our sides, and calling on us to help him and ourselves and one another. ... And so was brought home to the young boy ... the meaning of his life, that it was no fool's or sluggard's paradise into which he had wandered by chance, but a battlefield ordained from of old, where there are no spectators, but the youngest must take his side, and the stakes are life and death. And he who roused this consciousness in them, showed them at the same time, by every word he spoke in the pulpit, and by his whole daily life, how that battle was to be fought; and stood there before them their fellow soldier and the captain of their band. The true sort of captain, too, for a boy's army, one who had no misgivings and gave no uncertain word of command, and, let who would yield or make truce, would fight the fight out (so every boy thought) to the last gasp and the last drop of blood. Other sides of his character might take hold of and influence boys here and there, but it was this thoroughness and undaunted courage which more than anything else won his way to the hearts of the great mass of those on whom he left his mark, and made them believe first in him, then in his Master.[6]

This description of educator Thomas Arnold calls to mind no one so much as Elliott's father. With such similar father figures, it is no wonder that Elliott and Hughes felt a rapport; however, the coming year's adventure could fairly be described as "a sluggard's paradise" for Elliott.

Among the other passengers who were "very kind and good" to Elliott were the newly married James and Sara Delano Roosevelt, distant cousins "who pass for my aunt and uncle." James had courted Elliott's sister Bamie, a generation younger than he, after the death of his first wife Rebecca. Bamie did not reciprocate his interest, but introduced him to her friend Sara Delano. The couple was so enamored of Elliott that they would invite him to make their rooms in London his "headquarters." In January 1882 he would be godfather to their baby, Franklin Delano Roosevelt.[7]

As in his Texas days, Elliott kept a journal, this one called "The Golden Gate Gazette" or "Oceanic Oracle," and filled with utter nonsense like the following:

Beautiful potato thou art doomed to fade
Thy heart be severed by the ruthless spade.
Thou wilt but slumber 'til winter's fled
But spring will call thee from thy earthy bed.
Then shalt thou bloom in light of day
Wooed nightly by the moon's soft ray
Till on my plate the welcome sight
Shall stimulate my appetite.

Why are some of the men who board this ship like a
    Normandy Potato?
Because [they] are thick-skinned and hardhearted, though they
have eyes they don't use them, and generally speaking you find
them very green. (Our correspondent must be suffering from a
severe attack of indigestion. — Ed.)

"A Potato Sprout"
I've tasted 'em mashed
And I've tasted 'em sweet.
A la Maitre d'Hotel
They cannot be beat.
When in a Puree
Before competent Jury
Of French *connoisseurs*
Or real Yankee Hoosiers.
All very fine, but
In the Irishman's hut,
If the man of the stew
Answered you true
Most surely he would say

That if done in his way
Boiled, baked or fried
Or potato-pied
He'd vote they were best
By the old 'ooman dressed,
With a little salt to savour
And a bit of pork to flavour
O! Potato thou art fair
Pinkey eyes and peachy hair.
How I've watched you 'gin to sprout
Does your mother know you're out?

What silent still! My *pomme de terre*
Such rudeness I have never seen.
Upon my soul, I'll eat you up
Here, Boy! The Oleo-Margarine!

Oval her face, and passing fair,
But one can't have forever here
    The things that we love best.
The cruel hours divide the time,
From 7 at night, till morn at nine,
    And then she will appear.

Appear again in many forms,
What ere it be my bosom warms.
    Boiled, baked, quite brown and crisp
So on the deck I wander round
Impatient for the gong's soft sound
    My love! My sweet potato.

The Dromedary
The Dromedary is a camel that has got his back up twice.

Dear Sir,

Can you tell me why the hours of 4 to 6 & 6 to 8 in the evening, are called dog-watches, and oblige
Yours truly
Main-Mast

Possibly because they are <u>curtailed</u>. — Ed

Dear Editor,
When you stated in your last that the supply of liquors on board was inexhaustible you were misinformed. "Name your poison" has as often been heard of late that in spite of all my entreaties "Sarsaparilla" is all the "moon-eyed ones" will produce to assuage the sufferings of
Thirst Smoker
(It shall be rectified next voyage.)

What is the difference between a man in a bus and one in a passion?
One rides in a stage, and one strides in a rage.

A work of mercy — unhooking a young lady's dress, to enable her to sneeze.

Why is one of our passengers like a dog-rose?
Because he is a <u>Rose</u> felt without a thorn.

Lawyer. Did you not say that an incompetent man could keep a hotel as well as any one?

No, I did not. I said an Inn Experienced one could.

Elliott decided to spend the summer in Kashmir at the suggestion of the famous hunter John Rae Reid, who paved Elliott's way through India with letters of introduction and accompanied Elliott to purchase his guns. Reid even gave Elliott his "bearer" for a servant. "What shooting and what letters we both shall some day know! Dear little Mother don't think I don't long for and love you dearly too but it's all so queer and far off that there is hardly room on paper for affection, only description," wrote Elliott, always solicitous of Mittie's feelings. "I'll love you double demonstratively when I get home."[8]

Elliott was every inch a Roosevelt in the joy he found in life and people. "I may go through a list of my friends among the passengers and find none who have not been charmingly good and kind. … I have enjoyed every moment. Delighted in the trip as if it had been a yacht instead of the finest vessel it seems possible to build. Revelled [sic] in the soft gentle breezes of the first part and gloried in the gales of the latter part of the voyage."[9]

Upon Elliott's arrival in England, the first people he visited were Mittie's two brothers James and Irvine Bulloch, Confederate naval veterans who chose to emigrate rather than live in a Yankee-dominated nation. Captain James Dunwoody Bulloch was a blockade runner who was also involved in the Confederate secret service. Irvine, it was said, had "fired the last shot" aboard CSS Alabama.[10] "… As the tug came to the pier who should I see but dear old Jimmie Bulloch all ready to receive me; pretty soon Uncle Irvine's blooming face loomed through the fog of a regular old time Liverpool day and a chorus of affectionate greetings, much to the amusement of the surrounding crowd, took place. … I came to the dearest little nest of a home you can possibly fancy or picture to yourself. …

PHOTOGRAPHERS
TO THE QUEEN

*James Dunwoody
Bulloch, circa
1880. Courtesy
of The Houghton
Library, Harvard
University.*

Dear Mother how I have longed that you might have been there to enjoy Uncle Irvine's absurdities. ..."[11]

Elliott was beloved of his aunts as well. Years later, when Eleanor was a student at the Allenswood School in England and only a little younger than Elliott when he made his trip, she visited the widow of Elliott's uncle Irvine Bulloch in Liverpool.[12]

My father had always talked to me about her, and between my father and his "Aunt Ella" had existed a very close tie. He wrote her long letters, at regular intervals, which she always answered, and on her regular visits home they always renewed their intimacy by long talks which had been a habit of his boyhood. I had had letters from her, and this visit meant a great deal to her, for it brought her "Ellie Boy," as she called my father, back in the person of his daughter.

In London, Elliott found himself in such demand that the only meal he took at his hotel was breakfast. He corresponded with his sisters as well as his mother. "Corinne's letter arrived today and told of Thee and Alice's return, the two dear ones," Elliott wrote. "I know they will be a grand success in New York, I like to think now of my dearly loved family all together at home in 57th Street."[13]

While in London, Elliott spent most of his time in the company of his shipboard friend Sir John Rae Reid, who "went all over with me getting my outfit, wished to give me some hunting and shooting before I left the country, and was so very kind to me in all small and big ways that I felt the very least I could do was to tell him he was perfectly free of my house and home in return."[14] Since she was a gracious southerner, there is no record of Mittie objecting to her son's "letter of introduction to your good graces."

Elliott was still in England when he received a pair of snowshoes from Theodore, but he spent Christmas aboard a train racing through France with two British officers who had made careers in India. After spending a freezing December night in the "delightful but cold" crossing from Dover to Calais, Elliott settled into his "Pullman car" at 12:30 and embarked on a marvelous traveling holiday.

"We slept until ten o'clock having coffee in bed at Paris at 8 — Breakfasted at eleven on board, passed through France all day, dined, our Christmas dinner, also on board at 7. ... We began with stories and ended with songs so that our little stateroom ... was most jolly. Dinner 25th

Dec. 1. Soup — 2. Soles with mushrooms — 3. Roast beef — 4. Potatoes and peas — 5. Chicken and salad — 6. Plum pudding with fire!!! 7. Cheese, pastry, biscuit, and to end with coffee and cigars," wrote Elliott, taking a truly epicurean pleasure in living. "I got two bottles of *vin Macon* at that pleasant little station so we drank heartily to all the 'dear ones at Home' all the while going forty miles an hour."[15]

Elliott's arrival in Egypt brought with it a flood of memories of his visit there as a twelve-year-old. "The same swarm of native boats and boatmen overrunning the ship .... native villages, and the near views, of the natives themselves, all so vividly brought back the Nile days."[16] Late that night Elliott boarded the ship at Suez, and the next morning he was relaxing on the deck in his pajamas, sipping coffee and smoking his pipe, taking in the wonderfully exotic scene. "The bold rocky mountains in the distance seeming actually to rise out of the sea, and the possession and reading of 'The Burial of Moses' threw me into quite the right state of mind to run the next day out into the Red Sea."[17]

A typical day for Elliott began with the announcement "Bath ready Sahib," then an hour with his pipe and a book, or perhaps a stroll around the deck, while still in his pajamas. Then he would dress for breakfast at nine o'clock, after which he would return to his pipe and the study of Hindustani. After lunch, "a book, conversation, afternoon walk, etc., bring us to a six o'clock dinner, then music and pipes put us to bed at eleven," Elliott wrote to Mittie, summing up the experience as "monotony but certainly pleasure."[18]

"Pleasure" seems hardly a strong enough word to describe this experience; "a year of total self-indulgence," in Blanche Cook's phrase, is closer to the mark.[19] "So queer, unreal, and withal so delightfully luxurious," Elliott wrote to his mother. "I would not trust myself to live here. There is no temptation to do anything but what you please and so many ways of doing it that one never tires." This observation was prophetic; Elliott must have realized that a man of his background could say the same thing about New York. Still, he missed his family: "The only regret is that you, the dear girls, and Mr. and Mrs. Brother are not here too. How we should revel in the sights, sounds, *smells* even!"[20]

"It is a very barren spot, only one very artificial and discouraging attempt at a garden even, in the entire place," wrote Elliott, always conscious of beauty, or lack thereof, in his surroundings. "But the rocky boldness of the scenery and beauty of the sunset, skies, distant hills, and near water, more than make up, or did at least that day, for what evidently is considered the horrors of desolation."[21]

Even inclement weather was a pleasure to Elliott. "Our voyage over the Indian Ocean was in the teeth of a strong N.E. wind, a big sea for this part of the world at this time of the year, but still much enjoyed and gave an opportunity for a good deal of reading. ... I slept on deck and was happy from start to finish."[22]

Elliott made friends with everyone he met. In Aden, he became acquainted with a Lieutenant Colonel Goodfellow, who "took me under his special care."[23] While aboard ship, "a good deal of quiet attention was shown me ... and the letters of introduction which Colonel Goodfellow, Major Harcourt and Cotton gave me, very kindly called me a 'most agreeable gentleman' but still I was no great swell until the ship arrived in harbor here. Then while all the world was bustle, worry and disorder, up the companion way with pleasant faces beaming with delight, came my friends Clark and Kittredge. ... Nothing but pleasure, for who could not be pleased with two such kind friends to meet you in a strange land."[24]

What comes through again and again in these letters is how little it took to make Elliott happy. It was said that for Theodore Roosevelt "life was the unpacking of an endless Christmas stocking." It was no less so for Elliott, at least until the last few years of his life. From their father the boys absorbed the idea that fun could be found in the smallest details of

Elliott, around the time of his "sluggard's paradise," circa 1880. Courtesy of The Houghton Library, Harvard University.

life. "Can I be anything but pleased with Bombay?"[25] Elliott asked about a city that most westerners find entirely displeasing. "All together my first step in India, including a ball last week, is a great success and pleasure," wrote Elliott in a letter to Mittie describing the many dinners and "tiffins" (lunches) held in his honor.

"At seven Aya brings me my coffee and cigarette and I sit on the veranda lazily taking in all the beauties of the early morning — at my feet directly under me is the race track and the horses are being taken round for a morning spin," wrote Elliott, recounting the beginning of a typical day in India. "On the field, beyond the belt of waving green trees yonder, stretches the ocean; as the mist slowly rises, see the boats lazily drift along. To sit and read and think for an hour here is perfect happiness."[26]

Elliott must have wondered at times if he was dreaming, with "the delicious perfume, the delicate dishes and still more delicate wines, the quiet service — no sound of boots for the boys go without them, and the clothes make no noise. ... I cannot describe it, it was all too Arabian night-like."[27] But describe it he did, although he wondered how he could do justice to the fabulous life he was leading. "How I can write you accounts of these doings I really cannot see, how can my feeble pen portray the oddities, the orientalisms, the strange scenes and queerer people. But by taking up one subject at a time I will try to give you an idea of what I am so entirely enjoying."[28]

Elliott was fascinated by the lives of the Brahmin caste. "The Noblemen in the city of any pretension to power or wealth live entirely as if it were a city in a city. ... They often ... have regular pitched battles and sieges of each other's palaces within the city walls, and if it were not for the gun shots which the English residents without the walls can hear, they would know nothing of it." He was never without traces of the Roosevelt social conscience. "All these noblemen probably boast estates ... sometimes by oppression of the poor 'reyot,' they derive incredibly large incomes."[29]

Elliott dined with one of these noblemen, Sir Salar Jung. "Up we dashed to the door leaving hats and wraps in the carriages. We passed through long lines of motionless blacks holding flaming torches ... into an inner court canopied by heaven." Elliott was overwhelmed by the palace, which was alight with "hundreds of wax candles in many-colored glass lamps." His dinner companions on either side were two "saids" who had received English educations and "were remarkably full of knowledge and imparted their knowledge freely and yet modestly, conversed very intelligently about the position of England not only in India but all over the world; her difficulties and troubles, as well as her greatness and power seemed to be quite familiar to them."[30]

After dinner, Sir Salar Jung, "this delightful noble eastern prince," saw to it that Elliott was given a tour of the palace, which Elliott found "orientally beautiful .... One of the rooms, for example, is entirely China, superb and costly, even chairs, tables, walls, ceilings, chandeliers, both large — I can answer for one being a fine one."[31]

While Elliott "dined with princes of royal blood" and took "confidential breakfasts with Prime Ministers," he most enjoyed the company of a young Mrs. Fraser, "my perfect ideal of what a Scotch woman might be. … She is 5 ft. 10", my height just and strong and beautiful. … Golden hair and light pink color." Just twenty-two, she had been married to Col. Fraser four years already, and it was the colonel who would "gratify my great ambition for a tiger hunt which will give me food for many a letter to you dear ones at home I fancy. It was as you know the height of my ambition from a sporting point of view."[32]

Young as he was, the discontent of many Indian people under British rule was not lost on Elliott. "This is a picture of a native state, under, unwillingly, British protection," he wrote to Mittie. "England in power — natives high and low discontented."[33] Throughout her life, Eleanor Roosevelt savored these letters and read them over and over; could she have influenced FDR in his disagreements with Churchill over colonialism?

"How easy," her father had written so long ago, "for the smallest portion to sit down in quiet luxury of mind and body — to say to the other far larger part — lo, the poor savages. Is what *we* call right, right all the world over and for all time?"[34]

🐝8🐝

"Old Indian Fever"

When Eleanor Roosevelt was a little girl, her father asked her to name the best-tasting drink she ever had. When she answered that her favorite drink was pink lemonade, he conceded that while pink lemonade was good, he never could forget a drink he was given in India.[1] "A dish for Paradise — Rose water and milk left in the dew all night and beaten up with a silver leaf in the morning just before breakfast"[2] until it was thick and frothy. In fact, everything about that breakfast at Sir Salar Jung's was memorable: "A fairy meal with a touch of Hell in it every time they gave us curry."[3]

These unforgettable experiences of eating and drinking could not have been the only recollections with which Elliott entertained his small daughter. "The more I see of India," he wrote, "the much more ready I am to lift up my hand and hold my breath for the future development of the world."[4] When Eleanor Roosevelt devoted her life to projects that in her view contributed to "the development of the world," she was acting on her father's legacy. Elliott inherited *his* father's consideration for work-ingmen and servants; this is one reason he was so much loved in India. When he heard one of his servants tell another that his master never called anyone "a damfool," he felt that he had passed "the great test."

"I often think, don't you, that true judgment comes from below," he wrote to his mother. "I can only say the hospitality met with by me on all sides from everybody has made a pleasure trip out of my India travels." Col. Fraser's "Methusalistic head servant" thanked Elliott "on the part of the other fifty-nine servants of the Colonel's establishment" and told him "that any of them 'would die for me on any account of my smiling face.' However oriental and untruthful, it meant a pleasant state of things for me."[5]

Elliott was enchanted by India, with its variety of flowers, "the whole air heavy in the morning, the dew itself seeming scented by them. Yet not the close, hot, stifling, sickening sweet of the lower tropical jungle and plain, but a cool, fresh, invigorating air that tempted me to stroll over the beautiful hills, and I should indeed have enjoyed our favorite nature if you my little companion had been with me too," he wrote to Mittie.[6]

On his hunting trip with Colonel Hastings Fraser, Elliott again was aware of the Indian underclass, "the coolie guides, (they are a separate caste in each village), live without the walls and have very few rights if any. … They were followed and bullied too I warrant by a guard of police who marched ahead of Col. Fraser on his riding elephant, he is too big for anything smaller," Elliott wrote to Mittie. "Their wild odd songs, the sound of the hurrying of the many feet, the glare of the torchlight all combined in a strange way to impress me with life in India. The motion is not bad, in fact I slept comfortably most of the time. It is wonderful how long the men can carry and the rate they go at."[7]

Like his brother, Elliott was fascinated by animals and particularly enjoyed the elephants that carried him and his friends. "They are such jolly old brutes though so careful and almost human in their actions, picking up loose stones in the way and throwing them aside. …"[8] Elliott was living "the strenuous life" long before Theodore, for hunting tigers was a rugged experience, but "who cares when breathing fresh air and hard as iron after it all?"[9]

Elliott must have felt as though he was living one of the Mayne Reid stories he and his brother loved while growing up, for on a typical hunting day:

> The tiger has been marked down and surrounded. The beat to drive him out takes place. If successful the glorious excitement of the battle royal, for it is a regular battle, if not and he breaks through the line of beaters or cunningly, for your tiger is a knowing one, — slips off … again we track and beat in the hot sun; the thermometer goes very high now, this is trying work but at it we keep until evening, then the return to camp: if successful what a hub-bub and joy if not a quieter but none the less glad return. How jolly the tub again and pipe. … An appetite which only open air can give for the good things … The evening is just settling down over the still hot dusty tired-looking country The neighing of the horses, the trump of the old Hatties [elephants], the calls, songs and laughter of the men, come on the soft evening breeze in a quiet hum very pleasant to hear from the distant business camp; our tents are under some grand banyon trees in the shade. …[10]

The letter that must have given Elliott the most pleasure to write was to his "brave, old Heart of Oak Brother" about shooting this particular tiger, one of the largest ever seen in those parts. "Three hours after the blood had been running she weighed 280 lbs. Her length was 9 feet 1½ inches, height, 3 ft., 7 in." Elliott had "finished her … with a spare shot from the Bone Crusher — by George, what a hole that gun makes."[11]

Mittie missed Elliott terribly. "Everything in your billiard room reminds me so of you, precious boy," she wrote Dec. 7, 1880, "painful as it is, I am so glad it does. I love you my child & pray that you will be careful

& do not risk too much." "My darling Son," she wrote that evening, "I posted a miserable note to you this morning much dispirited, but it had been commenced so I finished it up & sent it. Poor dear Teddie tho' he rejoices with you in your prospects for your hunt longs to be with you & walks up & down the room like a caged lynx. When Alice appeal[s] to him, he smothers her with kisses and tells her he is perfectly happy with her but sometime he must go off with his gun instead of poring over *Brown versus Jenkins*."[12] On another occasion, "Teddie when reading your note to him stalked about like a caged tiger; his eyes gleamed and he longed to be with you."[13]

Along with the social conscience of his father, Elliott inherited the Bulloch appreciation of "a soft evening breeze," "the wonderful contentment that comes with a cool drink in the shade on a warm summer evening," "… a big pitcher of cooled beer and soda water, which has been in a wet blanket and fanned all day. Each one of us has his own pitcher and it *is* good, with nothing to think about but how good life can be, especially with several servants to wait on you."[14]

Elliott was careful to send greetings to the servants back home: "Remember me to Dora [his nurse], Mary Ann, Jane, Hannah, Ann, Dorothy, etc. etc. Thomas and David … " Servants in the Roosevelt household were regarded as members of the family — if not equal in social position, beloved nonetheless.[15] Even so, Elliott was the only member of his family to recall them in his letters, and this touched them, Mittie told her son.[16]

When Elliott finally parted company with the Frasers, he decided to go on by himself. "It might to some I suppose be very lonely but to me I confess that, if I cannot have one of my dear *own* people … above all Thee, that I like the idea of being alone."[17] He still could hardly believe his charmed life: "… Such beauties of scenery, climate and perfect sport. The feeling is that of a little King really."[18]

Elliott developed a limited fluency in Hindustani, due to the fact that he was traveling alone save for his faithful servant Ajaib. "I can't leave this my favorite and most amusing character," Elliott wrote to Mittie, and was touched to hear himself referred to as "a human Sahib."[19] Ajaib saw to it that Elliott need worry about nothing but his pleasure in the hunt. "I have no care, do nothing but once a month settle accounts with him," wrote Elliott. "The rest of the time I shoot — and he cares for everything."[20]

Ajaib was one more pleasant accessory to Elliott Roosevelt's epicurean delight in life. "Ajaib at the tent door smiling welcome, bath, towels, Kahnsamer [sic] good dinner, and so ends the history of a day's march," Elliott wrote from the Pir Panjal Mountains. "As I write now, seated at the table at my tent door, the rushing of the stream at my very feet sounding soothingly to my ear, the sunlight creeping higher and higher on the opposite mountains as the sun bids us good-night for another twelve hours, the quiet of evening settling down over every thing forms a scene of great attraction to me."[21]

Mittie's letters to Elliott were characteristically affectionate. "Do take care of yourself — but enjoy every moment and may you be guided at every step of your great trip. I love you my child. ... "[22] She kept him updated on Theodore's activities: "On Saturday the 20th being Alice and Teddie's first month anniversary — Teddie goes immediately after an 8 a.m. breakfast to his Law School and back in time to take Alice for her drive and every now and then he comes home for lunch an hour in the afternoon. ..."[23] She admired her daughter-in-law: "[Alice] is full of bright clever witty sayings."[24]

Mittie's family was entertained by the most prominent figures in the Social Register:

Alice & Teddie have just come in from a dinner at Mrs. Francklyn [sic] Delano's [FDR's namesake uncle].[25] Coleman Drayton took her in[26] & Teddie took Mrs. William Astor and sat between herself & Mrs. Coleman Drayton. They dined last week with Mr. & Mrs. John Astor.[27] Mrs. Astor took in Alice & Teddie tho' taking in Mrs. Robert Goelet[28] … Tomorrow Mrs. Leavitt gives Alice a Lunch & Mrs. W.E. Dodge gives her a Lunch in a few days. Mr. & Mrs. William Astor sent Teddie & A. Patriarch Ball tickets this time also. Alice is so very sweet in the house, so sunny — I wish you could see her.[29]

Thanksgiving evening Mittie sat at her bureau at 6 West 57th Street and provided Elliott with a vivid description of the holiday:

My dearest Son — We have all returned from the family dinner at Uncle Jim's. We sat down twenty-one. I wished so my darling boy was in sight but I hope he is with Uncle Jimmie and Irvine. Teddie sent Johnny Long his turkey and cranberry and we lunched off of Rhode Island turkey with Auntie and Uncle … Teddie leaving after milk and bread only to rush off to see a football match between Yale & Princeton. … Aunt Lizzie had a beautiful dinner. Alice sat by Uncle Jim and looked perfectly lovely in a pink dress trimmed with pearl beads. During the evening she received a telegram from her father greeting them both and saying that their health had been drunk at the Thanksgiving Dinner at Chestnut Hill. Mr. and Mrs. Lee come tomorrow for ten days, Mrs. Lee to finish Alice's trousseau (dresses) and then, too, she is longing to see Alice. … Mr. Martyn [and] Mr. Sedgwick called whom I thoroughly enjoyed — oh! It did make me think so much of my baby boy that I would so love to be with.[30]

While Elliott chronicled his adventures for his mother, she informed him of the excitement back home. Bamie and Corinne rented a room at 77 Beacon Street in Boston for an extended stay with Alice's family, and "Sunday, Dec. 5th — Theodore, Alice and I have just come home in the rain from church, and where do you think we sat? Well, thereby hangs a tail [sic]. After leaving church last Sunday having all of us been in our old pew, on Monday or Tuesday I had a letter from Mr. Mortimer the Treasurer saying that an application had been made to buy our pew and on acting found has offered it to us for $4,000. Of course I replied that we could not buy it but asked if we could rent another pew. ... I had a lovely note from Dr. Hall saying how 'deeply distressed' he was that our pew should be bought out. ..." Dr. Hall offered Mittie a pew in the gallery, "but it was so far back he feared it would not answer. Last night it was decided we should try two seats back of the Francklyns in the gallery. If we liked these we could occupy them until May 1st ... Our nice little sexton of our old aisle was so kind about it all. ..."[31]

Mittie occupied herself with more than pew sales, however. She continued to move in literary circles; she spent Thanksgiving in Boston with Theodore and Alice and "dined with Bob Grant (author of 'Little Tin Gods' and 'The Frivolous Girl')[32] & was introduced by him after to the St. Botolph's Club, like our Century, meeting James the novelist [and] Edward Everett Hale, then [Theodore and Alice] went to Albany to select their rooms — in a Boarding House two pleasant ones Alice thinks."[33]

"My own dearest Son, I love you so devotedly and I do wish you the happiest of New Years," wrote Mittie from her "morning room" at 6 West 57th Street. "Thank you my best beloved child for your tender constant thought of your Mother. ... Sweetest pet darling Son I have received & welcomed your dear letter from the Pullman car ... with your description of the xmas dinner & your traveling companions. ..."[34] "Teddie came home to lunch which we had cozily together & at half past three we drove in his cart to the Riverside park which I had never seen before. The afternoon was lovely & the Hudson a blue calm — the sailboats frequent & exquisite — the sunset exquisite looking, as Teddie said like the coastline of some distant shore. ... It was so queer taking in as I had to Mr. Newbold [whose estate adjoined that of James and Sara Roosevelt in Hyde Park] into dinner. ... Teddie enjoyed talking with Willie Astor[35] politics, books & sparring matches."[36]

In late April and early May of 1881, Elliott was beset by another illness from which he would never entirely recover. For the rest of his brief life, he would periodically be confined with what he called his "old Indian fever."

"I have been kept here for a week by fever but am on my feet again and off again in a day or two for my hunting grounds," Elliott wrote from Srinigar; characteristically, however, the focus of this letter to his mother is on the kindness of the natives who took care of him.[37] But more than two months later he wrote again to Mittie, this time from Thuldii:

Not having been able to get rid of that beastly fever I got in Srinigar, it combined with its different effects to bother me more or
less the entire summer and several times laid me up, but the day
I wrote Aunt Annie on the 17th of the month it took your little
son and laid him on his back where he has been until two days
ago ever since; I fear really very sick, as now I am so weak that
the very slightest thing tires me so completely, so much so that
after the two days march, the coolies carrying me on a litter too,
I have had to stop a day here to rest. ... I am so thin and pulled
down that I cannot even walk the 'marches' much less do any
shooting. ... I acknowledge that to really shoot in this country
one must work very hard and exert to the utmost ones abilities,
and just now after my fever in May and the way it hangs on I am

not equal to it at all. ... I write this beastly scrawl on my back half eaten by flies; half beaten by a poor coolie who is under the impression he is keeping them off with a towel. ... Fancy for fifteen days I have eaten only rice and milk, having no stomach for anything else. ... Since I wrote you I just marched up the Indus Valley to this part of the country, was taken sick and am going immediately back to Kashmir to rest and recuperate.[38]

Even in his distress, Elliott was solicitous of his mother. He was "flabbergasted" by Corinne's engagement to Douglas Robinson and insisted that he needed to come home for the wedding. "The only thing which does not give me entire satisfaction is the lack of information about Corinne's marriage and the apparent feeling that I must not come home to it. In all of my letters I say this must not be and if I am not present it will be a *life long* disappointment to me,"[39] he wrote to Mittie. "... If the baby gets married why just let Bammie and me try and be as much trouble and as loving in our singleness, the two of us, as the four were before. ... Dear Mother perhaps you and I might spend six months wandering around Europe if you felt like it next summer?"[40]

"I do not know what to say to you about your coming home, if only for the wedding," Mittie replied. "It is a short affair & you come a <u>long</u> distance & if to return the expense will be great!"[41] Mittie was pleased by Corinne's acceptance of Douglas Robinson. "... I enjoyed the drive & the nice long walk with Douglas. I am growing very much attached to him. A long engagement has been just the thing for Corinne, for now I think she loves Douglas & desires to be with him & is easy & familiar & he's certainly devoted to her."[42] This would indeed be a successful marriage, and Douglas would in time come to Elliott's aid.

A few months later Mittie wrote of Teddy and Alice:

They seem very happy. She's very loyal to me. Always takes a stool & sits by me when we go into our lovely home like Library after dinner. I was out with Teddy this afternoon and we sleighed nearly out to the Harlem Bridge. It was a lovely clear winter afternoon & I enjoyed being with dear Ted. I think of you always when I am out with him & think of our drives together & hope we will have some more.[43]

"My beloved and dearest Elliott, I long so to hear from you," Mittie wrote August 7th, "our last letter from you date of May 17th Srinigar."[44] By August 20th Elliott recovered sufficiently to travel. "I am rapidly getting well," he wrote to Mittie from Semaggar, "every day feel stronger and better." No thoughtfulness shown to Elliott while on his travels ever passed unshared with his mother. "All the people I knew here have been very kind and the Doctor gave me this, his delightful bungalow to live in, so as not to be near the damp ground as I should have to be in tents. … Tho' I leave so soon, still I am mending so fast, I hope to yet hear the crack of the old rifle once more before going."[45]

Mittie was horrified that Elliott had been ill in such a remote area. "Oh my precious boy you must have suffered so much when way off in those cruel mountains of Little Thibet when no one of your own by you. …"[46] But a couple of weeks later, on September 5, Elliott felt well enough to reassure his mother. "I am just in from a few days camping and shooting. I stood it very well and I may call myself again entirely recovered," he wrote. "The rest here and the forced exercise has kept me a fund of strength, I am glad to say, enough to run me up again as rapidly into health as it rudely and quickly dashed me out of it."[47]

Elliott continued to make friends along his journey — one in particular who must have reminded him of the other men in his family. "… Tomorrow I start from here to go out of the valley via Rawl Rudie and the murren road, about fifteen days marching; my companion will be the Padre of the post here, the Rev. Mr. Carruthers — a cheerful pleasant old Scotch gentleman. One of those older men with childlike simplicity of manner and character. Yet the other day I saw him knock a huge strapping fellow, who had insulted him, down as neatly, as well as Teddy could have done." With Theodore Roosevelt for a brother and Thomas Hughes for a favorite author, it's no wonder that Elliott got along with this fellow.[48]

Everyone wrote to Elliott — Theodore, Mittie, Corinne, Bamie, Aunt Anna Gracie (who wrote him sixty-one times), Aunt Ella Bulloch. "At present I have thirty-two! letters to answer,"[49] he exclaimed; and yet Elliott seems to have worried that he would be forgotten by his family, that their lives would go on pleasantly enough without him. "I am horribly afraid years after this," he told Corinne about her upcoming wedding, "all of you speaking of it will forget all about the boy who was not connected with so much of the pleasant time."[50] Mittie gave Elliott a detailed description of Corinne's wedding, during which Mittie carried "pale pink roses" and Theodore "whimpered" a bit.

> Corinne received twenty-five bouquets — she will have to tell you from whom — one was from Percy King. ... Alice had five. ... Corinne's flowers were piled on a table near and she looked very sweetly in her white muslin dress trimmed with some birthday lace — Alice in her wedding dress of satin and white flowers in her hair but no veil. ...[51]

Elliott and Theodore felt a great deal of brotherly affection for Corinne's new husband. "Why if you don't take him," Elliott wrote Corinne from India, "you and old Nell will keep house in some cozy country corner all by ourselves."[52] Corinne probably would have been perfectly contented with this arrangement, for she loved her brothers at least as much as she loved her husband. "Dear Elliott has been such a loving, tender brother to me," she wrote to Douglas. "If you were my brother or cousin, how freely I could say I love you dearly. That kind of love I give absolutely."[53]

A bearded Scotsman of extraordinary kindness, Douglas Robinson was willing to be patient with Corinne, and with all the Roosevelts. Elliott appreciated Robinson's thoughtfulness with Mittie, who grew more eccentric after the death of her husband. Elliott marked his twenty-first birthday by pledging himself to her service. "Remember Father left me particularly to care for you and at any time you want me no other mortal thing shall keep me from being with you," Elliott promised Mittie, proud of the responsibility Theodore Sr. had conferred upon him.[54]

Elliott referred to her as "my special charge"; he, in turn, was her "comfort child."[55]

On September 29, Mittie and Bamie went to New York to meet "Teddie" and Alice, returning after a seven-day voyage from Liverpool, followed on a subsequent vessel by Mittie's brother Irvine Bulloch and his wife. "Daniel is packing sponge cake, grapes & bread; Katrina packs chicken, eggs & butter & we take this country produce to make merry over these dear ones," Mittie wrote Elliott from Tranquility, the family home in Oyster Bay. "T. says, 'Uncle Irvine is the kindest and jolliest and Aunt H. [Harriott] so sweet and motherly. The Blessed old sea captain [James D. Bulloch] I am with all the time looking over his naval papers of which there are literally thousands. I am begging him to publish a work of the naval operations carried on in England in our late trouble as he alone possesses the matter for it.' They will probably go at once to visit the Lees, then visit us here & we will all be together after Nov. 2nd at 6 W. 57."[56]

Undoubtedly Elliott still felt overshadowed by Theodore, by this time a twenty-two-year-old New York state legislator and historian whose first book was about to be published. "Has not our Thee done well?" Elliott wrote from Kashmir[57] to his mother, who informed him of Theodore's colorful sartorial taste: "Teddie brought out from London with his dress suits two or three satin waste coats — purple, pale yellow & blue & one rich black silk one. We all prefer the latter, tho' the others if you wore them would be very handsome." She thanked Elliott for "electrifying me with the description of 'The Rogue Elephant.'"[58]

Elliott never wanted to be excluded from Theodore's life. When he heard that his brother and sister-in-law were building a house in Oyster Bay, Elliott wrote Theodore that he would like to buy property there as well, so that "we will *all* live there happily as in old times. ... It delights me beyond bounds to see the way you have 'gone in' for everything as the son of the dear old father should, and I will come back ready and eager to put my shoulder by yours at the wheel, Thee."[59]

Before he was ready to put his "shoulder to the wheel," however, Elliott basked in the sheer enjoyment of life. One of the most rhapsodic of what Eleanor Roosevelt's friend and biographer Joseph Lash referred to as "Elliott's incomparable compositions"[60] was written to Mittie from Colombo, Ceylon, December 2nd, 1881:

My own dear Mother,

If this gets to you at all in time a sweet Merry Christmas to you dear Home Ones all. To you my beloved little darling black headed Motherling — the beautiful centre of our Home worship — Darling Mother your children love you and not the least loving is the boy away out here. ... The ocean waves beat on the wall under my pillow as I write with a pleasant restful sound that is very agreeable. the clear blue sky, the sun sparkling on the white caps, the flying proas swiftly chasing one another about way out there on the blue water, the fishing boats, and fishing men, the sandy miles of glittering beach, the black stretches of rock, the reefs and breakers, the lagoons and still waters, the palm trees and jungle and the quaint songs of the boat men, the beauty of everything and the soft languor of the breeze. ... I could sit and alternately write and dream all day. ... To be in the shade of some ancient, half-ruined Palace or temple during the hot tropical mid-day in the heart of some tropical jungle, grown up since and hiding entirely the old ruin; which had its pride of life and its fall — hundreds of years ago — this is not today, it means past and all time in the past and it means future and an unlimited future. It means old fancies, old beliefs, old deeds, old history, old fiction, lived over. It means too, new thoughts, new cravings and fulfillments, new possibilities, new history, new men; if all are after all only dream men, it can't be helped. They are all noble, at least as much so as it is in the power of the brain which creates them to make them. You can't think evil when the only Being near is one in Whose presence but Good can be. A man who can't feel God in nature, and a man who can't think Christ in solitude, must be very unfortunate. What a wonderful thing it all is, mother, this God's and Christ's World.[61]

Elliott's hunting adventure nearly turned fatal in Ceylon when he shot an elephant in the eye and was chased through the jungle by the beast for two and a half hours, running at full speed the entire time. He managed finally to slaughter the elephant, however — "... It was only after I had put sixteen bullets into him that his great, crushing weight fell down in the bamboos" — and to kill yet another elephant.[62]

From Ceylon it was on to Singapore and then Saigon, where Elliott hunkered down in a typhoon. Saigon showed the influence of its occupiers;

"the quaint air of old France" in the Far East, "much shipping and an air of thrift and quiet comfort that reminded one more than anything else of a prosperous southern city in the old days, say in Louisiana." Then to Hong Kong and a detour to Canton, up the Pearl River in an "ordinary American river steamboat, really into China proper."

Back in New York, Elliott's aunt Ella Bulloch wrote him about a discussion she had with Theodore, who was about to journey to Albany for the opening session of the state legislature — Theodore's first experience as an elected official. Their talk, wrote Aunt Ella from her sister Anna Gracie's house on West 36th Street, was "mostly about you, darling."

'What a fellow that is!' I was so glad to find that Teddy too thinks so highly of your power of influence with others. He spoke of the differences between you in this respect with such noble generous warmth and said that where he would naturally wish to surpass other men, he could never hold in his heart a jealous feeling toward you. Then we talked of his book and his political interests. Thee thinks these will only help in giving him some fame, but neither he says will be of *practical* value, or giving him advancement, but says he must begin again at the beginning ... So that you will *both* in point of fact start your career together, he having gained this intermediate experience while you gain yours in a different way during your travels. Thee is a dear 'grand' old fellow in very truth ... Sometimes he reminds me so much of you. ...[63]

Since Elliott was hardly sure of what his "career" would be, he could not have been comfortable knowing that he and his brilliant brother would "start together," their respective progress endlessly compared by their family and friends; but the brothers were always outwardly supportive of each other, and there is no record of either one having been less than supportive inwardly.

Even so, Elliott wrote to tell Theodore how proud he was of him, "in your life so useful and so actively led at home. Will it be any help to have me one of these days go round with you to back you in your fights, old man?"

Do take care of yourself now for everybody's sake, the little wife's (to whom give my best love), the family's, and mine. I tell you, Thee, I shall need you often in your good old strong way to give a chap a lift or for that matter if I am on the wrong road a *blow* to knock me back again.[64]

This was an easy (although doubtless heartfelt) sentiment for Elliott to express during this extraordinarily happy chapter in his life; he would hardly welcome the "blow" when it came.

With the approach of Christmas, Mittie grew nostalgic. "Do you remember once I sat in your lap while we opened our Christmas presents? The bell kept Daniel running to & fro & he was veiled with mystery as he would carry up parcels not intended for me to see."[65]

As Elliott's world tour neared its conclusion, Mittie, still using black-bordered mourning stationery, wrote Elliott from her "morning room": "My own dear darling Elliott to say I long to see you gives you no idea of my ardent wish to do so. I would be the last one to spoil your trip — but for my sake I am glad that April will bring my Beloved child back. ... I will be on the lookout for your box or boxes & unless being injured by being unpacked everything shall remain for you to distribute with your mother seated holding one of your dear hands. Everything that came with the tiger skin is packed away. ..."[66]

On Christmas Day Mittie wrote:

Dearest Elliott,

Happy Merry Christmas to you my dearest Son wherever you are. I have read the beautiful Christmas Hymns from your little Hymnal with Teddie, Alice & Bamie at prayers. Later I read the Collect, Epistle & Gospel for the fourth Sunday of Advent & Christmas day with Corinne. Yesterday I was tumultuously busy with sending out all of our Christmas presents & receiving the various packages for the children. ... I have not yet wished my most darling boy the Happiest New Year which I do from the bottom of my heart and tho' I rejoice at the idea of seeing him in April yet I can not bear him to return unless he has done and seen all he wishes to do & see. I was so happy to read your letter to Teddie of Nov. 18th telling of your day in the jungle with the tracker, the lovely morning & the deer. I do hope you have been able to keep the Buck's head! I think I know your letters almost by heart. ...[67]

Mittie took great pleasure in Elliott's trophies. "I am so delighted to learn ... [that] the tiger skull had the full compliment of teeth & I am having the head mounted with the mouth open," she wrote Elliott September 29, 1881.[68] Later: "... The tiger skin is placed before the fireplace in the Library mounted on a lining of dark cloth. ... The skin exactly placed over the skull & the great terrible tusks & teeth showing. ... I am very jealous that you gave some of your precious trophies away in Bombay when I value even a tail of a mouse that is my darling Elliott's trophy!"[69]

Elliott had done "sporting work worthy of the Roosevelt name," he wrote to Theodore. "It is the life, old man. *Our* kind. The glorious freedom, the greatest excitement. ... How everything here would have pleased your fondness for the unusual and the dangerous."[70] Elliott knew that for sheer enjoyment of life, nothing would ever compare with this sojourn in India — and yet, when he walked into the parlor of 6 West 57th Street after having been gone sixteen months, at least one member of his family knew that something was terribly wrong. After a private dinner with his Aunt Annie, she went to church and asked God "to cure" Elliott — but of what, we do not know. "Ellie is very ill" is all she confided to her diary. This perceptive woman had helped to raise the Roosevelt children, and Elliott was the one she loved best; she knew him as well as he allowed himself to be known. Whether his illness was mental, physical, or spiritual she does not say, but she may have suspected that it was a combination of all three.[71]

Elliott was a Roosevelt, however; and for all their consciousness of "the joy of living," Roosevelts did not give in to illness or live for pleasure. It would never be "our way," Elliott wrote to his eldest sister, "for that means life for an *end*."[72]

Life for an end. What could that be for Elliott? He had no clear idea of his mission; the one person who seemed to need him was his mother. He slept in a small room next to hers, and she loved taking care of him, in her mildly distracted way. "Now when my little mother feels cold at night, she comes in and puts an extra blanket on me, so that I wake up perfectly roasted and when she is warm, she comes in and takes the covers off me so that I wake up frozen."[73]

Elliott felt unworthy of the honor he accepted March 20, 1882, nine days after his return, when he took on his responsibility as godfather to two-month-old Franklin Delano Roosevelt at St. James Chapel in Hyde Park. Mittie convinced him that it was his duty to accept.

Elliott also felt needed at the Orthopedic Hospital, and especially at the Newsboys' Lodging House, as Theodore found when he stopped by. "As soon as they saw me, they mistook me for you," he wrote to Elliott, describing the cheering that went up from the boys. "I thought it pretty nice of them; they were evidently very fond of you."[74]

Elliott, circa 1882, around the time he became godfather to Franklin Delano Roosevelt. Courtesy of The Franklin D. Roosevelt Presidential Library.

Had Elliott lived in a subsequent era, he may have gone into full-time social work; but in 1881, the business of a man was business. Douglas Robinson offered him a partnership in his real estate firm, and the name of the office was changed to Robinson, Russell and Roosevelt. Each morning, Elliott commuted by horse-drawn carriage to 106 Broadway to take his place in the business world.

While his heart's desire was for the people he loved to depend on him, Elliott was only twenty-two, and another part of him shrank from responsibility in any form. What he really wanted was not to be a good businessman, but a devil-may-care man-about-town. What young man would not have found it difficult to make a sudden transition from facing down tigers in the Far East to shuffling papers in a real estate office? He had been the dashing hero of his family, the envy of his smarter, more talented, more aggressive brother. Elliott still wanted to be the center of attention, to exercise his charm in public, to shine in a forum in which people he admired would be impressed by his romantic experiences. It was at this juncture that he immersed himself fully in the world of what his daughter euphemistically called the "sportsman," becoming one of the most active and popular members of the Meadowbrook Country Club on Long Island, where he "rode to hounds," played polo, and became something of an expert on horses.

"He never could learn to control his heart by his head," wrote his daughter. "With him the heart always dominated." Any "end" that could truly excite Elliott would have to be emotional rather than intellectual.

His heart was about to be overwhelmed.

9

"Even the Flowers Are Happier at Being Your Servants"

Anna Rebecca Hall was never one to question her surroundings or her appointed role. Like most confident people, she knew exactly who she was and thought a great deal of it. Anna knew that she was beautiful. While she underwent the obligatory "grand tour" of Europe in her teens, the poet Robert Browning saw her sitting for a portrait and asked if he might be allowed just to gaze at her.[1] She touched something in Elliott Roosevelt's sensitive soul when he met her at a party given by Sara Delano's sister Laura at Algonac, the Delano estate.

Anna knew that she was an aristocrat. She was descended from both the Livingstons and Ludlows, whose estate at Tivoli on the Hudson was deeded to them by Charles II, James II, and George I. Her mother Mary Ludlow Hall and her father Valentine Gill Hall, Jr. were as earnest and reserved as Elliott Roosevelt's parents were gracious and fun-loving.

"My father, Elliott Roosevelt, charming and good-looking, loved by all who came in contact with him," (Eleanor was always quick to add this) "had a background and upbringing which were a bit alien to her pattern. ... I doubt that the background of their respective lives could have been more different. His family was not so much concerned with Society (spelled with a big S) as with people, and these people included the newsboys from the

Anna Rebecca Hall, circa 1884, wearing a necklace made of claws from a tiger Elliott shot in India. Originally the necklace was a gift to Elliott's mother, Mittie Roosevelt. Anna inherited the necklace from her mother-in-law. Courtesy of The Franklin D. Roosevelt Presidential Library.

streets of New York and the cripples whom Dr. Schaefer, one of the most noted early orthopedic surgeons, was trying to cure."[2]

Elliott and his siblings made a conscious effort to follow their father's example of concern for the poor. When Theodore Sr. died, The Rev. Henry C. Potter of Grace Church in New York scolded his congregation by noting that of all the wealthy men in the country, only two, Theodore Roosevelt and a recently deceased citizen of Philadelphia, went out of their way to spend time with the forgotten poor in their cities.[3] Theodore's children were careful to be a credit to their father's memory, and it was not long before they inherited his "do-gooder" reputation.

This trait in Elliott was not entirely foreign to Anna; the Halls considered it incumbent upon their station in life to make themselves available, at least from a distance, to the poor — but the enthusiasm with which Elliott went about it may have caused Anna to be even more drawn to him.

Anna's father took his religion seriously, but not in the same way as Elliott's father. Valentine Hall was an autocrat who ruled his family the way he conducted his Sunday School class at Gramercy Park's Calvary

Church, keeping strict attendance records and stressing rectitude, perhaps at the expense of forgiveness.[4] His father, the first Valentine Hall, came to Brooklyn from Ireland and developed such a genius for real estate that his fortune enabled his son to be accepted as a Hudson River aristocrat alongside the Roosevelts, Livingstons, and Ludlows. At age twenty-one he was a partner in one of the largest real estate firms in New York City (in which Elliott Roosevelt would one day be employed) and married the daughter of another Irish immigrant partner. His business, Tonnele and Hall, was extended "unlimited credit,"[5] but this Irishman's orbit consisted of the piece of Sixth Avenue he owned from Fourteenth to Eighteenth Street.

The younger Valentine Hall's inheritance enabled him to eschew the business world and to indulge an interest in theology, going so far as to keep a clergyman along with the rest of the hired help on the premises for the purpose of learned discussion.[6] When Hall was not debating metaphysical issues, he micromanaged every area of his estate, including the running of his home, a mansion called Oak Terrace, at Tivoli. He assumed the task of raising his children and treated his wife Mary, daughter of a New York City mercantile family, as another child.

Mary Ludlow Hall could trace her New York ancestry as far back as 1640, and by 1699 the family was in politics, a Ludlow serving in the Assembly of the Province of New York. Mary was the daughter of Edward H. Ludlow, a doctor, and Elizabeth Livingston, whose family was even better off financially and socially than the Ludlows. "The wealth and connections, the public offices, the splendid war records, and the numerous family relationships created around the Livingstons a special aura which survives even today," writes historian Jerry Patterson. He then quotes Ward McAllister, who in 1892 drew up the list of "The Four Hundred": "All my life I had been taught to have a sort of reverence for the name of Livingston, and to feel that Livingston Manor was a species of palatial residence that one must see certainly once in one's lifetime."[7]

Elizabeth did not like the hours a doctor was required to keep, and forced her husband to give up the practice of medicine and invest instead in real estate. Having accomplished this, Elizabeth had no interest in bringing her husband's business into her home. When some associates of Mr. Ludlow came to his house on what is now Park Avenue South to see him about a business matter, she turned down the lights and informed them, "Gentlemen, my husband's office is on Lower Broadway." They left without asking questions. "She was *character*," Eleanor Roosevelt said of her maternal great-grandmother. "I was terrified of her."[8]

Well she might have been, for Elizabeth Livingston Ludlow had no tolerance for weakness. When she was very old and her great-granddaughter was very young, Mrs. Ludlow's female descendants would visit her on Sunday afternoons. One day, when her daughter Mary Hall pleaded illness, Mrs. Ludlow would have none of it and sent her granddaughter Maude and great-granddaughter Eleanor home to fetch "Molly," as Mrs. Hall was called. Molly meekly dragged herself out of her sickbed. "A picture of this iron-willed lady shows a plain but strong mouth," observes Joseph Lash, "and if the upper half of her face is covered, the mouth and chin are those of Eleanor Roosevelt."[9]

It has been lost to posterity what the attraction could have been between Valentine Hall, Jr. and the daughter of Edward and Elizabeth Livingston Ludlow. Hall was too much of an ascetic to enjoy the genteel life of leisure he chose. When he needed money, he asked his mother. Eleanor Roosevelt, whose keen (albeit little-acknowledged) sense of humor led her to relish ridiculous anecdotes about the idle rich, enjoyed telling the story of her Grandfather Hall's dependence on his mother's largesse while building Oak Terrace.

She would go to the wardrobe and rummage around and emerge with a few thousand dollars. ... because in Ireland it would be perfectly normal to keep your belongings in whatever was the most secret place in your little house. You would not deposit them in a bank, and this was what … my great-grandmother evidently had carried into the new world and proceeded to do. … As neither of her sons ever added to the fortune but both of them seemed well-provided for, I think it is safe to say that the original immigrant great-grandfather must have made a considerable fortune.[10]

Anna's father made her take walks every day with a stick in the crook of her arms to hold her shoulders back and ensure upright posture. Uncomfortable as this training was, it bore fruit in stately bearing.[11] The lesson was not lost on Anna: discipline was key to everything. Failure, imperfection of any kind, could only be the result of a lack thereof.

The Hall sons, Valentine III and Edward, eventually — one is tempted to say inevitably — became alcoholics. The daughters, stunning debutantes all, were known as "the beautiful Hall sisters." The sisters closest in age to Anna were named Edith and Elizabeth, but they called themselves "Pussie" and "Tissie" and indulged a talent for self-dramatization, particularly in matters concerning the opposite sex. Pussie was especially unstable; once when traveling aboard an ocean liner with fifteen-year-old Eleanor, she made such a production of despair over the latest in her series of failed romances that the terrified Eleanor took her constant threats of suicide seriously and never left her side throughout the voyage, so convinced was she that Aunt Pussie was going to kill herself.[12]

When Anna was seventeen, her father died without leaving a will, and she, rather than her mother, took charge of his estate, although the court administered his property. Anna was considered the strongest character in the family, taking more naturally to balancing budgets and keeping accounts than her mother would have. Anna and Tissie, as the oldest of the children, had been most directly influenced by their father's ideas and example. "Anna Hall's upbringing," writes historian Kenneth S. Davis, "seemed designed to destroy resilience of character, tolerance, and flexibility of mind."[13] Davis's discerning analysis bears quoting:

> [Hall] had impressed deeply … his own narrow view of a woman's proper role in that banal society into which they had been born, his own high and rigid standards of personal conduct, and also the religious piety by which these standards were allegedly sustained. The results, so far as Anna was concerned, would seem to show in photographs taken of her in her wedding year. These give the impression of a certain cold primness overlaying a beauty otherwise passionate, the latter manifested in her rather full pouting lips and enormous eyes. But passion is not all; there is also in those eyes a kind of tense, hurt look, as if they were windows opening on a soul drawn too painfully taut between poles of Right and Wrong, giving her a hard but brittle integrity.[14]

The effect of the unbalanced view of religion in the Hall family is disturbing. "In the Roosevelt household religion was seen as the affirmation of love, charity, and compassion; in the Hall household at Tivoli it was felt that only a ramrod-like self-denial was acceptable to God," writes Joseph Lash. "While the Roosevelts welcomed 'joy of life' as the greatest of heaven's gifts, the Halls considered pleasure of the senses to be sinful and an affront to God."[15]

Anna was deeply influenced by the popular literature of the period (although there was strict supervision over what she was allowed to read) in which wayward, passionate men are reformed by the influence of holy women. Unlike Elliott Roosevelt, who wrote humorous verse and short stories by the hour to pass the time, Anna is known to have made only one attempt at creative writing. This was a story about the reformation of a decadent English lord by a noble and innocent young woman of his own class.[16] (Could Anna Hall have viewed a member of any other sphere with sympathy?)

In 1869, Louisa May Alcott wrote with amusement and a note of disapproval about the ecstatic reception given "a certain yellow-haired laddie"[17] on his visit to America. This was Edward, Prince of Wales. Isaac Hull Brown, longtime sexton at Grace Church and *major domo* at all of New York City's fashionable parties, supervised a reception for the prince at the Academy of Music on East 14th Street, for which "invitations were sought like passports to paradise," writes one historian, "and the most august families did not hesitate to beg and bribe for them."[18] There was no group more desirable or attractive to upper-class Americans than the British peerage. Elliott Roosevelt was Anna's ideal man — the only thing he lacked was Englishness. He was handsome, well-traveled, slightly dissolute, aristocratic, and weak. This idealistic young woman of course had no way of knowing how quickly the charm of his weakness would fade.

Anna and Elliott had one important thing in common — they were both surrounded by love. "She was made for an atmosphere of approval, for she was worthy of it," a friend remembered. "Her sweet soul needed approbation."[19] Only one person is known to have found Elliott resistible, and that is his brother's second wife, Edith Carow. Even as children Theodore was always welcome to play with Edith, whereas Elliott was not.[20]

Anna Hall was regarded as a woman of exquisite beauty,[21] both physical and spiritual — at least in her own little world, "the Second Avenue set," as the old families of Stuyvesant Square and Gramercy Park were dubbed, and the pleasant milieu of the wealthy families who lived along Fifth Avenue starting at Washington Square, and Madison Avenue from its beginning at 23rd Street all the way to Central Park. This was a lovely atmosphere of brownstones and carriages, ballrooms, parlor games, sentimental songs, cotillions, house parties in grand mansions, servants, and — for those with the social conscience Elliott was introducing to Anna — service.

Anna and Elliott would be married in December 1883, but in January of that year he was still addressing her as "My dear Miss Hall":

… I am looking forward with the greatest pleasure to a charming visit and thank you now more than I can say for inviting me. The country after the city weather we have been having will in itself be heaven. And when I think where in the country I am going I feel myself a very fortunate man. I am making up in part for the future holiday laziness by being horribly busy now. Give my kindest regards to your mother and sister. Also to the little lady your baby sister, if she will receive my love.

With many thanks for your goodness I am

Faithfully yours, Elliott Roosevelt[22]

There is much that is touching in their formal and old-fashioned courtship. "My dear Mr. Roosevelt,"[23] began a letter from Anna,

Thank you many times for your lovely philopena present. I think it was wicked of you to send me anything, yet I must tell you how much pleasure it gave me. I would try and thank you for your note, but feel it would be useless. Let me only say that I fully appreciate your kindness.

Hoping to see you, Believe me,

Yours very sincerely,

ANNA R. HALL

11 West 37th Street

Monday, March 12th

Under Elliott's influence, Anna began volunteering at the Orthopedic Hospital that was so important to the first Theodore Roosevelt. Elliott usually met her there to escort her home or to squire her around the city.

Dear Miss Hall,

It will be, I hope, so delightful an afternoon that I will be at the hospital at half after four instead of five, it being so much more pleasant an hour for driving than the later. I trust that you can get through your work there by that time. Accept these few flowers and wear them for the little children to see. They say that the "lovely lady" always has some with her. Even the flowers are happier at being your servants I am sure.

> With regard I am
> > Faithfully Yours
> > ELLIOTT ROOSEVELT
> > 6 West 57th Street
> > Friday[24]

Elliott proposed to Anna in the setting where they had met — Algonac, the Newburgh mansion of the Delano family — at yet another party given by Laura Delano, this one on Memorial Day.

Elliott may have told Theodore before the engagement was formally announced, for in February 1883 Elliott wrote an essay about Anna in the form of a letter to his brother. It is remarkable for what it reveals about his literary talent, his values, and his depth of feeling:

My Love

When my worship for women began I can not tell. May be when the devoted Auntie showed me by a practical forbearance and how great a power a religious belief in a good woman's heart might have in making a throne where no earthly elements of great happiness ought be. Or perhaps when the poor little mother turned to me on that night and called me her loving son and only comfort. May be when as the years have gone by and I have seen the two sisters unselfishly and with thought often only for us boys, the brothers, feel that in us and in our interests, our lives, lay their great enjoyment year after year. Or in seeing Aunt Annie Gracie live year after year for her husband & her loved relations, we the children & her sisters & brothers. But this certainty with every distrust and hatred of what ordinarily goes to make up the life and character of the generality of women that I have met, with a contempt of which I had well learned to have for the thoughtless or worse than that even, really bad women who made the history, big or little, in the world. At last I met one, a Sweet Heart, a True, loving, Earnest woman who <u>lived</u> the life she professed. Womanly in all purity, holiness and beauty, an angel in tolerance, in forgiveness, and in faith — My Love, thank God our Father — and in her true promise to be my wife I find the peace and happiness which God has taken from me for so long. It is not that I did not see the good in woman For I have seen that and most willingly acknowledged it in some — but so many more proved themselves the other sort. In how many beautiful faces which should be God's reflection does the Devil put his stamp & way down in the soul also.

Anna, however, had

… A heart part of God's own kingdom come to Earth. And a mind and life in the contemplation of which I find the quiet repose of certain trust in <u>Truth</u>. This is my sweet girl, my darling

Anna. A child in years, A woman in experience & knowledge. A Christian in deed & fact. No one could say a word against her, but her own sweet humility denies her the power of thinking herself free of faults. In every action of the beautiful young life she commands the admiration and love of those around her. Her beauty of body and grace of figure is only a shadowing of the perfect loveliness of the mind within the frame. God's great goodness in giving me the love of this dear woman, and her companionship through life, is great. She seems to me so pure and so high an ideal that in my roughness and unworthiness I do not see how to make her happy. How can any single love make up for the lavish admiration of the many. How can I who have been but a wanderer and a self-amusing dilatante [sic] ever command the love for ever of so earnest & true a woman, be my efforts ever so honest and my success as men count it even the average of beyond. Dear old Brother Thee I enjoy & <u>love</u> you.[25]

As extravagant and Victorian as this is, it is also true that Elliott's prose is the invention of a remarkably romantic and passionate nature.

"You must be very pure and very true now that you have secured the right to guard, love and cherish so sweet a girl as Anna," Theodore responded.[26]

When the engagement was announced a few months later, the Roosevelts responded with characteristically affectionate joy.

"He loves you with so tender and respectful a devotion, that I, who love my darling brother so dearly, cannot but feel that you as well as he, have much to be thankful for," wrote Corinne to Anna.[27] Bamie, no doubt remembering the death of their father, told Anna that Elliott was "such a tender, sympathetic, manly man" that she had turned to her younger brother "in many sad moments for help and strength."[28] Theodore, who had strong convictions about the institution of marriage, assured "Dearest Old Brother … it is no light thing to take the irrevocable step you have just taken, but I feel sure that you have done wisely and well, and we are all more than thankful to have so lovely a member added to our household circle."[29] James and Sara Delano Roosevelt each sent notes offering "warmest congratulations." James kept Elliott abreast of one-year-old Franklin's progress. "Your Godson thrives and grows. I have just been teaching him now to climb a ladder in a cherry tree."[30]

The following summer was among the happiest months of Elliott's life. The "Tivoli Crowd" that lived along the Woods Road made his and Anna's life an endless round of parties in their honor. They read aloud, played tennis, took "jolly drives" in the country. On weekdays Elliott came to New York City where he and Theodore often spent entire nights talking.

"No letter from you after spoiling me so in regular chats on paper has quite upset me, and the postman has caught on the joke for he smiles and shakes his head at every delivery with no Tivoli letter," wrote Elliott on stationery from Robinson, Russell and Roosevelt. "I hope you are all well dear and that it was only lack of time and not headache that prevented your writing to the impatient and wistful though ardently loving Boy, down here. How I wish tomorrow morning were here for then I must surely get a note."[31]

"My darling beautiful Sweetheart," Elliott wrote six weeks later from the brokerage firm:

> Your dear note brought such satisfaction to my longing heart. …
> My Love how I wish for you and my whole <u>Being</u> seems up in the
> charming quiet country while the body of Elliott wakes and worries away down here. As I sit at my desk now in the few moments
> taken from the "office" hours a pretty picture of your lovely face

in its halo of waving soft hair comes up before my eyes and "I will be true," "I do love you," I seem to hear again — bringing to me a great peace, and such a joy in the heart of your devoted Boy — My darling Love so dear. ... Last night the two Parish girls spent with us ... I am afraid I was not very good as a host, I longed so to be back at Tivoli seated next to my sweet girl. ... Do you not think the violets a good idea for my ushers' scarfpins, or do you think of some other better idea?[32]

His closing salutation was even more ardent than usual:

> Good bye my own true Love.
> With faithful and tender devotion I
> am your Lover
> Elliott

Around this time Elliott began spending time in Hempstead, Long Island, a perfect venue for his gifts as a "sportsman." Anna was proud of Elliott's athletic prowess, and he kept her informed of his triumphs. "The 'Meet' at Jamaica yesterday afternoon was a very pretty one and we had a glorious run. ... Mohawk [Elliott's hunting dog] did grandly and gave me a good place in the first flight from start to kill." Later he and his friends "dined quietly at the kennels," after which he relaxed "cozily over the big wood fire gazing into the flames and wishing for and thinking of my Sweet Heart."[33]

Although Elliott was indeed a great sportsman, he ran the risk of seriously hurting himself in the pursuit of pleasure, and much later an injury incurred in a frivolous undertaking would have a disastrous effect. In the meantime, he wrote to Anna:

You will have to hurry up and marry me, if you expect to have anything left to marry. It seems to me that I get from one bad scrape into another. That beastly leg gave me so much pain that I went to the Doctor and I'm in for it this time, I'm afraid, not to get on a horse for a week and not to walk about more than is absolutely necessary. Oh! My! Poultices! Ointments! And three evenings alone by myself at 57th Street with my leg in a chair.[34]

The "Indian fever," whatever it was, never left him. "My old Indian trouble has left me subject to turns like I had Monday from change of weather or some such cause,"[35] he wrote Anna from 6 West 57th Street, about a seizure or fainting spell he suffered at Tivoli. On his way back to New York he felt "pretty bad" and apparently had some difficulty making the trip; fortunately he encountered friends who took care of him. "Herm Livingston and Frank Appleton[36] were on board and very kind so I pulled along very well."[37] "I'll be at work down town tomorrow and am really all right again today. I would not let the Mother know or Bammie. But Douglas spent last night with me and the boys have been very good and the servants took good care of me. I thank you for your dear anxiety about me pretty Baby, but it's all right again. … How I wish you were here to read to me, that tender sweet voice I love so dearly. … Next week I'll work until Friday afternoon and then get off to follow my little Sweet Heart wherever her wayward pretty feet have led her. If back to the old house at Tivoli I shall be very glad … only I must see you dear I can't stand it longer and it is very hard to stand it as long as it is."[38]

Elliott had a tendency to depression — "melancholia" it was called in those days — that either precipitated his physical problems or was a result of them. "I know I am blue and disagreeable often, but please darling, bear with me and I will come out all right in the end, and it really is an honest effort to do the right that makes me so often quiet and thoughtful about it all." Anna was troubled by this and invited him to open his heart to her. "Please never keep anything from me for fear of giving me pain or say to yourself, 'There can be no possible use of my telling her.' Believe me, I am quite strong enough to face with you the storms of this life and I shall always be so happy when I know that you have told and will tell me every thought, and I can perhaps sometimes be of some use to you."[39]

Elliott must have seemed to Anna the most wonderful man in the world. His sparkling eyes conveyed a warmth and radiance that was not unusual in the Roosevelt family, but were unlike those of most people Anna had encountered. He was handsome in the way of a man on a Victorian valentine, with his hair parted in the middle and his mustache waxed at the tips. Not the least of his attractions was the strange illness; the sadness that came over him at times — the hint of some secret torture — gave him a vulnerability that made him irresistible. "If you do not show [your fears] to me," she remonstrated, "how am I to learn to help you?"[40]

Sitting at his desk at 106 Broadway, Elliott regularly passed the time by composing beautiful notes to Anna:

My dearest Girl,

Thank you for my letter which I found on my desk on arriving. Each morning Darling if I could only tell you how great a pleasure your daily letters are to me. I long so for you and miss you so that I feel almost as if I could not stand the separation but for these short "paper chats" which put the sunshine into the day for me. Oh! Dear little True Love, how my breast beats with the thought and the hot blood rushes to my head as I picture again the meeting on Saturday.

Belmont and Appleton were in today to fit me to come to Meadowbrook on that day for our opening "Meet." But that is my happy day of the WEAK [sic]. And nothing can keep me from my Baby girl. Ah! I'm happy Sunday too. Don't think me selfish if I want you all to myself ... I feel love starved little one. How I shall kiss the kind hand that wrote to me "<u>Your</u> <u>ever</u> <u>loving</u> Baby." You were royally toasted last night at Clive Dodge's dinner which by the way was a real success and very jolly. ... I have had a long talk with Theodore about his Western investment. He has a good thing I believe, he certainly has sound judgment. He looks very well and had fine sport. Shot a buffalo and three fine stags. I dine with him tomorrow night and suppose we are in for an all-night talk.[41]

Faith was important to Anna, or at least the trappings of religion — and here Elliott suited her as well. Elliott's small New Testament was his "comforting and joyous though silent companion" throughout his travels, and he invited Anna to share his pleasure in it. "Darling if you care to, we will read some of my favorite chapters and verses in the little Testament together."[42]

"All my love and ambition are now centered in you," Anna wrote to Elliott, "and my objects in life are to keep and be worthy of your love, to aid you in the advance of all your projects in life, and to lead myself and you in leading a life worthy of God's children."[43]

"Anna can I show you the truth and strength of my tender, deep love for you? I wonder if you feel how much a part of my life it is, how strong and good a part?"[44] "Thank you Sweet Love for your little letter which I found on my desk — it makes so great a difference in my day to receive one. ... Don't bother to write me when you are not feeling like doing so, only when you do feel like it send a line for it fills my joy and I am wondering all day what you are doing."[45]

Elliott didn't have to wait long; the next day he wrote Anna:

Your sweet letter to me has made me a very happy man all day. It has the ring of your content about it and when my Baby Girl is so, I too have a feeling of deep quiet joy that perfectly satisfies and rests me. My Love my one great wish in life is to make you happy and in so far that I do so is my life a success. I look forward to tomorrow afternoon and seeing you again with great impatience. ... Dear one tomorrow 4:00 train seems so miserably far away. I am going up now for half an hour with the little children of the Orthopedic. ... I went immediately to Alice and Thee's where during dinner we talked over their plan for the winter ... the wedding to come in December, and a great deal of the beautiful and dear bride of that happy day. After dinner Thee went to drill his company (8th Reg[iment]) and I left Alice to go early to bed and went down myself to call on Mrs. Gracie on 36th Street. ... Had a very agreeable evening returning to Thee's at 10½ to a talk over business and political matters, his book, wife and various affairs which last until after one this morning — and was very satisfactory. ... The little house on 45th Street, our "Home" to be is looking very pretty and oh! My darling what a happy boy I shall be when I bring you into it. I thank our kind God for it all.[46]

Like most (although by no means all) young couples of their time and place, Elliott and Anna adhered to the strict moral standards of nineteenth-century courtship, and their feelings for each other were all the more intense for their containment. There was, however, a turning point of some sort in their relationship one night two months before the wedding, when Elliott finally let Anna in on some of his anxiety. "I do so hope you will not have any more horrible nights, and no more dreams which make my boy so wretched," she wrote the next day after Elliott

Elliott, circa 1883, the year he married Anna. Courtesy of The Franklin D. Roosevelt Presidential Library.

left for Manhattan.[47] Her sympathy may have allowed for a physical closeness they had not known before. Elliott wrote a letter that next day as well, reminding Anna that nothing could ever change what had transpired the previous night.

"My heart has been sorrowful today, and the week before me looks very long and dreary. … Do not forget last night, we can neither of us ever recall [undo] it. *I* do not wish to and never shall, being oh *so* happy and proud as I think of it, and the heart beat loyal and true my sweet, that pressed to yours." He concluded with the salutation, "My dear love, God bless you, your lover Elliott."[48]

Anna, always less intense and more guarded than Elliott, ended her note, "Devotedly, Anna R. Hall," and made no mention of physical contact.

The next day Anna thought better of her previous formality and signed that day's letter, "*Your ever loving* Baby." Even so, she convinced herself that whatever had passed between her and Elliott had been a sacramental experience.

"Yesterday, somehow I felt nearer Christ, as though he were really going to take me into his army and make me his. It made me so *peaceful* and happy. I felt as though all my struggles would be ended. ... Remember that you are God's child and he will do what is best for you. ... It is wrong for us to be unhappy when he has given us each other — what more can we ask for!"[49]

Elliott rejoiced in Anna's demonstrative (for her) letters, and yet his deep and enigmatic sadness remained. "Do be happy, my beloved," she urged him.[50] In an attempt to please her, Elliott affected a lighter tone. He could not decide on a wedding present. Would she like diamonds? Or perhaps "a little *coupe* or Victoria [carriage]?"[51] This was a most important question as the first of December, the designated wedding day, drew nearer.

Anna's mother seems to have been aware of Elliott's melancholy, and she too believed that the answer was to lean close to God. In a letter written to Anna on the night before the wedding, Mrs. Hall wrote: "I pray you and Elliott to enter your new life with your hearts turned to God. Go to Him tonight before retiring and in His presence read your Bible and kneel together and ask Him to guide you both through this world which has been so bright to you both, but which must have some clouds, and dearest Anna and Elliott for my sake, and for both of your dear fathers' sakes never fail to have daily prayers."[52]

On his honeymoon, Elliott found time to answer his mother-in-law's note on behalf of himself and his bride.

"Your kind letter we received today and both your children, for I feel for Anna's sake you will consider me one now too, are deeply and truly with you in the spirit of what you say. We both knelt before the Giver of every good and perfect gift and thanked him the source of perfect happiness for His tender loving kindness to us. Dear Lady do not fear about trusting your daughter to me. It shall be my great object all my life to comfort and care for her."[53]

But the "dear lady" suspected that she had every reason to fear. Elliott was clearly a believer, and he had the gentleness of a dove; but the corollary wisdom of a serpent eluded him. Anna's mother, like Elliott's father years before, apparently sensed that this young man, so full of kindness and winning ways and even of spirituality, nevertheless had a susceptibility to demons that no one, least of all himself and his bride, had the perspicacity or knowledge to combat.

⊰ 1 0 ⊱

"SOCIETY WITH A BIG S"

To stand today at the corner of 21st Street and Park Avenue South, with its pizza restaurants, Korean-owned grocery stores, and trendy night spots, is to feel very little of the presence of the past — until one notices Calvary Church. If one tries hard enough, it is almost possible to imagine a cold but clear December day in 1883 when a virtual traffic jam of elegant carriages lined the street, carting guests to the wedding of exquisite Anna Hall and dashing Elliott Roosevelt.

Containing a collection of some of the world's most beautiful stained-glass windows, the edifice is a remnant of a time when well-to-do and socially conscious citizens made their churches into centers of social service. It was appropriate that Elliott Roosevelt, whose altruistic father had owned a home two blocks away, would be married here; it was suitable as well that the rite would be performed by The Rev. Henry Satterlee, whose energy in caring for the particularly needy was eclipsed only by the vision he would bring to overseeing the construction of the National Cathedral in Washington, D.C.

Perhaps it was fitting also that this tragic marriage would begin in a church with a beautiful yet dark interior, which even now adds a melancholy aspect to the music and liturgy.

Even so, it is not difficult to understand why the wedding was called "one of the most brilliant social events of the season" by *The New York Herald*. "The bride was every bit a queen and her bridesmaids were worthy of her."[1] Elliott had been best man at Theodore's wedding, but for reasons lost to posterity, Elliott chose his childhood friend Percy King for the honor.

The "sportsman" and the "queen" were about to embark on an undertaking that they took with the utmost seriousness but for which neither of them was suited, at least not at this point in their development. Did either of them sense this? In the shadow cast by his father and brother, Elliott never felt worthy of much, and he must have felt himself extraordinarily blessed as he turned at the altar and saw his bride, in her long satin dress, coming toward him.

What of Anna? As she was escorted up the aisle by Edward Ludlow, her maternal grandfather, did she look at her groom, or at the statue of Christ above him? Did she seem rather like a marble sculpture herself, holy and remote?

William T. Youngs gives a wonderful evocation of what came next:

Outside the air was crisp and clear. In the street the young couple and other guests climbed into fine carriages. Drivers urged horses forward, and soon the wedding procession rolled onto the busy confluence of Broadway and Fifth Avenue. Flanked by elegant hotels, this was the most fashionable crossroads in New York. A tall white-gloved policeman from the elite "Broadway Squad" waved a rattan stick over the traffic, guiding the carriages through the favored crossing with a bandmaster's crisp precision. Signaled on, the coaches moved up Fifth Avenue, where New York society was made tangible in monuments of stone: A.T. Stewart's column-studded marble palace and the Astor mansions, their solid walls built on profits from western furs. Here stood

Formal wedding portrait of Anna Hall Roosevelt, December 1883. Courtesy of The Franklin D. Roosevelt Presidential Library.

New York's most fashionable clubs: the Calumet, the Knickerbocker, the Union, and the Manhattan. The wedding guests knew them well; these clubs, this avenue were their private realm within the city.[2]

As the carriages headed north, then west on 37th Street, Elliott and Anna prepared to receive their guests. The house could hardly have seemed more serene and genteel with its rose bowers and chamber orchestra. Elliott and Anna were their enchanting selves as they moved among their guests discussing the theater (this was the age of Charlotte Cushman and the great tragedian Edwin Booth, also a Gramercy Park resident), their travels and mutual friends.

At last Mary Hall and Mittie Roosevelt said goodnight to the bride and groom and sent them off to begin their married life.

That night, Mittie wrote to Elliott from 6 West 57th Street:

> My darling Elliott, a more happy Mother does not exist after the faithful remembrance of the idolized son shown lately by the telegram received so immediately after the wedding. …
> I wished to run out of the pew & kiss & hug & never leave you when you stood to receive the sweet bride. …

Her next line is poignant in light of what would ultimately happen with Anna and Elliott: "I wish you great blessings & long happy lives."[3]

When Elliott had returned from his trip around the world clearly ill, Mittie had put him up in a small room adjacent to her own in order to take care of him. Her extravagant affection he took with a "caressing" humor, as a friend described it.[4] If he came in late, she left notes by his bedside: "My darling son, I have missed you all evening. Sleep well, darling, and call Mother if you wish her."[5]

Mittie shared Elliott's joy, but it was difficult for her to give up Elliott to his bride, more so than it had been for her to let go of Theodore.

Darling Elliott my own beloved child you have your Mother's deep love & blessing. "Blessed are the peacemakers" — You are a great lesson to me my son, my comfort child. What I am to do without you! God knows only. I am sure of your love & Heaven's blessings rest upon you in all your ways — & it is perfectly right that you should marry your dear Anna ...[6]

Mittie missed Elliott terribly. "… With no boy to peep in the door between ourselves, the only hopeful thing in your old room is the little crib waiting for a little new baby! … Uncle Ellie who I thought loved children never comes to his godson," wrote Mittie in an uncharacteristically scolding tone, referring to Corinne's newborn son Theodore Douglas Robinson.[7] "Our dear baby is heavily breathing with bronchitis and is truly miserable with fever. Corinne is so unhappy about him. …[8]

"Happy New Year my dearest Son is your Mother's fervent wish," Mittie wrote to Elliott six weeks before she died. "I miss your prayers with me more than I can say."[9]

Two weeks after Elliott's wedding, Mittie wrote, "After taking a nap I had waked up so homesick for you that I must just write you this line to tell you of my ardent mother love. … Please come down some evening to O[yster] B[ay] to see me."[10]

These early days were very happy for Anna and Elliott, although Anna was often unwell, even on their honeymoon. "I am so glad dear Anna got better with the journey & continues to be so. I hope this Honeymoon trip will be the means of restoring her to health & resting both of you," wrote Mittie.[11]

"I have just returned from the station having missed the ten o'clock train, so that I feel very cross, as I had planned a long shopping day," Anna wrote to Bamie the following summer. "Perhaps it is just as well as I am feel-ing very miserably & my bed is so comfortable."[12] "Doing nothing," Anna would confide to Bamie two months later, "is very attractive to me."[13]

Elliott attempted to settle into the life of a good young businessman by working for the Ludlow firm, owned by his mother-in-law's family and the premier real estate business in New York City. The home he and Anna shared was a brownstone in the Thirties with a full compliment of servants, and while they did not live ostentatiously (unlike some of their even more well-to-do friends), neither were they given to denying them-selves, with Anna ordering her gowns from Palmer in London and Worth in Paris while Elliott indulged his interest in hunting and horses. "Wasn't it nice that Elliott and Winty Rutherfurd won the doubles at Polo?" Anna asked Bamie, unknowingly invoking a name that would be pivotal in her daughter's life.* "I am so pleased for him."[14]

As Elliott pursued his sportsman's life at the Meadow Brook Country Club, he reminded Anna that even these short separations were painful. "I sat cozily over the big wood fire gazing into the flames and wishing for and thinking of, my Sweet Heart and True Love so sadly far away," he wrote to Anna, who was visiting her family at Tivoli. "I came back to town the early train by a.m. and will have a quiet evening with the Mother. A long sad and heartfelt longing for you as my companion for the night. With tender love dear believe me, faithfully your boy, Elliott."[15]

Elliott and Anna were charter members of "the swells," as the newspa-pers referred to the younger and livelier members of New York's upper class; indeed, they were among "the howling swells" that feared the exclusive Patriarchs' Ball had become too democratic![16] (A clarification is in order here: it was felt by "the howling swells" that many among New York's upper class had compromised their morals by benefiting from the mach-inations of Boss Tweed and the notorious Tweed Ring. Those of sterling character wished to keep from being guilty by association with those trai-

Anna and Elliott, in this photograph taken circa 1885, were charter members of "the swells." Courtesy of The Franklin D. Roosevelt Presidential Library.

tors to their class who were not sufficiently scrupulous.) Certainly no one, at any time or in any place, in real life or in a fairy tale, could have been better looking than Anna and Elliott. *Town Topics*, an arbiter of propriety and good taste, criticized American girls for their slovenly posture compared with young English ladies, but noted that Anna Hall Roosevelt was one New Yorker who was always graceful and stately, and the periodical recommended her as the one to emulate.

Despite her statuesque bearing, Anna was not always stiff and starchy. Unlike her dour and puritanical father, she enjoyed life. To be sure, it was a quiet enjoyment, well within the dictates of decorum — but it was enjoyment even so. A welcome guest in the great houses of Fifth Avenue, at the loveliest social occasions in Newport, Bar Harbor, Tuxedo, Meadow Brook, and various favorite vacation spots in Europe, Anna loved the opera, tennis, dancing, amateur theatricals, cotillions, meetings of various charitable organizations, horse and dog shows, and everything else connected with "the season." Anna's deepest happiness was found in what her daughter called "Society with a big S."

For Anna, none of it was trivial. It was all beautiful and graceful, and she fit in like a perfectly cut piece in a delicate jigsaw puzzle. A society columnist described Anna as "fair, frail and fragile, and therefore a good illustration of beauty in American women." Helen Cutting Wilmerding, a schoolmate of Eleanor's and the daughter of a friend of Anna's, remembered, "The proud set of the head on the shoulders was the distinctive look of the Halls."

Anna was pride personified. She was, after all, born and reared to take her place in this setting. This was "a closed society to which one either did or did not belong,"[17] recalled Mrs. Winthrop Chanler. If anyone belonged, Anna Hall Roosevelt did. She was "a leader in the exclusive circles she adorns."[18] She knew exactly what she was, and liked it a lot.

Elliott had all kinds of things he was going to do. He joined a local Republican club and flirted with the idea of running for office. He wanted to write a book about his adventures in India. But so much of his time was taken playing polo and going to parties that finally he accepted his dreams for what they were — dreams. Those daydreams were, after all, "pure pleasure"; to live them out would have required that he occasionally do things that were not pleasurable.

When sorrow came to Elliott, it never came in small doses. Eleanor maintained that the pain of the people Elliott loved became his own pain as well. The family anticipated the arrival of the second of Mittie's grandchildren, the first child of Theodore and Alice, but Elliott and Anna were married all of two months when Elliott was shattered and bewildered by the blow his family suffered on Valentine's Day, 1884. He took after his mother, and she was his friend and champion, as their many letters attest. When Mittie died of typhoid fever on the same day and in the same house as Alice (from Bright's disease following childbirth), Elliott wondered what cosmic fate was being played out at 6 West 57th Street.

When Corinne and Douglas arrived the night before, they were startled by Elliott's pale face and staring eyes. "There is a curse on this house," Elliott said as he opened the door. "Mother is dying and Alice is dying too."

Theodore, who had worried through a foggy night ride on the train from Albany, arrived an hour later, at 11:30 p.m. Alice, twenty-two years old,[19] died eleven hours after Mittie, whose four children were at her bedside. Mittie was forty-eight.[20]

Elliott's father gave him an ideal to emulate, but his mother understood him. "Mittie — slight, humorous, creative, emotional, and very Southern," writes one author, "Thee — large, serious, motivated, self-contained, and very Northern."[21] His father in all likelihood suspected Elliott's weaknesses and would have attempted to guide his son with the compassion he showed all people, but Mittie felt right at home with the sort of man Elliott was — a throwback to his pleasure- and leisure-loving Georgia forebears. With her "splendid dash and energy,"[22] demonstrative, affectionate nature, vivacity and equestrian expertise, Mittie was nearly a female version of Elliott. Now he was without the two people who gave him life and who might have helped to redeem his later life.

Mittie's last few months had been filled with delights connected with the marriages of Theodore and Elliott, whom she called her "comfort boy" and of whom she had remained solicitous. "Uncle Jimmie tells me of your accident. ... I am most anxious to hear from you just how your ankle is & exactly what you are doing for it. ..."[23] "My sprain is nearly

Anna Hall Roosevelt, circa 1884, wearing tiger claw necklace inherited from Mittie. Courtesy of The Franklin D. Roosevelt Presidential Library.

well again, quite well enough for me to ride again," Elliott answered her. "Had a jolly two days at Tivoli. My Sweet Girl was perfectly charming and so beautifully loving and good to me. She delighted in her present of the pin from you and wears it in the evening every day. Keeping the soft white lace about her neck, together."[24]

"I am anxious to learn from some of the family how Anna enjoyed Oyster Bay and what they all thought of her. She is very lovely,"[25] wrote Mittie. "Give my love devotedly to Anna & tell her to love your mother. Will you?"[26] Mittie was pleased that Anna wore the necklace made with claws from a tiger Elliott shot in India, a gift from Elliott to Mittie, and then from Mittie to Anna.[27]

Mittie was likewise overjoyed with Theodore, who had been full of happy plans for building a home for Alice and himself and the several children they planned on having, to be called "Leeholm," after Alice's family. (Not until several years later would he take up residence in the house, renamed "Sagamore Hill.") "Sunday at West Point Aunt Annie and I walked all over Teddie's place down to the Cold Spring side, finding his stagnant pond & his spring (a sunken barrel with the largest bull-frogs 'sitting in slime & with no thoughts — ready to yell tonight.') Teddie was there yesterday with his architect Mr. Rich & with the surveyor afterward. Today went in town to see about his western trip."[28] "As the time draws near I do dread parting with Teddie & Alice — the end of December they go to Albany for three months, if not more. I shall dread being in the house without them. Alice has endeared herself to me, she is so companionable & always ready to do what I ask her. I do love her & I think she loves me,"[29] wrote Mittie Roosevelt of the young daughter-in-law who would die the same day as she.

Mittie occasionally displayed a mordant sense of humor, as in this letter to Elliott concerning a mistaken newspaper item:

I must tell you the latest engagement — Can you guess — Miss Fanny Morris to — Mr. George Cabot Ward! Strange as it seems, I do believe it to be a very happy engagement tho' Mr. Ward has only been dead sixteen to eighteen months!

But Mittie's sensitivity was not far behind: "Fanny wrote me a lovely letter which I would like you to see, so perfectly calm & quiet."[30]

"She became, in years immediately following the war, a figure of real consequence, or at least within the limits imposed by gender and the social order," writes David McCullough, in a memorable tribute:

To her already stunning physical beauty was now added the luster of success. She became a personage, quite as much as her husband, one of the great ladies of New York and one to whom society could naturally turn for example and leadership. She, the southerner, the outsider, ranked with Mrs. Hamilton Fish ... and the two Mrs. Astors as one of those "gentlewomen of such birth, breeding and tact that people were always glad to be led by them ... whose entertainments claimed most comment, whose fiat none were found to dispute," to quote a contemporary author, Mrs. Burton Harrison. ... In the "graciousness of her manner and that inherent talent for winning and holding the sympathetic interest of those around her," wrote Mrs. Harrison, "I have seen none to surpass her."[31]

For all her idiosyncrasies, Mittie had something that certain of the Astor and Vanderbilt women lacked — a deeply loving nature, remarkable kindness, and a sense of what is truly important. "My precious child I love you with all my heart — in fact a very tenderly loving heart & most softhearted when Ellie is in question. I mean the darling boy who is and has been such a comfort boy to his mother."[32] Elliott would never truly recover from her loss.

Elliott was also to lose the companionship of his brother for over a year, for Theodore was so dumbfounded by his double loss that his sisters feared he was losing his mind. "He feels the awful loneliness more and more," Corinne wrote to Elliott, "and I fear he sleeps little for he walks a great deal in the night and his eyes have that strained red look."[33]

Theodore had to get away from familiar surroundings and to be alone with nature. He deposited his baby girl into the care of his reliable sister Bamie and took up a rancher's life on property he had purchased in the "Badlands" of the Dakota Territory (later North Dakota). Theodore traveled west, "not thinking to recover from his loss," writes biographer Peter Collier, "but merely to live what was left of his life in its afterglow." But then a most unexpected thing happened — the strange environment began to have a healing effect. "The landscape of the Badlands had a mournful beauty that drew out his inner torment like a poultice."[34]

After great pain a Roosevelt trait was, finally, to feel "the pull of breath / better than death."[35] But Theodore was always more resilient than his brother, and now Elliott was without the company of three key Roosevelts and under the spell of a well-meaning but self-important young beauty.

After all, how could he not be in thrall to her? Almost everyone was. "She never entered a room as others did — she seemed almost to float forward, with upraised hand and cordial greeting," remembered a friend. Her "presence was a blessing"; her smile was "the sweetest play of light upon the features, ... an expression of sweetness and sympathy sometimes so intense that one knew it was never to be forgotten."[36]

Anna may have had "sweetness" and "sympathy" to spare — these qualities, however, would not always be apparent to one person who was about to enter Anna's idyllic world: her daughter.

*Winthrop Rutherford, after failing to rescue Consuelo Vanderbilt from an arranged marriage to the Duke of Marlborough, married Alice Morton, daughter of Vice President Levi P. Morton. Late in life, Rutherford married a second time — to Lucy Mercer, who a few years earlier had been the catalyst for a crisis in Eleanor Roosevelt's marriage.

⧎ 11 ⧎

"LITTLE NELL"

The year Eleanor Roosevelt was born, the tallest building in New York was Trinity Church on Broadway. Every business day, when the hour struck, men would pause together in the street and synchronize their watches to the clock in the church's spire. Few structures were more than five stories high. New York Harbor was dotted with white sails and gigantic iron merchant ships; there was no Statue of Liberty in the harbor, but the arm holding her torch was sitting for all to see on East 24th Street, near the home of Herman Melville in the Gramercy Park district so important to the Roosevelt family.[1] Castle Garden, where immigration officials busily sorted out bewildered people, was as noisy as the "lunatic asylum"[2] on nearby Blackwell's Island, later known as Welfare Island and, after the death of Eleanor's husband, Roosevelt Island.

Eleanor's arrival was not without anxiety — the sudden loss of Theodore's wife two days after her child was born was a fresh wound — but Elliott and Anna kept fear at arm's length as they excitedly awaited the arrival of "precious boy jr." — who turned out to be a girl. Bamie took charge of the baby and her mother and spread the news of the arrival of the small daughter.

Elliott's beloved aunt Annie Gracie was reminded of the day Elliott was born. With characteristic tenderness she wrote:[3]

Bamie's telegram at 11:30 this morning brought us the joyful news. I am overjoyed to hear of itty girl's (not itty "precious boy jr") safe arrival and just long to have her in my arms. How well I remember when I held you darling Ellie for the first time. My heart beat so I could hardly hold you! And you were so rosy and so beautiful! Kiss Anna for me.

The little girl was named Anna Eleanor Roosevelt, after Elliott's eldest sister. She would never be called Anna or call herself Anna.

From the start there was a deep connection between Eleanor and Elliott. To him she was "a miracle from Heaven."[4] She was every inch a Roosevelt rather than a Hall or Bulloch — with her tendency to earnest virtue, large, mild eyes, somewhat oversized mouth and teeth that seemed "to have no future,"[5] as her aunt Edith would famously observe.

"I was a shy, solemn child even at the age of two," wrote Eleanor, "and I am sure that even when I danced, which I did frequently, I never smiled. My earliest recollections are of being dressed up and allowed to come down into what must have been a dining room and dance for a group of gentlemen who applauded and laughed as I pirouetted before them. Finally, my father would pick me up and hold me high in the air. All this is rather vague to me, but my father was never vague."[6]

During Eleanor's earliest childhood, Anna and Elliott were very happy in each other's company. While visiting her family in Tivoli, Anna wrote her husband, "I am crazy to hear from you and wish you were here. We could have such nice times going around together." Eleanor received mixed signals from her parents. She worried her mother just by being who she was — "She is so old-fashioned," Anna would complain — but her parents were so enraptured with each other that their daughter must have felt included in their circle of love. Eleanor may have been "shy" and "solemn" when she was two, but when her father tucked her into bed on her fourth birthday, she told him, "I love everybody and everybody loves me."[7] "Was it not cunning?" thought Elliott.

Elliott gave his daughter the endearment by which Eleanor Roosevelt would define herself— "Little Nell." It is impossible to overstate the significance of this appellation. One of Elliott's favorite books, Charles Dickens's *The Old Curiosity Shop*, is the story of a child, Little Nell, who keeps house for her grandfather, who is hopelessly addicted to gambling. When they are forced to flee a demonic landlord, the little girl and the helpless old man wander throughout England pursued by their vicious creditor but pitied and sheltered by various eccentric and tenderhearted characters. Though only a child, Little Nell is the parent in the relationship. "Dear, gentle, patient, noble Nell," Dickens eulogizes.[8] There is a still deeper element to the "Little Nell" cognomen. Elliott had been called Nell as a boy; "Little Nell" was a sacrament of his identification with her.

"What you are in life results in great part from the influence on you exerted over the years by just a few people," wrote the elderly Eleanor Roosevelt.

The first were my mother and father. I suppose it is natural for any person to feel that the most vivid personalities in early youth were those of his parents. This was certainly so in my case. My mother always remained somewhat awe-inspiring. She was the most dignified and beautiful person. But she had such high standards of morals that it encouraged me to wrongdoing; I felt it was utterly impossible for me ever to live up to her! My father, on the other hand, was always a very close and warm personality. I think I knew that his standards were nowhere nearly as difficult

According to Eleanor, her mother "looked so beautiful. ... [a] vision which I admired inordinately." Photograph circa 1890. Courtesy of The Franklin D. Roosevelt Presidential Library.

to achieve and that he would look upon my shortcomings with a much more forgiving eye. He provided me with some badly needed reassurance, for in my earliest days I knew that I could never hope to achieve my mother's beauty and I fell so short in so many ways of what was expected of me. I needed my father's warmth and devotion more perhaps than the average child, who would have taken love for granted and not worried about it. ...[9]

Eleanor loved to watch both of her attractive parents dress for their busy social lives. Her mother "looked so beautiful ... I was grateful to be allowed to touch her dress or her jewels or anything that was part of the vision which I admired inordinately."[10] Observing her father was fun, too. "He would take me into his dressing room in the mornings, or when he was dressing for dinner, and let me watch each thing he did."[11] This included waxing the tips of his moustache, and perhaps turning up the cuffs of his pants in the fashion of men in the 1890s. Of course his pants were creaseless — everyone recognized creased trousers as homemade; creaseless pants were tailor-made.[12] He usually wore a brown derby and patent-leather shoes, a dark gray frock coat, and of course a boutonniere — violets during the day, a gardenia for the evening.

Although Elliott occasionally affected a cane, the fact that he was a Roosevelt probably kept him from being a full-fledged "dude." "A dude was a dandy — any man who wore exquisite clothes, and we children were inclined to laugh at him as he sauntered down the street with a cane and spats and ... a light overcoat with plaid buttons which spread fan-like, as it left his waistline," wrote New Yorker Charles Hanson Towne. According to Towne, the term "dude" became common parlance around 1880, when Elliott was twenty. New York historian Jerry Patterson writes that, "The cane was important ... because it had connotations of the British gentry. The dude took his cane into the drawing room when visiting ladies. The fashionable and much-admired posture for a male caller was seated, leaning forward, his chin resting thoughtfully on the gilded head of the cane. Though worshipped and emulated by young men, especially junior clerks in stores and offices, the dude was always faintly ridiculous to other American men and subject to derision even by his contemporaries."[13] Elliott's friends De Lancey and Woodbury Kane, William Whitney, Frank Gray Griswold, and William Jay definitely qualified as "dudes"; perhaps these were the men for whom baby Eleanor danced.

Another ingredient that kept Elliott from being a "dude" was his rugged sportsmanship. He hurt himself constantly. "Elliott's eye is much better,"

Anna wrote Bamie from Bar Harbor. "That is it doesn't hurt him now at all but he cannot see with it very well. He is going to play polo in the doubles at Newport. He is improving so much lately that he thinks he will be perfectly well by next week."[14]

Elliott continued to send thoughtful notes to people he loved, for no other reason than to let them know he was thinking of them. "My dear little girl," he wrote Corinne from his office at 11 Pine Street.

I had such a nice talk with Mr. Rainsford [Rector of St. George's Episcopal Church in Manhattan] coming in on the train today. He says that you are the best educated and most attractive woman he has met & that Douglas [is] to be proud of such a wife [and I of such] a sister. He don't know [sic] how really proud I am of you, does he Sweet-Heart? And think of having a brother like Thee too! Dear Sister I am coming out some day soon to see you. Precious girl take good care of your self. Anna & I talk & think of you all the time. Anna & baby Eleanor send love & kisses. The latter says "Ess" every time I ask her if she loves "Aunt Corinne." Anna sent a lot of lilacs into the orthopedic children this morning. I left them & the children were delighted.[15]

Eleanor spoke French before she spoke English — her parents engaging a French governess — and all her life Eleanor was fluent in French, a language she loved. To speak French was considered one of the essential accomplishments for a girl of her station in life, but Eleanor did not learn to cook or sew until one of her mother's aunts discovered her lack of skill. "I surmise that my mother was roundly taken to task," wrote Eleanor.[16]

Anna was seldom "taken to task," but she was something of a taskmistress herself. "You would be unhappy if you were a man," little Eleanor told Aunt Pussie, her mother's sister, "because your wife would send you

"Scolding Father," April 30, 1889." Courtesy of The Franklin D. Roosevelt Presidential Library

down to town every day."[17] There is a picture of Eleanor, five years old, with her small index finger raised. Elliott wrote in the upper left-hand corner, "Scolding Father."

Elliott was used to people scolding him, but Eleanor was "afraid of being scolded, afraid that other people would not like me."[18] Elliott never scolded his little girl, though; "I knew only that he was the center of my world, and that all around him loved him."[19] Eleanor's mother, on the other hand, seems to have been a perpetual scold. "... I can remember standing in the door, very often with my finger in my mouth — which was, of course, forbidden — and I can see the look in her eyes and hear the tone of her voice as she said: 'Come in, Granny.'"[20] "Eleanor, I hardly know what's going to happen to you," Anna said to her daughter. "You're so plain that you really have nothing to do except *be good*."[21]

Perhaps Eleanor was inclined to be solemn with Anna. "I was always disgracing my mother," she remembered, and this by doing nothing — just by her uncomfortable appearance.[22] Would she have been so solemn with Aunt Annie Gracie?

The other Elliott in Eleanor's life, her son, believed that "a sense of Victorian Gothic guilt colored much of her thinking throughout her younger years. She tended to remember deaths in her family — and they were many — instead of births and the simple everyday rewards of living." Certainly her son was correct in that Eleanor's belief that she "must have been a more wrinkled and less attractive baby than the average," is "without a shred of evidence in any photo album."[23] Eleanor claimed to have been given this impression "from all accounts"[24]; however, the only negative account on record is her mother's. "Baby has grown fatter and seems very stupid and has absolutely no hair," Anna wrote to Bamie.[25]

"Although Mother regarded herself as having been almost exclusively her father's daughter," wrote the second Elliott, "I think that she was more the product of her mother's stern upbringing."[26] While her father would disappoint Eleanor, it was her mother who cast the darkest shadow over her childhood. "No one can make you feel inferior without your consent," was the venerable Eleanor Roosevelt's counsel. Anna was the first one to make Eleanor feel inferior.

What was Anna to make of this alien child who, it was clear, was not going to fit the mold of "the beautiful Hall sisters"? One wonders what their relationship would have been like had Anna lived to see Eleanor grow up, for when the latter wrote her memoirs as First Lady she made no attempt to hide her disdain for the conformity that defined Anna's world.

> My mother belonged to that New York City Society which thought
> itself all-important. Old Mr. Peter Marie, who gave choice parties
> and whose approval stamped young girls and young matrons a

success, called my mother a queen, and bowed before her charm and beauty, and to her this was important. In that society you were kind to the poor, you did not neglect your philanthropic duties in whatever community you lived, you assisted the hospitals and did something for the needy. You accepted invitations to dine and dance with the right people only, you lived where you would be in their midst. You thought seriously about your children's education, you read the books that everybody read, you were familiar with good literature. In short, you conformed to the conventional pattern.[27]

"Old Mr. Peter Marie" is described in *The First Four Hundred: Biographical Sketches* as "broker, amateur poet, collector of fans and snuff boxes, and cotillion leader."[28] So it was important to Anna that he called her a queen. Indeed.

Eleanor added, "My father, Elliott Roosevelt, charming, good-looking, loved by all who came in contact with him, high or low, had a background and upbringing which were a bit alien to her pattern."[29]

There was one pattern they did share — love of the pleasures associated with "the idle class." Elliott wanted to indulge his wife. Of course, his inheritance made it unnecessary for him to work, but on those occasions when he attempted to settle into a job, his motivation was to enable Anna to live even more luxuriously. "I must get wealth, for my little wife's sake."[30] But it never took. He had no taste for the business world.

Had Elliott not been beset with ill health, alcoholism, and the shadows of his purposeful and productive father and brother, he would likely have settled happily into a life much like that of his acquaintances Sidney Dillon Ripley and James Vanderburg Parker. Ripley's money had been accumulated by his grandfather, president of the Union Pacific Railroad, and he was himself treasurer of the Equitable Life Insurance Company, owned by his wife's family, but he rarely put in a day at the office. Like Elliott, he lived in Hempstead and "he was mainly occupied with horses."[31] When he died in 1905, his *New York Times* obituary stated, "Mr. Ripley held largely aloof from business, as well as from public affairs."[32] James Parker was a lifelong bachelor and perennial guest of Mrs. Astor's. A book at the time described him as having "inherited a large fortune which has enabled him to be a lifelong man of leisure."[33] As one historian of the period recounts:

> In their own circles there was little criticism of men if they chose not to work. ... Middle-class businessmen, and journalists, too, sneered at "Society loafers," but their wives thought loafers charming cotillion partners, and their daughters dreamed of marrying one. Hostesses like Mrs. Astor depended on unemployed or underemployed males as escorts, dinner partners, and cotillion leaders. Today, such gentlemen are known as "walkers," and they are as indispensable to hostesses now as they were then. Mrs. Astor always had such men in her entourage, which meant they were invited to every party she gave and escorted her when Mr. Astor was absent, which he usually was. In the next generation ... Mrs. Cornelius Vanderbilt, who inherited Mrs. Astor's social supremacy, used to keep a card index of "men who can lunch," which implied that they did not have a job and were thus free for her two-hour weekday luncheons, and another file of "men who dance."[34]

When Eleanor was three, her Uncle Theodore remarried, this time to his childhood friend Edith Carow, and resumed work on the rambling house near Oyster Bay, Long Island, begun during his marriage to Alice Lee and abandoned after her death. He called it "Sagamore Hill," after the chief of the Mohonk Indian tribe that had once prevailed on the land.

W. KURTZ.   MADISON SQUARE

Elliott was a member of the New York Militia at the time his daughter Eleanor was born in 1884. Courtesy of The Franklin D. Roosevelt Presidential Library.

Elliott, too, built a large home he called "Half-way Nirvana," on ten acres in Hempstead, twenty miles away. Here Eleanor played with animals and had a kitten of her own — an angora, but she called the little cat "angostura." Perhaps Elliott envisioned his estate one day overflowing with children and pets and animal skins and trophies, as Theodore's would be — but much as he loved his family, he was no more comfortable with the thought of being a *paterfamilias* than he was in the role of businessman. He was still lost without his own father.

He was happy to be a godfather, however, and laughed when, on a visit to "Springwood," the home of James Roosevelt and his family,

Elliott's godson Franklin carried Eleanor around the nursery on his back, playing "horsey." Eleanor always insisted that she was a morose child and that this ride was undertaken "probably under protest," but the impression she had of her own solemnity was implanted by her mother. When the little girl came in to afternoon tea wearing a starched white dress and stood shyly in the doorway, her mother apologized to Sara Roosevelt and called, "Come in, Granny."

"She often called me that, for I was a solemn child, without beauty and painfully shy and I seemed like a little old woman entirely lacking in the spontaneous joy and mirth of youth," wrote Eleanor. But this cannot have been true all the time, for in Elliott's presence she chattered away and "even danced for him, intoxicated by the pure joy of motion, twisting round and round until he would pick me up and throw me into the air and tell me I made him dizzy."[35]

By the spring of 1887, Elliott's marriage was in trouble, as his "melancholia" began to get the upper hand. Elliott quit the Ludlow real estate firm and decided to take his wife and daughter to Europe for a lengthy interlude. Anna hoped that this separation from his drinking cronies would distract him and refocus his energies and ambitions, but Anna, "instead of anchoring him in a domestic life," as one historian observes, "exaggerated his self-indulgent traits by her own frivolity."[36]

On the first day out, May 20, Anna, her sister Tissie, three-year-old Eleanor and her nurse, and Elliott were floating through fog aboard *Brittanic* when that formidable vessel was struck by the smaller *Celtic*, which was on her way in to the same port from which *Brittanic* had put to sea.

Unlike Theodore, but very like his godson Franklin would become, Elliott was an expert sailor who hoped to transfer this enthusiasm to his wife and daughter; but on this day he would rescue Eleanor from an experience that kept her aloof from all things nautical for the rest of her life.

Celtic hit *Brittanic* twice, the first time bouncing off but then crashing nose-first ten feet into *Brittanic's* side. Several people were killed and at least one newspaper reported that a child was beheaded. Anna, however, took the experience with preternatural calm, writing to Bamie, "The strain for a few minutes when we all thought we were sinking was fearful though there were no screams and no milling about. Everyone was perfectly quiet. We were among those taken on life boats to the *Celtic*." Whatever happened was enough to traumatize her three-year-old daughter, however. One suspects Joseph Lash's description is closer to the mark:

> The sea foamed, iron bars and belts snapped, and above the din could be heard the moans of the dying and injured. Grownups panicked. Stokers and boiler men emerging from the depths of the BRITTANIC made a wild rush for the lifeboats until the captain forced them back at the point of his revolver. The air was filled with "cries of terror," Eleanor's among them.[37]

Eleanor would remember looking down into the face of her father as he stood in a pitching lifeboat with his arms outstretched to catch her. Not even his endearments and entreaties could keep her from grasping the sailor who held her over the side. He finally managed to force her small hands to let go, and although the drop into Elliott's arms could not have lasted more than a second, the memory of falling next to the side of the huge sinking ship was frightening enough that when, as an adult, Eleanor finally braced herself against her fear of the water and learned to swim, she considered it a milestone. "You must do the thing you think you cannot do," was the mature Eleanor Roosevelt's perennial counsel — but much to her husband's chagrin, one thing she never could do was love the sea.

Anna and Elliott knew that they must go ahead with this extended stay in Europe for the sake of Elliott's physical and mental well-being, but

Eleanor, around the time of the Brittanic *disaster, circa 1887. Courtesy of The Franklin D. Roosevelt Presidential Library.*

Eleanor, with all the might of a three-year-old, refused absolutely to go near the water. They felt that they had no choice but to leave her behind, and they called upon Elliott's aunt Anna Gracie, who loved all children and especially loved Eleanor just as she had doted on Elliott.

"We took a cab and called for our sweet little Eleanor and brought her out here with us," Aunt Annie wrote to Corinne.

> She was so little and gentle & had made such a narrow escape out of the great ocean that it made her seem doubly helpless & pathetic to us. ... She asked two or three times in the train coming

Aunt Anna Gracie, circa 1885. Courtesy of The Houghton Library, Harvard University.

out here, where her "dear Mamma was, & where her Papa was, & where is Aunt Tissie?" I told her, "They have gone to Europe." She said, "Where is Baby's home now?" I said "baby's home is Gracewood with Uncle Bunkle & Aunt Gracie," which seemed to satisfy the sweet little darling. But as we came near the Bay driving by Mrs. Swan's she said to her uncle in an anxious alarmed way "Baby does not want to go into the water. Not in a boat." It is really touching. ...[38]

"That summer I remember; the pretty house and grounds at Oyster Bay, the bantam chickens which were called mine, and the eggs I brought in for breakfast," wrote Eleanor in the 1930s. "Occasional 'Br'er Rabbit' stories, told me by sweet and gentle Auntie Gracie, visits to Auntie Bye, my father's older sister, who, it seems to me, had a cottage in the woods nearby."[39] Tender and affectionate as Aunt Annie Gracie was, Eleanor must have wondered why she had been deserted by her parents, just as Elliott must have wondered as a boy why he had to be sent away so often. This would be the strongest tie that would bind Eleanor and Elliott: their status as outcasts — although they were not yet outcasts together.

For feminine companionship Anna brought along her sister Elizabeth ("Tissie"). Naturally, the Hall sisters were admired by all and enjoyed it thoroughly.

"We have had a glorious time. In England the girls took like wildfire and they really had a great success," Elliott wrote Bamie. The "two girls are having that kind of a dissipated time buying dresses, hats and the Lord knows what that I don't know what will become of mine or the Hall mother's credit if I don't get them into less tempting quarters soon. … Tissie was too jolly for anything, and Anna they fell down and worshipped. She certainly never has looked so perfectly lovely or seemed so strong and well." She didn't seem very well when she had "a headache for six hours" after Elliott "persuaded [her] to give up the Italian Lakes and arranged a very good September in Scotland. It is selfish of me I know but I think she will enjoy it too really when once there. …"[40]

Elliott and Anna did enjoy their six months abroad, but the trip to Europe did not change any of their old habits. After they came home, Anna and Elliott were often separated. She spent the summer of 1888 in Newport with her friends the Vanderbilts and Morgans; Elliott joined her there frequently, but they were by no means the inseparable couple they had been. While Elliott spent two weeks racing aboard the *Bedouin*, the boat of his friend Archie Rogers, Anna visited Theodore and Edith in Oyster Bay. "My dearest old Nellie Boy," she wrote:

I am waiting anxiously to see the papers to see if you reached New London safely. We are having lovely weather and are most comfortably settled. I am very lazy and don't come down until

Elliott at Meadowbrook Country Club, circa 1883. Courtesy of The Franklin D. Roosevelt Presidential Library.

nine o'clock and Baby has a splendid time. Yesterday she went to Lewis West's party and this morning is to play on the beach with Alice and then she has lessons with Aunt Annie. … Uncle Jimmie [Gracie] wants me to tackle Mrs. James [Sara Delano Roosevelt] for a large subscription to the Orthopedic [the hospital begun by Elliott's father]. I know I shall fail but of course will try. Write when you can. I know you are enjoying it and find the party sufficiently congenial. … Try and persuade Dr. Lusk to come to town by Sept. 1st. Tell him how worried I am. …[41]

In his memorial to Alice, Theodore had written, "When my heart's dearest died, the light went out from my life forever."[42] He was, however, experiencing a newfound joy in his second marriage. He took Edith to his ranch in the Badlands. "I have thought very often and very lovingly of you, my darling sister, since we left you alone in New York — that is, as much alone as it is ever possible for you to be," he wrote Bamie from "Medora, Dakota." "Tell Nell I have sent him the two goat heads from Mandan. ..."[43]

Theodore's family was growing. "Things came with a rush even sooner than expected. Edith was taken ill last evening at nine, and the small son and heir was born at 2:15 this morning," he wrote "Darling Bysie." "Edith is getting on very well; she was extremely plucky all through. The boy is a fine little fellow about 8 ½ pounds. ... Of course the nurse is not here yet. Aunt Annie spent the night here and took charge of Baby. Little Alice is too good and cunning for anything, and devoted to 'my own little brother'; she will not allow her rocking chair to be moved from alongside him. I am heartily glad it is all over so quickly and safely."[44]

Elliott once again took a position in his uncle's brokerage firm, but he could not seem to find any compelling mission in life. He wanted to live up to the example set by his father, but Theodore was already doing that to perfection. How could Elliott measure up to both his father and his brother?

⚜12⚜

"I Am Too Sad & Need No Friends"

Lives of great men all remind us
We can make our lives sublime,
And, departing, leave behind us
Footprints on the sands of time.

Henry Wadsworth Longfellow

If I should labor through daylight and dark,
Consecrate, valorous, serious, true,
Then on the world I may blazon my mark;
And what if I don't, and what if I do?

Dorothy Parker

Theodore Roosevelt was spending less and less time with his brother. While planning his wedding to Alice Lee, Theodore had declared that he would not have a best man at all if Elliott could not be there, but by the time of his second marriage this seems not to have been a concern. Perhaps because of Edith Carow's relative immunity to Elliott's charm, or perhaps because of Theodore's increasing disapproval of his brother, at his wedding to Edith, Theodore's best man was his new best friend, English diplomat Cecil Spring-Rice. Companionable and impeccably dressed, Spring-Rice bore a remarkable resemblance to Elliott.

Theodore was dismayed by the contrast between the atmosphere of Sagamore Hill and that of Half-way Nirvana. Elliott seemed to have everything to live for, yet he was depressed and drank heavily. "I wonder if it would do any good to talk to him seriously about his imprudence! I suppose not," Theodore wrote to Bye. "I wish he would come to me for a little while; but I guess Oyster Bay would prove insufferably dull, not only for Elliott but for Anna."[1]

For his part Theodore found life at Nirvana insufferably self-indulgent and pointless. "I do hate his Hempstead life; I don't know whether he could get along without the excitement now, but it is certainly very unhealthy, and it leads to nothing."[2]

Theodore nearly lost his more "healthy" life in competition with Elliott as they represented their respective country clubs, Oyster Bay and Meadowbrook, in a near-fatal game of polo, witnessed by Corinne. Theodore had learned to play polo in order to have some interest in common with Elliott, but at the climax of this game, "Theodore rushed after Elliott at terrific speed as he took the ball downfield. There was a thump of horseflesh as brother tried to ride brother out. Suddenly — no one saw how — Theodore was thrown, and knocked unconscious. … [He] neither moved nor stirred, and seemed like a dead man" long enough to disturb those present. Even so, Theodore made light of the incident as he described it to Bye: "We played polo every afternoon, almost, and Saturday had a match with the Meadowbrook. Our team consisted of Douglas, Farr, Jack Thorpe and myself; theirs, of Elliott, Frank Appleton, Dick Richardson and young Carroll. We beat them six goals to one; a pretty bad beat. Of course, they were only a scratch team. My duty was that of 'rider out,' as I had fast ponies; when fortunately there was only a couple of minutes left I got a tumble and was knocked senseless. ..."[3] Theodore's wife miscarried a week later; Elliott's reaction is not recorded.[4]

Elliott finally visited Theodore at Sagamore Hill. "... Elliott and Anna, with Eleanor, were here on Thursday; and I really think they have enjoyed themselves greatly, and it has done Elliott good," Theodore wrote Bye. There is no record of his having a man-to-man talk with Elliott, however; he seems to have joined Elliott in the sporting life. They went to the races at Huntington, where they entered their ponies "for the half and quarter mile dashes. ... Elliott won the half, I coming in fifth. ... Yesterday we had great fun playing polo. We also have tennis, rifle shooting, swimming, etc. ..."[5]

What stability Elliott may have had was lost when he finally destroyed his health irrevocably in an accident he suffered while engaged in a typically frivolous pursuit.

Elliott and his "sporting" friends, circa 1889. Eleanor holds Elliott's leg. Courtesy of The Franklin D. Roosevelt Presidential Library.

Elliott's friend James Montaudevert Waterbury was a "sportsman" like Elliott, with memberships in the New York Yacht Club and the Coney Island Jockey Club, among others. He was a Columbia graduate (class of 1873) and a manufacturer of cordage, but he lived chiefly for his amusements. (His son, the famous polo player Larry Waterbury, married Anna's sister Maud.) Waterbury held a practice session on his Pelham estate for an amateur circus to be performed by members of "society," with the proceeds to be given to charity.

Elliott broke his ankle attempting a double somersault. The doctor consulted believed it was only a sprain, and Elliott spent several weeks limping painfully under this misdiagnosis. Elliott was examined by a second doctor who, after declaring that the previous physician "ought to be hung" and telling Elliott that he was "on his way to getting a fine club-foot,"[6] re-broke and reset the ankle.

The discomfort was intense and lingering, and Elliott turned for comfort to his most sympathetic friend, his daughter, who was not quite five. Eleanor never forgot this conversation, "for we were alone in his room when he told me about it. Little as I was, I sensed that this was a terrible ordeal, and when he went hobbling out on crutches to the waiting doctors, I was dissolved in tears and sobbed my heart out for hours. From this illness my father never quite recovered."[7]

(Waterbury's party went on as planned, his 350 guests arriving at Pelham railroad station in a chartered train from New York, riding in coaches over torch-lighted roads to his estate, where in a sawdust ring, to the strains of Lander's ubiquitous society orchestra, "The grand entrée was made at half-past nine o'clock," wrote a society reporter. "Four gentlemen and four ladies mounted on matched Thoroughbreds, dashed from the anteroom and began to dance the grand quadrille on horseback." No wonder Elliott had wanted to be part of it. Several of his friends, including Winthrop Chanler, performed circus tricks.)[8]

Illness piled upon illness as drug addiction joined alcoholism. Elliott's cries could be heard throughout his home for days on end. For relief he took morphine and laudanum, two drugs prescribed as a matter of course in the late nineteenth century. Under the influence of these substances, Elliott felt free from pain, grief, scolding, competition, humiliation.

The hurt inflicted on Eleanor by Elliott's suffering went very deep. "As leaves moved to the wind," wrote her friend Joseph Lash, "she stirred to the thought of others in pain. If a playmate was injured she wept, and her father was the person she loved most in the world."[9]

Characteristically, on June 13, 1889, Elliott went to the Knicker-bocker Club and wrote a cheerful letter to Bye, asking her help even as he painted a glowing picture of life at Half-way Nirvana: "Under Anna's ready hand ... it is rapidly growing not only livable but cosey [sic] and comfortable. ... Anna is wonderfully well, enjoys everything, even the moving, and looks the beautiful girl she is. Little Eleanor is as happy as the day is long, plays with her kitten, the puppy and the chickens all the time, and is very dirty as a general rule ... I am the only 'off' member of the family and my foot is very bad yet. ... Do come to us on your return dear old girl, just for a little while if you can't pay us a long visit and help Anna out. I am no use on my sticks and there is so much that your cool judgment and good taste would help her in. ..."[10]

Elliott may have had selective perception, for in fact Anna's paralyzing headaches continued, and Eleanor, always sensitive to the suffering of her parents, sometimes became ill herself. "I am afraid to let Baby go to you on Monday," Anna wrote to Nannie Roosevelt, wife of Elliott's cousin John. "She does not seem very well and I am afraid she is too small to appreciate a magic lantern and would be frightened and cry. I thank you very much for thinking of her. I would have written you yesterday morning, but I woke up with one of my terrible headaches. I could not move or think."[11]

Elliott wrote a characteristically loving letter to "dear old Jack," the friend of his Wild West boyhood days: "I am so glad to hear of your happiness in the birth of the second little daughter. She will be a sweet one indeed if she grows up like her lovely mother. ... Anna sends love and so does Baby Eleanor. ... We are so glad all is well with you and yours old man. With a great deal of love, yours ever, Nell."[12]

Elliott had turned increasingly to drink for solace following the death of Mittie, but the disease had reached an advanced stage by the time his second child and first son, Elliott Jr., was born. "Of his arrival I have no recollection whatsoever," wrote First Lady Eleanor Roosevelt of this little brother,[13] but at the time she dictated a letter to Elliott from her Grandmother Hall's house in Tivoli. She asked what the baby looked like, as she was told by some that he looked like a bunny, by others that he was more

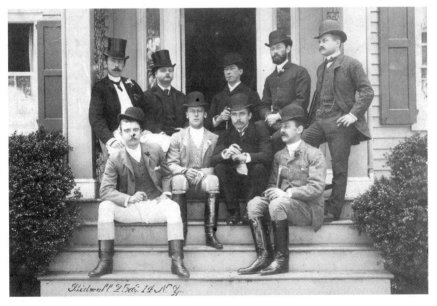

Elliott, derby slightly askew, "with his riding club." A few of the gentlemen are unidentified, but listed, in no particular order, are Stanley Mortimer, Winthrop Hoyt, W. Thorne, A. Ladenburg, J.F.D. Lavier, and "Richardson." Circa 1889. Courtesy of The Franklin D. Roosevelt Presidential Library.

like an elephant. She told Elliott that she hoped her brother did not cry, but if he did, she instructed her father to have the nurse "give him a tap, tap." Elliott always came first with the little girl, and so this, her first letter, was addressed to him; her greetings to everyone else were secondary. "I love you very much," she assured her father, "and mother and brother too if he has blue eyes."[14]

The birth of her son widened the emotional gap between Anna and her daughter. Perhaps it was the strength of the immediate bond that mothers have with their sons; perhaps it was just that this new baby did not look at her with disapproving eyes for "scolding Father." Whatever the cause, Eleanor knew that she had been consigned to the back of her mother's heart. As Blanche Cook writes:

> Always correct and generally aloof, Anna Hall Roosevelt was not a woman of spontaneous emotion. The problems in her marriage caused her to become even more walled off from her feelings, as she struggled to ignore as much as she could and hoped always to notice less, to care less, to feel less hurt. Since to love a child is to open oneself to the most profound feelings, little Eleanor could only have seemed a threat to Anna's quest for composure. From the first she was the recipient of her mother's coldest attentions.[15]

Elliott, a very emotional man, must have wearied of his wife's "quest for composure." Pussie, her less composed sister, also wrote to Elliott while "Totty" — the Hall family's nickname for Eleanor — stayed at Tivoli. "Eleanor and I are writing you this letter together, so you must excuse the writing. We are both so glad that she has a little brother. Totty is flourishing, she has quite a colour, and tell Anna the French lessons are progressing, although I am afraid the pupil knows more than the teacher. ... It is so gorgeous up here now, the trees are one mass of red and gold. I was so glad you were not in the hunt the other day, when Mr. Mortimer was hurt. What a risk it is every time. But *oh!* What fun!! How I wish I were a man. I am afraid I am tiring you with my nonsense."[16]

Elliott had always enjoyed being a man, but now that he was staying in the city and leaving his wife alone, he fretted that she might too much enjoy being a woman, and he accused her of betraying him. "Poor darling old Elliott," she tried to reassure him. "Please don't worry darling. Start off firmly making up your mind that you will be happy. Say to yourself that *you* know I am true, & that you will trust people. It would make you feel so much happier if you truly could, & I tell you there is *nothing* to fear. Please believe me — And as to success, remember that you are God's child. I seldom worry when I tell him everything, all my troubles."[17]

Elliott with Eleanor, his friends and dogs at "Half-way Nirvana," circa 1889. Courtesy of The Franklin D. Roosevelt Presidential Library.

My mother is the lady on the right," wrote Eleanor Roosevelt, on donating this photo to the FDR Library in 1954. "Note the tennis costumes." Eleanor identified those pictured as, "C.H. Becker, Hudson, Kennedy," and "C.L. Fritz." Photograph circa 1890. Courtesy of The Franklin D. Roosevelt Presidential Library.

The last sentence is a reference to Anna's increasing distress over Elliott's frequent illnesses and erratic moods. His lifelong physical problems now intensified — the old "Indian fever," the headaches that had made him "cry out" during his days at St. Paul's. Eleanor Roosevelt believed later that her father might have suffered from a brain tumor.[18] Travel — the nineteenth century's answer to all distress — had been prescribed and, while it provided temporary respite and a renewal of good intentions, Elliott's troubles were being absorbed increasingly into one all-encompassing sickness: alcoholism.

"Elliott has had a really hard illness during this last week," Theodore wrote "Bysie" June 17th from Sagamore Hill. "He has had two abscesses on his neck; they prevented him from swallowing, and drove him nearly mad with pain; to complete matters he got a severe attack of rheumatism.

He looks ghastly, can not even sit up in bed, and has been kept under the influence of anodynes; but the doctors say he is now improving rapidly and will be down stairs in a few days. Aunt Annie is with him."

Theodore played polo with the Roosevelt brothers' friends Mr. Underhill, the Thorpe brothers, and Harry Myers, and then they all decided they would go to visit Elliott. "Today we all drove over in the high phaeton to see Elliott, but I am the only one they would let into his room."[19] One week later, Theodore wrote again to reassure Bye. "Elliott is now very much better, but still extremely weak; he has had a hard trouble with such a combination — an abscess, rheumatic gout, and inflammatory rheumatism." And one week after that, "Elliott is very much better, I lunched with him Wednesday and he is now able to go out driving. ..."[20]

Elliott probably tried to tell himself that he was God's child, but given the fact that he was also Theodore Roosevelt's brother, it does not seem to have been much consolation. Theodore's run for mayor of New York in 1886, while it did not get him elected, had made him one of the youngest and most admired celebrities in the city. Elliott looked at his brother and then saw himself, a pain-wracked, hard-drinking, drug-dependent nervous wreck, and could no longer face his family. Despite his love for "Little Nell" and "Baby Joss," as Elliott Jr. was called, as autumn turned to winter he hid from them in Manhattan even on weekends.

"Dearest Elliott, I was so depressed when the carriage came this afternoon with Douglas [Robinson, Corinne's husband] in it & without you. I actually sobbed alone in my bed and am beginning again now as I write ... I am anxiously waiting for a letter from you tomorrow," pleaded Anna. "I shall never feel you are really your dear old self until you can give up all medicine and wine of every kind. I believe the latter has really led to your great difficulty in giving up morphine and laudanum. That is I believe it irritates and makes your ankle worse, as well as ruining your stomach. Do dearest throw your horrid cocktails away & don't touch anything now you are off for your health you have no business and nothing to trouble you — I wonder if this last is asking too much."[21]

Elliott deserted his family even at Christmas, going to Bermuda ostensibly for a "cure," but it was unheard of for a Roosevelt to spend Christmas alone. "I am so terribly lonely without you. I do hope you are really getting well. Not simply playing Polo and having a splendid gay old time," wrote a bewildered Anna. "Perhaps your letter will tell me all." Anna became very ill Christmas morning to the point of hemorrhaging, but she forced herself to get out of bed at some point and open presents with Eleanor. "It was very lonely," she wrote. "Then I kept quiet all day, but went to the News Boys dinner, where all the boys cheered you."

The next day she finally received a letter from Elliott. "Eleanor came wandering down when she heard the postman to know if there was a letter from you and what you said. I told her you would not be here for two weeks, & she seemed awfully disappointed but was quite satisfied when I told her you were getting well. ..."[22] In his missive Elliott admitted to being "a little homesick."

When he finally returned, his family was upset to see that he came back no better. His sisters hesitated to invite him to their homes, so erratic was his behavior. On January 24, 1890, Theodore wrote to Bye from Washington: "Darling Bye, It is a perfect nightmare about Elliott: I am distressed beyond measure at what you write. No wonder you dread having him to dinner. Can he not be persuaded either to go to Metcalfe [Elliott's friend from his Texas days], or else to some first-rate surgeon who can put him under control — being told of the case beforehand — and make him take a rest cure, or a long ocean voyage with a young physician always in attendance?"[23]

In her strong-older-sister fashion, Bye took Elliott and his family under her wing. Elliott wanted to go back to Europe for a while — had not travel always been prescribed when he was unwell? — and take his sis-

*Elliott in Austria
with Eleanor
and Elliott, Jr.,
circa 1891.
Courtesy of
The Franklin
D. Roosevelt
Presidential
Library.*

ter with them on a tour that would, it was hoped, divert him and renew his marriage. Eleanor and Elliott Jr. accompanied their parents on what was instead, as Joseph Lash has written, "a restless, troubled journey that ended in disaster."[24]

Theodore, who had no use for Elliott's doctor — after all, what good had he done? — felt that the time had come to force the issue. "Half measures simply put off the day, make the case more hopeless, and render the chance of a public scandal greater," he wrote to Bye in April 1890.

I have been *very* glad to get both your recent letters; you are very good to keep us so constantly informed. Yesterday I received a perfectly ordinary letter from poor old Nell himself, it made me feel dreadfully to read it. In response I put in a line or two of ... advice as I knew how; but of course it will do no good. He *must* leave that fool Lusk and put himself completely in the hands of some first rate man of decision ... and unless he goes to a retreat he ought to be sent on some long trip, preferably by sea, with a doctor as companion. Anna, sweet though she is, is an impossible person to deal with. Her utterly frivolous life has, as was inevitable, eaten into her character like an acid. She does not realize and feel as other women would in her place. San Moritz would be in my opinion madness; he must get away [from the] club and social life. For you to go to Europe with them, under their guidance, would in my opinion be simple folly. Somebody must guide them; merely to follow them round would be nothing.[25]

Meanwhile, *Frank Leslie's Illustrated Newspaper* profiled Anna as a "Representative Society Lady," featuring a woodcut made from a photograph of Anna in all her finery. The article put the best face on the family's circumstances.

The beautiful face that looks out from this page ... is that of one of New York's most popular young matrons. Mrs. Elliott Roosevelt is a sister of Miss Tissie Hall, and of Mr. Valentine G. Hall, Jr. [actually, the 3rd], the gifted amateur actor. Mrs. Roosevelt, who has been married perchance a half-dozen years or less, is a shining light in the brilliant galaxy of young married women of Gotham. She is of the delicately blonde type, with large, light-blue eyes and a profusion of fair hair. She has a beautiful complexion and a very handsome figure a trifle above medium height. Youthful as Mrs. Roosevelt is, she has a lovely little daughter, a dainty little maid named Eleanor, and about five years old. During all the years of her married life Mrs. Roosevelt has maintained the belleship conceded during her girlhood, and she is now recognized as a leader in the exclusive circles she adorns. ... Mr. Roosevelt, for whose health's sake New York is to lose so charming a member of society as his wife during the coming season, has been a semi-invalid ever since the now famous amateur circus given by Mr. James M. Waterbury last spring. During one of the rehearsals, Mr. Roosevelt fell and seriously injured his ankle, and now is to go abroad for treatment of the obstinate hurt. A part of Mrs. Roosevelt's summer has been divided into long visits paid to Newport, Lenox, and other fashionable resorts, and to the beautiful old family country seat of her mother at Tivoli-on-the-Hudson. ... Mr. Roosevelt is a cousin [sic] of Mr. Theodore Roosevelt, who, having tasted the surfeiting sweets of society, first dived into politics and then soared into authorship.

Readers of *Frank Leslie's* were told that, at the Long Island home of Elliott and Anna, "gay house-parties of guests, fox-hunts, teas, and races are the order of the day, and there Mr. and Mrs. Roosevelt will probably remain this year until they have to spend the winter abroad."[26] But in fact, life in New York was increasing in misery for Elliott and his family. Not knowing what else to do, they sailed for Berlin, from whence Elliott wrote to Bye, who had decided not to "follow them round": "For Bye only/ Dearest old Bye, Your sweet note to me and your letter to Anna have both been received. You were very good to us as you always are. ... Continue it all to her, our noble beautiful Anna. But I am not going to speak of this all again even to you. I am too sad & need no friends."[27]

⊰ 13 ⊱

"Something Dreadful Awaiting Us"

Anna was cheerful as she wrote to Bye from Berlin, the family's first stop on their "restless, troubled journey." She described what began as a typically Rooseveltian sojourn, visiting friends running the gamut from Buffalo Bill to German royalty. The former, touring Europe with his "Wild West Show," nearly caused a catastrophe by inviting Elliott to join him in a toast. Elliott's friend Count Sierstorff intervened by telling Bill that this would go against doctor's orders, simultaneously removing the glass from Elliott's hand.

After watching the garrison parade and the cavalry drill as guests of Counts Sierstorff and Bismarck, Anna, Elliott, five-year-old Eleanor, and baby Elliott Jr., called "Joss," journeyed on to Bavaria, where Anna reported that Elliott's foot was finally feeling better and that when he was not contending with "awful attacks of depression," seemed to have no trouble sleeping.

"Elliott is really studying German now, and I hope he will take some interest in it. Eleanor is beginning to speak a little but teaching her to read is hopeless. She is as good as gold," wrote Anna, who felt the need to remark that the people around them in Reichenhall were "all of a class that no one would think of meeting."[1]

At this time Elliott did Eleanor a tremendous favor by inoculating her for life, perhaps unwittingly, against his particular illness.

We often went to the cafes, and the older people drank steins of beer with the delicious looking foam on top. I saw little German children drinking it, too. I begged my father to let me have one of the small mugs, as the other children. He refused for a while and then said, "Very well, but remember, if you have it, you have to drink the whole glass." I promised without a suspicion of the horror before me. When I took my first taste, instead of something sweet and delicious, I found I had something very bitter which I could hardly swallow. I was a disillusioned and disappointed child, but I had to finish the glass! Never since then have I cared for beer.[2]

The family spent one month in these less than congenial (to Anna) surroundings, then traveled to Munich and Oberammergau, where they saw the Passion play. Then on to Venice, where another aristocratic friend, Count Arco, was not so helpful as Count Sierstorff had been. "Elliott was an angel up to Wednesday night," wrote Anna of this visit, "then I think he drank champagne for dinner, although he denies it." Shortly afterward she walked in on Elliott while he was consuming watered-down brandy. "I was furious and said so. It affected him at once. ... I am sure it is the first alcohol he has touched in two months."

Anna was often ill during this period, but she forced herself not to let Elliott out of her sight, even when he was with his friends, "except when they were shooting." She worried about money: "I don't know how it is, but we don't seem to be able to travel under $1,500 dollars a month."[3] They had gone over Elliott's trust fund allowance and were depending on the family endowment.

In Venice Eleanor experienced what would become one of her most treasured memories. "I remember my father acting as gondolier, taking me out on the Venice canals, singing with the other boatmen, to my intense joy. I think there never was a child who was less able to carry a tune and had less gift for music than I. I loved his voice, however, and, above all, I loved the way he treated me. He called me "Little Nell," after the Little Nell in Dickens' *Old Curiosity Shop*. Later he made me read the book, but at that time I only knew it was a term of affection, and I never doubted that I stood first in his heart."[4]

In another way Italy was a lifelong painful memory for Eleanor, for it was the scene of the only recorded time when her father ever really scolded her.

"He could ... be annoyed with me, particularly when I disappointed him in such things as physical courage — and this, unfortunately, I did quite often. We went to Sorrento and I was given a donkey and a donkey boy so I could ride over the beautiful roads. One day the others overtook me and offered to let me go with them, but at the first steep descent when they slid down I turned pale, and preferred to stay on the high road, I can remember still the tone of disapproval in his voice, though the words of reproof have long since faded away."[5]

In fact, his exact words were, "I did not know you were a coward."

For Eleanor love covered a multitude of sins — it never occurred to her, then or later, that on that slope a five-year-old had every reason to be frightened, that perhaps it showed the better part of valor for such a little girl to refrain from attempting to navigate a donkey down a steep hill, and that her father had no business calling her a coward. She would return to this incident again and again in her writings:

"You are not afraid are you?" The tone was incredulous, astonished, and the man looked down from his horse to the child on

her small donkey. The eyes were kind, but she sat shivering and hung back, looking at the steep descent. A steely look came into the man's eyes and in a cold voice he said: "You may go back if you wish, but I did not know you were a coward." She went back and the man went on sliding down the hill after the grown-ups — the nurse and the little donkey boy escorted the five-year-old girl along the dusty highway back to Sorrento, Italy.

No self-justification here — the one lesson Eleanor learned was summed up in the title of a magazine article in which she recounted the story: "Conquer Your Fear and You Will Enjoy Living."[6]

Echoing the day when Elliott, as a little boy on East 20th Street, gave his new overcoat to a child who looked cold, Eleanor was "very sensitive to physical suffering, and quite overcome by the fact that my little donkey boy's feet were always cut and bleeding. On one occasion we returned with the boy on the donkey and I was running along beside him, my explanation being that his feet bled too much!"[7]

Even though Elliott wrote to his mother-in-law that his wife's "great delight of course, as mine; is in Baby 'Joss,'" Eleanor is not reported to have been jealous; on the contrary, she doted on her little brother.

He gets stronger and fatter and rosier every day. I am afraid he is a son of his father, though, for he is not at all a "good boy." Eleanor is so sweet and good with him and really is learning to read and write for love of it making it possible to tell him stories which he cannot understand.

Elliott went on to tell "Dear Anna's Mother" how much he enjoyed

The little things such as Ellie's feeding the pigeons on the Piazza at St. Marks, the lovely music on the canal in decorative Gondolas by the band of the "32" Regiment, the delight that Eleanor and I have taken in the Lido shore, wandering up and down looking over the blue Adriatic watching the gray surf and catching funny little crabs![8]

Mrs. Hall received equally calm and happy letters from her daughter, still in Sorrento:

This is the most beautiful place, right on the bay with Naples, Vesuvius and Capri opposite and only a little way off Pompeii. Elliott takes both children sailing every morning, while I have an Italian lesson from the Priest here, and later in the afternoon we drive and then go on the water for the sunset.[9]

With Bye, however, Anna felt comfortable enough to admit how worried she was by Elliott's instability.

[Elliott] goes sailing every day and takes the children in the morning. I went one afternoon but cannot stand it. Elliott generally takes a nap in the boat in the afternoon. Last night I only got four hours sleep owing to a dear sweet letter from Aunt Annie which completely upset Elliott. Don't repeat this, but beg them to write brightly. Elliott is so nervous, everything upsets him. First he sobbed, then got furious and went out, said he would never go home, etc. and worked himself into a perfect fever of excitement.[10]

What was in this "sweet" letter from his much-loved aunt that so upset Elliott's equilibrium? Likely she encouraged him to overcome his difficulties, and in his confusion he felt criticized and inadequate.

The next morning, Elliott impulsively awakened Anna to tell her that he was taking Eleanor and her nurse on a twenty-mile trek up Mount Vesuvius.

Late that afternoon they still had not returned. Anna, sleep-deprived from anxiety over Elliott, wrote to Bye that she was "nearly dead" from her vigils keeping track of him. He was not drinking, but spent a great deal of time alone, taking a little sailboat into the bay at Sorrento and floating all alone for hours, alternately napping and watching the ancient and peaceful routine of the fishermen. He slept very little at night, although he tried; he could more often be found sitting on the piazza, perhaps finding comfort in contemplation of the sleeping village and the sea.

Anna was "dreadfully worried" that Elliott would go back to drinking, she told Bye. Every afternoon she watched him put to sea in his small boat, then worried that he might not return sober.[11]

While Anna composed her anguished letter, Elliott and his daughter rejoiced in each other's company, although Eleanor was anxious not to be called a coward again. Eleanor remembered standing at the summit of the volcano with her father, "and the throwing of pennies which were returned to us encased in lava, and then an endless trip down. I suppose there was some block in the traffic, but I can only remember my utter weariness and my effort to bear it without tears so that my father would not be displeased."[12]

Finally they arrived at the inn, long after sundown. Anna, one hopes, was too relieved to scold them.

As winter approached and the children caught cold, physicians suggested a less humid climate, and the Roosevelts headed for the Austrian university town of Graz. At first everyone's health improved in the "hardy, honest and healthy climate." Elliott presented a happy façade when he wrote to Theodore:

Tell Alice that Eleanor takes French lessons every day and tries hard to learn how to write so she won't be far behind when we return. Eleanor is learning to skate too, quite well. She has some little German friends with whom she coasts and plays snow balling all day. She really talks German very well. Little Boy understands both German and English but can only say "Nein" and "Mama" and "da-da" as yet. He is so fat and well. Eats all the time. He looks just like little Ted used to those days at Sagamore when I used to laugh so at his back view digging holes in the walk. And playing he was as big as the other children. Do you remember?[13]

Elliott and Eleanor, circa 1889, at "Half-way Nirvana," their home in Hempstead, Long Island. Courtesy of The Franklin D. Roosevelt Presidential Library.

Elliott loved his children and wanted to please his brother, but his devotion was incapable of protecting him from an overwhelming depression. "Elliott has been a perfect angel since he left Arles & he never tried to take anything more which I think shows how very much better he is & how much more control over himself. But Bamie I have *never* been so worried about him as for the past week he is settled into a melancholy from which nothing moves him," a distraught Anna wrote to Bye.

> He says you and Uncle Jimmy both told him he has irretrievably disgraced himself, which he knows you think true, so he says he cannot go home, & there is no future for him, besides which he feels that as long as he stays with us, he injures the children and myself. I was so worried I stayed another three nights fearing his mind would flee away. Yet he is as well in every way as you & I. He is the saddest object I have ever seen & so good and penitent. Ask Theodore to write him praising him for keeping straight & pulling himself together & you write me in the same vein. I am afraid he might suspect my telling you if you both write him. He also believes there is something dreadful awaiting us in the near future.[14]

Bye decided to sail to Europe and take charge of her brother and sister-in-law. "My dearest sister," wrote Theodore, "Edith and I have thought of you so much and genuinely wish we could be with you, for we know what a terrible trial you have to go through; but I will not speak more of this; for as it has to be done, why may all good fortune guard and attend you, dearest sister. ..."[15]

⌁ 14 ⌁

"HE WAS THE ONLY PERSON
WHO DID NOT TREAT ME
AS A CRIMINAL"

Anna Roosevelt was pregnant again. What she did not know was that she was not the only woman carrying a child fathered by Elliott Roosevelt.

Theodore, intensely happy fighting corruption on the Civil Service Commission in Washington, despite "the little runt of a President,"[1] received a letter from a New York attorney representing Katy Mann, a servant in Elliott's household who claimed Elliott had an affair with her shortly before taking his family abroad and that she was now expecting his baby.

This was the beginning of the end of Theodore Roosevelt's sympathy for his brother. "Alcoholism he believed to be a disease that could be treated and cured," writes Edmund Morris. "But infidelity was a crime, pure and simple; it could be neither forgiven nor understood, save as an act of madness. It was an offense against order, decency, against civilization; it was a desecration of the holy marriage-bed."[2] Theodore did not understand that adultery is part of the usual course of alcoholism.

Before Bye even told Elliott about what Theodore referred to as Katy's accusation, Elliott wrote Theodore another of his cheerful, chatty letters. Theodore remembered the brave, bright boy Elliott had been, contrasting him with the wayward, volatile man he had become. "Last week I received a most natural and affectionate letter from poor Elliott. It made me feel dreadfully; for it was exactly like his old self when he was at his best. It was terrible to think that it represented merely a momentary interval of well-being, and that the relapse must soon come, and that we can not tell what he will do when the fit is on him. It is horrible, awful; it is like a brooding nightmare. If it was mere death one could stand it; it is the shame that is so fearful. And in her last letter to Edith Anna blandly wrote that she hoped she would have <u>four</u> children! The wind of natural philosophy of disposition has been almost too much tempered to that particular dear lamb — sweet though she is in many ways. ..."[3]

At first Elliott denied in no uncertain terms that he had ever been intimate with Katy, and Theodore's sense of honor led him to believe his brother. Elliott wrote what Theodore described as a "simple, natural, truthful" letter, after which Theodore believed the family should challenge Katy. "It is a ticklish business," he wrote to Bye. "I hate the idea of public scandal; and yet I never believe in yielding a hair's breadth to a simple case of blackmail."[4]

You must be having a dreadful time, Bye. Even if Elliott does not drink he is sure now and then to have some of the attacks you spoke of, a dozen years of his life leave effects which cannot be gotten rid of in any short time. I am at my wit's end to know what to advise. It is useless to preach self-control, and yet it is the only real remedy. He must live alone and in a gloom unless he can learn to stand by himself when associating with pleasant company. If only he could have lived quietly at Oyster Bay! I suppose such a plan would come too late now; and the same with life in the west.[5]

"Did Douglas write you that the woman claims to have a locket and some letters of Elliott's? Of course she is lying," Theodore wrote to Bye, whom Anna had persuaded to join the family in Europe. "Whether she will make a public scandal or not no one can tell. ..."[6]

Elliott wrote another letter to Theodore insisting on his innocence, but suggesting that Katy be paid "a moderate sum" in hopes of keeping her quiet. "After writing you last I had directed Weekes [the Roosevelts' attorney] to tell the woman we would make no compromise, and she might do what she chose! An open war seemed inevitable. Douglas and I then told Uncle Jimmie [James King Gracie], but Aunt Annie knows nothing."

> Then came Elliott's letter authorizing a compromise. On this I at once directed the Weekes bros. [to] see if such a compromise, a final and legally binding one, could be made. ... We believe Elliott innocent, we regard it as mere blackmail; but remember what a hideous tale of his life we should have to testify to if put on the stand; and nobody can tell what he himself would do if put there.[7]

Theodore had his own future to protect. "I live in constant dread of some scandal of [Elliott's] attaching itself to Theodore,"[8] wrote Edith to her own sister. Theodore believed that Elliott had generated his own calamity: "It is a case of paying the penalty for past misconduct of another kind."[9]

"Elliott's letter was sane save for one characteristic touch where he said that 'he would have on his side the Weekes brothers ... the Sheriff, the Police and a host of friends'! It was a desperately sad and touching letter."[10] Theodore replied to "Dear old Nell":

If you and I were alone in the world I should advise fighting her as a pure blackmailer, yet as things [are] I did not dare ... The woman must admit on her own plea she must have been a willing, probably inviting, party. But she has chosen her time with great skill. During that week [in which she claimed Elliott seduced her] you were very sick, and for hours at a time were out of your head, and did not have any clear recollection of what you were doing. You wandered much about the house those nights, alone. She could get testimony that you were often wild and irresponsible, either from being out of your head or from the use of liquor or opiates. At present you are not in any condition to go on the stand and be cross-examined as to your past by a sharp and unscrupulous lawyer. So that however the suit went, it would create a great scandal; and much would be dragged out that we are very desirous of keeping from the public.[11]

Theodore knew that in any paternity suit involving a wealthy man and a woman from a less privileged background, the jury would automatically side with the woman "if she can make out at all a plausible case." Katy's case was sounding more and more plausible, since Elliott told Anna that he and Katy might have had sexual relations, but "he could not say for certain whether he had or had not done it"! ... "I am inclined to think he is guilty," Theodore told Bye reluctantly.[12]

That affair ... gives Anna a perfect right to a divorce. But she loses that right if she condones the offense by getting him back to live with her. If I were in her place I should never have made an effort to get him to come back; it was putting [herself] at his mercy. I should not only let him go, but tell him that I would not live with him for an hour if he continued to behave as he has been doing. I think the break with him had better come as soon and as openly as possible, if he will not consent to be shut up, it will be better for him, and infinitely better for us, if some frightful scandal arises from his connection with the country club, or otherwise, that it should be widely known that we regarded him as irresponsible, that Anna had left him with the children, and that we all stood by Anna. In a week — I cannot tell exactly when, as it depends on the President — I shall be home. I shall then get a legal opinion about divorce, or any form of legal separation from him, and also about shutting him up if we get a chance at him over here. I cannot advise another person whose whole view of life may be different from mine. All I can say is that Anna has no moral right to condone his offenses by again living with him; and that in her place I should come home with the children as soon as I was well. If she won't help herself we can't help her; if she will, we'll stand by her in every way. Any poverty would be better for the children than to be brought up in the degradation of association with Elliott.[13]

In a consultation with his lawyer, "without giving names," Theodore was told that "in such cases the jury was sure to give the benefit of the doubt to the woman; particularly if it could be shown that the man was given to free living, to drinking too much wine, going off his head, etc."

The character of the man is taken much into account [by juries]. If it can be shown that he was apt to get drunk, or to be under the influence of opiates, or to go out of his head and become irresponsible, it would tell heavily against him. ... even if innocent he after has to pay the penalty for his past character for lack of sobriety or for untrustworthiness. If any of the servants have been of loose character this also may count against him.

... Katy Mann says she can prove the other servants chaffed her about his being devoted to her, and asked her once if they had not heard his voice in her room. It is the greatest mistake to have any servants, men or women, save of unimpeachable character in this respect. Elliott must consider whether he is fit to go on a witness stand and be cross-examined as to his whole way of living, his habits in drinking, opiates, going out of his head and acting in a wild and foolish way, etc. You know what every one who knows him would have to testify to on these points; the more intimate they were with him, the more they loved him, the worse it would be. ...[14]

The heaviest blow fell after Katy's child was born, when either Katy's lawyer or Theodore employed a man named Cosgrove, a specialist on family resemblances, who pronounced the infant's features "decidedly Rooseveltian."[15] "K.M.'s story is true," wrote a horrified Theodore.[16] "Douglas and I go to see the baby tomorrow."[17]

Now the top priority was to silence Katy and to keep her silenced. Theodore discussed the matter with his brother-in-law Douglas Robinson and his uncle James Gracie and the three of them agreed to get Katy to settle for three or four thousand dollars "for the support of the child." Theodore wrote to Bye that "if after rational discussion you and Elliott are sure it is mere blackmailing and wish us to push the defense until the last gasp we will do it, public scandal or no public scandal," but wouldn't it be better for everyone, including Elliott, to give Katy "a moderate sum than have his reputation shredded in court"?[18] Theodore had made plenty of political enemies during his "warfare with the ungodly,"[19] and any exposure of a less than stellar example in his own family could leave his career in ruins. Of course he detested the thought of blackmail, but "Is it not better to be blackmailed than to have blazoned to the world the way [Elliott] has been acting when, as I firmly believe, not master of himself?"[20]

"If he would only go into a refuge, and get cured by staying there long enough, he would be free of the danger of being blackmailed for what he has not done because of the reputation he has gained by what he has done."[21]

In late February 1891 Elliott committed himself to a three-month stay in the Mariengrund Sanitarium in Graz, Austria. Theodore was unsure of what positive effect such a short stay would have, but he was in favor of the incarceration, which he declared would "serve to explain and atone for what cannot otherwise ever be explained."[22]

Three months will be useless as far as permanent improvement goes. If the worst comes to the worst, next fall let him come back, and we will put him in asylum here. It is altogether too late to fear sandal; if he isn't put in there will indeed be a hideous scandal some day.[23]

He reached the limit of his patience with Elliott, professing concern only for Anna and the children: "Consider her first: take her to wherever she can have a good doctor. Elliott is purely secondary."[24]

Theodore was baffled by Anna as well. His understanding was that Anna hoped Elliott would be "cured" in time for the family to sail back to New York for the beginning of the social season! "If only poor darling Anna could realize how things are, and did not have such a thoroughly Chinese [inscrutable?] moral and mental perspective!"[25]

Theodore was appalled and disgusted by the very idea that Anna could actually want to continue being a wife to Elliott after his infidelity, at least that she would want to do so before he could be made sober and punished into repentance.

Normally I regard it as little short of criminal for Anna to continue to live with him and bear his children. She ought not to have any more children and those she has should be brought up away from him. Rather than be with him she should separate, taking her children with her; he has no claim on them. ... Anna has no <u>right</u> to live with him henceforth.[26]

... Now, one thing is definite. The present dreadful existence must not drag on beyond Anna's confinement and convalescence. Now you are doing a noble deed — the deed of a true, brave, loving woman — in standing between Anna and the horror of voluntary association with Elliott. But you would be guilty of mere blameworthy folly if you permitted yourself to lead the life a moment longer than it is absolutely necessary; that is a moment longer than Anna's health permits her taking the children and coming home, leaving Elliott if he will not come home to go where he can be treated for a year and over. ... If Anna plays the fool, and is false to her duty to her children, and persists in being with him as he now is — and it would be impossible to overpaint the shameful immorality of her continuing to live with him — then you must leave her to her fate, and come home yourself.[27] ... Make Anna understand that if I am telegraphed for I come to act decisively and at once. If Elliott will not go into an asylum then make Anna take the children and come home with you as soon as she can travel. ... Let him make a scandal if he wishes. I don't like a scandal; but there are some things infinitely worse. If he threatens to go off alone, let him go. He is evidently a dangerous maniac. Let Anna come home with the children <u>at once</u>, then we can proceed against him to have more provision made for their support.[28]

Theodore's officiousness in the private lives of Elliott and Anna was based in part on the knowledge that Elliott could be dangerous; he also deferred to Bye's judgment. "Let me know by letter or cable what you wish me to say or do."[29]

Bye convinced the doctors to let her stay with Elliott while he attempted his latest "cure." "Elliott has kept perfectly straight," Bye wrote to Edith less than a month after his commitment. However, he "is as utterly impossible in every other way as usual which naturally leaves me with no confidence as to what he will do when not in this very quiet spot — it apparently never occurs to his mind for one instant that he is in any way responsible for anything he does, or, for what he brings on Anna. ..."[30]

"Darling Bye, I hate to think of you in your time of worry and real anguish over Elliott, and to be able to be of no possible assistance myself," wrote Theodore. "Edith and I talk over it all the while. It is a perfect nightmare. ... Elliott must be put under some good man, and then sent off on a sea voyage, or made to do whatever else he is told. Half measures simply put off the day, make the case more hopeless, and make the chance of public scandal greater. ..."[31]

Elliott seems at this time to have had a curiously compartmentalized sense of reality. He wrote to Anna's mother describing scenes that may not have been recognized by those around him: "Sometimes in the afternoon Anna and I drive a jolly little pair of ponies we found at a Livery Stable down along the banks of the Seine or through the grand old forest. ... [We] read for two hours at a time while the children play. ... Mother dear I will take care of your sweet Daughter my own darling Anna you may be sure that no accident shall come to her through fault of mine. She is my only friend my precious Wife. The children are so happy and little Boy gets more enchanting every day. Eleanor too I think. Give my love to all. ..."[32]

Meanwhile, Theodore's correspondence with Bye increased in intensity, to the point that he composed careful letters to Bye intended for Elliott's benefit ("Best love to Anna and Elliott"), while furtively writing separate and frank messages intended only for their sister. "I shall write you every week; my letters will generally be taken up merely with what we do here; whenever I wish to write you what you may show Anna, it will be on a separate sheet."[33]

I have written you the enclosed so that if Elliott is suspicious you can show it to him. Dear girl, it is horrible beyond words to think of what you are going through. Your letter was heartbreaking. I wrote Elliott at once, as you desired; I intended to make the letter as tender and firm as I possibly could; I have not the slightest idea how it will affect him. It may drive him even more crazy. It is all a nightmare of horror. I fear the Katy Mann affair is but the beginning. ... If we could get Elliott back on this side we could shut him up at once without the slightest difficulty. If you can get him back to Gratz [sic] of course that is the best for the present. If he will do nothing, and gets worse, and you can not get any doctor to shut him up, then when Anna is well it will be necessary to consider seriously if you and she and the children must not, in mere justice and not to uselessly sacrifice your lives, leave him. I think that after a very short career alone he would be confined somewhere and then we could have a hold on him at last. What do you mean when you say he threatens awful things? He has long talked of suicide.[34]

Elliott insisted on taking his family back to Paris, even though Anna was expected to give birth in less than two months. "He was perfectly furious the whole day because the doctor told him Anna must break the journey at least three perhaps four times," wrote Bye. "He said it was all 'Poppycock' and they could go right through it was so much trouble stopping with children. And so it goes all the time."[35]

Elliott was in such a hurry to get back to Paris that he, Anna, and Bye left ahead of the children, who were brought along by Elliott's valet Stephen and his wife, the children's nurse Albertina. All four of them got off the train at one stop, but Stephen re-boarded the train with Elliott Jr., not realizing that Albertina and Eleanor were left behind. "Such excitement on the part of the nurse, for of course, she had neither money nor tickets!" Eleanor remembered. "Such terror for me and exasperation on the part of the station master! Finally, after much telegraphing, we were put on a train and met later that night by a worried but decidedly annoyed father and mother in Paris."[36]

Anna and Bye moved into a house in Neuilly, near Paris, for the rest of Anna's confinement. Elliott went back to a new sanitarium, the Chateau Suresnes in France. Eleanor needed to be out of the way.

"In those days children were expected to believe that babies dropped from Heaven, or were brought in the doctor's satchel," wrote Eleanor. Anna placed Eleanor in a convent school nearby. This seems an odd choice considering that the little girl, only six years old, shared neither the language nor the religion of the other children, and even if she had, she would still have been desperately lonely, separated from everyone she knew. As if the child's situation were not painful enough, on the carriage ride to the convent, Eleanor's mother, instead of reassuring the child of everyone's love, took the occasion as an opportunity to insult her.

"I must have been very sensitive, with an inordinate desire for affection and praise — perhaps brought on by the fact that I was fully conscious of my plain looks and lack of manners. My mother was always a little troubled by my lack of beauty, and I knew it as a child senses those things. She tried very hard to bring me up well so my manners would in some way compensate for my looks, but her efforts only made me more keenly conscious of my shortcomings."[37]

There is no record of Anna noticing her daughter's thick blonde hair or large blue eyes with their trusting expression, and if she did, apparently she was not a believer in what came to be called "positive reinforcement." Before parking Eleanor with the nuns, Anna gave her a long, scrutinizing look with this parting shot: "You have no looks, so see to it you have manners."[38]

Like Elliott, Eleanor felt disgraced, abandoned, exiled, and utterly unable to win the approval of the one person who could have made such a difference.

The only thing that matters to a child is love, and Elliott gave her that; but now Elliott was busy self-destructing. If Eleanor had nowhere to turn for love, she could at least find some way to be noticed.

The little girls of my age in the convent … had a little shrine of their own and often worked hard for hours beautifying it. I hoped to be allowed to join them, but was kept on the outside and wandered by myself in the walled-in garden. Finally, I fell prey to temptation. One of the girls swallowed a penny. The excitement was great, every attention was given her, and she was the center of everybody's interest. I longed to be in her place. One day I went to one of the sisters and told her that I had swallowed a penny. I think it must have been evident that my story was not true, so they sent for my mother and told her that they did not believe me. She took me away in disgrace. Understanding as I do now my mother's character, I realize how terrible it must have seemed to her to have a child who would lie![39]

"You have no looks, so see to it you have manners." Photograph circa 1891. Courtesy of The Franklin D. Roosevelt Presidential Library.

Even in that era, when few people had heard of a child psychologist, it would not have taken one to discern what was going on. But Anna did not.

"I finally confessed to my mother, but never could explain my motives. I suppose I did not really understand them then, and certainly my mother did not understand them."[40] What kind of mother would not understand this?

> I remember the drive back as one of utter misery, for I could bear swift punishment of any kind far better than long scold-ings. I could cheerfully lie at any time to escape a scolding, whereas if I had known that I would simply be put to bed or be spanked I probably would have told the truth. My father had come home for the baby's arrival, and I am sorry to say he was

causing my mother and his sisters a great deal of anxiety — but he was the only person who did not treat me as a criminal![41]

Just as Elliott had always known that he would never measure up to Theodore, Eleanor knew that she was outside the realm of her mother's approbation. Elliott and his daughter drew closer because he saw her vulnerability and she sensed his.

Anna's relationships were complex, if not confused. She called plaintively for Elliott while in labor with their third and last child, their son Gracie Hall. Theodore was dismayed "that Anna should have been so foolish as to insist on Elliott's being sent for when her baby was being born," but there is no question that she loved Elliott profoundly. She loved Eleanor ("My mother made a great effort for me")[42] although they never made a connection emotionally.

"Dear Mother," Elliott wrote Anna's mother after Hall was born June 28, 1891, "all is over and Anna our darling girl is well & the Boy is the biggest thing you ever saw and kissed me like a little bird the first hour of his life. ... Her pains and all did not take three hours. ... Bamie was very sweet & the doctor a *wonder*. The little wife looks so sweet & *well*. Good bye Mother ... Try to love and trust your devoted son-in-law. ..."[43]

Meanwhile, Theodore too received a "dumbfounding" letter from Elliott, he told Bye, "no allusion to his delirium tremens, sane in tone."

I am disappointed [in Anna]. ... Personally I shall advise her most strongly not to go back and live with Elliott after he is out of his temporary confinement, but to tell him he is either guilty of the K.M. affair, or has behaved so outrageously that it is impossible to say he is not guilty, and that she will not condone his offense by living with him until he has by two or three years of straight life shown the sincerity of his repentance; and if he bothers her she can and will get a divorce. Show her this.[44]

Anna holding baby Hall, 1891. Courtesy of The Franklin D. Roosevelt Presidential Library.

One more appalling discovery finally hardened Theodore's heart against Elliott.

Bye informed Theodore that, during Anna's confinement, Elliott began yet another extramarital affair, this time with the elegant and worldly Florence Bagley Sherman, an American divorcee living in Paris.[45] Bye did not tell Anna about this development, but she did tell Theodore: "… The last hideous revelation hangs over me like a nightmare," he replied.[46] Anna was even more distraught by Elliott's secretiveness, his lengthy and mysterious absences. This famously gentle man even became violent with his wife, frightening her into a frantic loss of control that was as uncharacteristic for her as Elliott's behavior was for him.[47] Theodore longed to talk sense into both Elliott and Anna, but could not afford to leave his wife, who was about to give birth herself. (This would be their daughter Ethel.) Six days after Hall was born, Theodore wrote to Bye:

> My own dearest sister, the strain under which you are living
> is like a hideous nightmare even to hear about. Your last letter
> in which you describe Anna's hysterical attack due to Elliott's
> violence, is the most frightening of all. His curious callousness
> and selfishness, his disregard of your words and my letters, and
> his light-heartedness under them, make one feel hopeless about
> him.[48]

As far as Theodore was concerned, Elliott had reduced himself to the level of "a flagrant man-swine."[49] One officer of the Boone and Crocket Club showed Theodore a visitors' book in which "was inscribed, below Elliott's name, 'Mrs. Maxwell Eliot'; spelled thus, with the queer low cunning which runs through E's most insane or foolish moments." The official "colluded to seeing the two, remarking, as a joke on himself, that he had by mistake once addressed 'Mrs. Eliot,' as 'Mrs. Roosevelt.' Nice man, our brother. ..."[50] There could be no alternative but to lock Elliott up, dry him out, and punish him into reformation.

Anna must be made to understand that it is both maudlin and criminal — I am choosing my words with scientific exactness — to continue living with Elliott, or suffering him to live with her, in the present fashion, a moment after she gets well enough to travel and take the children with her. Do everything to persuade her to come home at once, unless Elliott will put himself in an asylum for a term of years, or unless, better still, he will come too. Once here I'll guarantee to see that he is shut up ...

Make up your mind to one dreadful scene. Use this letter if you like. Tell him that he is either responsible or irresponsible. If irresponsible then he must go where he can be cured; if responsible then he is simply a selfish brutal and vicious criminal, and Anna ought not to stay with him an hour.

Do not care an atom for his threats of going off alone. Let him go ... What happens to him is of purely minor importance now; and the chance of public scandal must not be weighed for a moment against the welfare, the life, of Anna and the children. I enclose a letter to Anna, give it to her unless you deem it better not to do so; and choose your own time about doing it. Read it over.

If he can't be shut up, and will neither go of his own accord, nor let Anna depart of his free will, then make your plans and go off some day in his absence. If you need me telegraph me, and I (or Douglas if it is impossible for me to go on account of Edith) will come at once. But remember, I come on one condition. I come to settle the thing once and for all. I come to see that Elliott is either put in an asylum against his will or not, or else to take you, Anna and the children away and to turn Elliott loose to shift for himself. You can tell him that Anna has a perfect right to a divorce; she or you or I have but to express belief in the Katy Mann story and no jury in the country would refuse a divorce.[51]

The situation went from bad to worse to worst. Bye reported that Elliott was tormented by delirium tremens, that he told Anna that he would cut her off without a cent if she left him, and that he had threatened to disappear on a long voyage as soon as her baby arrived. "He is evidently a maniac morally no less than mentally," wrote Theodore. The thought of Anna destitute with three children led Theodore to initiate a lawsuit for their protection, in which Elliott would have to be declared incapable of taking care of his property.

Theodore continued to insist that the first priority was to keep Anna and Elliott apart while Elliott was sunk in "hopeless misconduct and outrageous behavior."[52]

It makes little difference about her taking the first step rather than him, and coming back here with the children, where we can protect her and them. Read her this, and tell her again that it is no less criminal and foolish for her to go on living with him. She must come home at once. Let him plainly know that he has no hold on her. He hasn't any, if she will only act with moderate spirit and sense. On yours and my testimony alone any court would decide in her favor. Don't yield an ounce to his threats; keep a lookout that he doesn't try to kidnap one of the children. Refuse point blank to let him have them; let Anna slip away with them if necessary, having engaged her passage on a French line steamer. If he can't be confined for Heaven's sake let him go off alone; the sooner the better.[53]

Over the July 4th weekend, Katy demanded $10,000 from the Roosevelts. This was "so huge a sum," Theodore wrote Bye, "that negotiations are for the moment at a standstill."

Frank Weekes [Bye's lawyer] thinks Elliott could be declared judicially insane by proceedings begun here now, even if he does not come back; and that Anna could certainly get a decree of limited divorce, giving her the custody of the children, and her own property, and alimony from him. Harry Weekes is more doubtful about the insane part; and says he feels very awkward, as representing Elliott in the matter. ... Perhaps I do not tell you enough of our ordinary lives; but really everything seems absorbed in writing about the tragedy. The three children are too darling for anything. I brought them home a hammock, and some fireworks for the Fourth. Yesterday I took Alice and Ted for a rapturous run down Cooper's Bluff. ...[54]

On July 21st he wrote to Bye that Frank Weekes "advises me that I have no power whatever to compromise in the Katy Mann affair. I suppose it will all be out soon. We have therefore told Aunt Annie. Corinne and Douglas have been with her and Uncle Jimmie the last few days, and I have had some ... hard fighting to do ... I think it better that the Halls should be informed in full of everything."[55] "... I wish it all done through the lawyers, without my seeing the woman ... as personally I think it unnecessary and probably unwise."[56]

Theodore may have recalled the lament of Job, "that which I have greatly feared has come upon me," when on August 17, less than a month after his prediction, the following article appeared in *The New York Sun*:[57]

ELLIOTT ROOSEVELT INSANE
His Brother Theodore Applies for a Writ in Lunacy

A Commission [has been] appointed by Justice O'Brien of the Supreme Court to enquire into the mental condition of Elliott Roosevelt, with a view to having a committee appointed to care for his person and for his estate. The application was made by his brother, United States Civil Service Commissioner and ex-Assemblyman Theodore Roosevelt, with the approval of Elliott Roosevelt's wife, Anna Hall Roosevelt …

Theodore Roosevelt avers in the papers in the case that the mental faculties of his brother have been failing him for nearly two years. He says he saw him frequently until Elliott went to Europe in July 1890, and he had remarked the gradual impairment of his intellect. His conversation had been rambling and he could not tell a story consecutively … During the winter of 1890 he had several bad turns. He became violent and on three occasions threatened to take his own life. He had to be placed in surveillance. Mr. Roosevelt says he is "unable to say how far the result is due to indulgence in drink or other excesses." He alleges that the property of his brother in this State consists of real estate, bonds, stocks, and is worth $170,000.

The *Sun* prided itself on its veracity ("If you see it in the Sun, it's so," was the paper's motto), but at that time there were thirty-nine daily newspapers in New York City, and variations on the story above were printed in all of the tabloids with large circulations. "But one reporter has spoken to me," Theodore told Bye, "and I simply told him that it was not a matter in which the public had any concern."[58]

The next day, *The New York Herald* was even less circumspect:[59]

ELLIOTT ROOSEVELT DEMENTED BY EXCESS

Wrecked by Liquor and Folly, He is Now Confined
in an Asylum for the Insane near Paris
Proceedings to Save the Estate
Commissioners in Lunacy Appointed on Petition of His Brother
Theodore and His Sister Anna
With His Wife's Approval

The eminently honorable name of Roosevelt had never before appeared in stories of this kind. It was deeply painful for Theodore to publicize Elliott's shame, but he felt that the plight of Elliott's immediate family left him with no choice. "The only thing to do is go resolutely forward," Theodore wrote to Bye, while realizing, "It is all horrible beyond belief."[60]

Theodore insisted that his attempt at damage control was for the sake of what remained of Elliott's reputation, as well as for the protection of Elliott's wife and children. "If he is not utterly irresponsible then his moral condition is one of hideous depravity."[61]

The petition was drawn up by Weekes, with especial care; it said in substance that the insanity was produced or aggravated, to what extent could not be definitely told, by excessive alcoholism. It would be a great mistake to confine ourselves to alleging *merely* alcoholic insanity — there may be much more — otherwise the inquiries about his epileptic fits are meaningless. So we allege insanity, and say it is probably *mainly* alcoholic.[62]

Elliott tried to neutralize his shame. He wrote an indignant missive to the editor of the *Herald*'s European edition, and his denial was printed in the paper's August 21 New York issue:[63]

You publish in your edition today a most astounding bit of misinformation under the title "Is Mr. Elliott Roosevelt to be Adjudged a Lunatic?" I wish emphatically to state that my brother Theodore is taking no steps to have a commission pass on my sanity with or without my wife's approval. I am in Paris taking the cure at an *establissement hydrotherapeutique,* which my nerves shaken by several severe accidents in the hunting field, made necessary. My wife went home at my request to spend the summer with her mother, Paris not being a good place for children during the hot months. I hope you give this letter as great prominence as you today gave the invention — or worse — of your misinformant.

Elliott Roosevelt

Paris, 18 August 1891

"Elliott's letter in the *Herald* was astounding; still more astounding was the fact that the asylum authorities had allowed him to send it,"[64] Theodore told Bye.

In fact, for the rest of his life Elliott maintained to those who would listen that his family had "kidnapped" and incarcerated him against his will.

"I am firm in my belief that Anna should come back to America as soon as she can travel," Theodore continued to insist, "then she can take prompt legal measures, if necessary, to get her own money. She can live part of the time with her mother. Any poverty would be preferable to the dreadful moral degradation of a longer life with Elliott. ... You and I must appear on Anna's behalf to testify for her in any suit."[65]

If I were in your place I would not try to prevent his going off alone, or writing to any one he chose; or making a scandal; let it come; any thing is better than the present condition. Once he forces the issue, humiliating though the publicity will be, we shall undoubtedly win. Let him understand that we have not the slightest fear of any thing he may do; and a continuance of the present condition would be far worse than any scandal. If you have by your presence made Anna stand up a little for her rights, you have indeed done well.

In the margin he insisted: "Let Elliott know that the Katy Mann affair gives us a complete hold on him if Anna chooses to use it. He has no right to get drunk in his own house; and his wife could refuse to live with him if he does."

As Elliott's confusion deepened, his wife floundered and was ashamed of doing so. Desperately worried about Elliott, she was dumbfounded when he wrote letters in which he attacked her and declared his devotion, simultaneously. "His letter is certainly that of a mad man. First he flings the most abominable charges against me. Then he says I am a Noble Woman & he trusts me entirely. What do you think I ought to do[?]" Anna inquired of Edith. "Ask Corinne and Douglas. ... I have tried to write Elliott as though I had not seen [the newspapers]. Do you think this deceitful? Not right?"[66]

Alcohol addled Elliott's conscience to the extent that he could accuse Anna of the very offense he had committed against her, insisting that he could not be sure that he was Hall's father. Should she demand a retraction from Elliott, or should she go along with Theodore's plan, in which "I would try and prove him a dangerous lunatic. And yet his letter is so hopelessly sad & I long to help him, not to make him suffer more. And yet I feel I ought not on his account pass this over again. ..." Before Anna would send a letter to Elliott, she let Bye read it first.[67]

The Robinsons and the Gracies had never approved of the lawsuit against Elliott, and Uncle James Gracie tried to stop it from going any further. "Uncle Jimmie has certainly played the fool," Theodore wrote to

Bye. "I fear we have an ugly fight ahead. If we fail, Anna must move at once for divorce. Uncle Jimmie may as well understand this."[68] By October there was still no agreement, but Theodore felt that events were making the situation plain even to Elliott's defenders.

> I am for some reason not sorry that Anna had the row with Aunt Annie. ... Douglas is not as stiffbacked as he looks; Elliott's last letter to Anna made him weaken greatly; though when I asked him what he proposed he had no plan to offer. I have tried telling Aunt Annie and Uncle Jimmie everything; they tell an untruth if they say they do not know all; from now on I shall respond to questions, and be very pleasant, but volunteer nothing. ..."[69]

The physicians were unable to agree. Anna believed the contention between Theodore's lawyers and Elliott's made Elliott's condition even worse. At this juncture Elliott hardly seemed capable of carrying out any financial threat against his immediate family, and so Theodore considered dropping the case, but not until after trying to make a new man out of Elliott.

"This morning I had a dreadful letter from Elliott. The horrible part is that it is quite a sane letter, but with a hideous lack of moral sensibility about it."[70] "His letter to me was terrible and harrowing to a degree, especially because while claiming to be sane he seems totally unaware of the hideous moral turpitude on his part which such a claim of necessity implies."[71]

Theodore journeyed to his ranch in North Dakota, the place where, in deep distress, he had once found peace. Now that peace eluded him. "The horror about Elliott broods over me like a nightmare," he wrote "Darling Bye" from Medora, on stationery that reads: "Joseph A. Ferris, Dealer in Dry Goods, Notions, Groceries." "... He and poor Anna and the children and all of us have a hideous time before us. Moreover his letters are so unspeakably terrible! They are so sane, and yet so utterly lacking in moral sense. … His next few letters will doubtless be particularly dreadful."[72] "After much thought I remain unalterably fixed in my belief that the only possible hope for our dear old brother lies in his going into some retreat or asylum," Theodore wrote to Bye, "and I hope exceedingly that he and Anna will themselves see this."

He must go in; if he delays, it can be but for a few months, and then he will probably have to be put in under duress and perhaps after some terrible disgrace. It is idle now to think of appearances; they are gone already. Almost everyone now believes he is in some retreat or under medical care; and most people who knew him, in business or during the last year know he is out of his head. For the sake of his own reputation he must go into some retreat; that alone can put him right. If he does so it will serve to explain and atone for what can not otherwise ever be explained. He now suffers and Anna suffers every disadvantage in the eyes of the public, and in their own hearts, which can attach to residence in a retreat; and they gain not one of the advantages. Elliott must realize this if he hopes ever to save himself — and the time is but short in which he can do it — and Anna must realize it too if she is not willing to barter a moment's foolish respite for some terrible future catastrophe. Another thing on which there is need of the plainest speaking. Elliott and Anna must live apart. They have no right to have children now. It is a dreadful thing to bring into the world children, under circumstances such as these. It must not be done. It is criminal. There is but one hope, and every month's delay weakens that hope. Let Elliott go into an asylum, in England if possible. Or else in France.

Your brother, Theodore Roosevelt[73]

By the end of November, Theodore's anguish caught up with him physically and he collapsed with bronchitis. He rallied briefly, then fell ill again in December. His wife sent him to bed for eight days, his longest illness since his childhood asthma. Upon recovering, he spent a typically joyful Christmas with his "bunnies," then asked President Harrison for a leave of absence to take care of urgent family business.[74]

On January 9, 1892, Theodore embarked on what a later generation would call an "intervention." He sailed from New York to find Elliott and knock some sense into him, literally if need be. "Elliott had always worshiped him," writes Theodore's biographer Edmund Morris, "had always craved his authority."[75] The family waited in sickening suspense for the outcome of the confrontation.

For an entire week Theodore never left Elliott's side. "One can imagine the scene: Day after day, hours and hours on end," writes Blanche Cook. "What would Father think of you? Consider your dear sainted mother. You bring disgrace and disaster upon the entire family. Your wife. Your children. Our good name."[76]

"Won! Thank Heaven I came over," wrote a relieved and exhausted Theodore to "Darling Bye" January 21, 1892. On his last day in Paris, Theodore

... found E. absolutely changed. I had been perfectly quiet, but absolutely unwavering and resolute with him; and he now surrendered completely, and was utterly broken, submissive and repentant. We signed the deed, for two thirds of all his property (including the $60,000 trust); and agreed to the probation. I then instantly changed my whole manner, and treated him with the utmost love and tenderness. I told him we would do all we legitimately could to help him to get him through his two years (or thereabouts) of probation; that our one object now would be to see him entirely restored to himself, and so to his wife and children. He today attempted no justification whatever; he acknowledged how grievously he had sinned, and failed in his duties; and said he would do all in his power to prove himself really reformed. He was in a mood that was terribly touching. How long it will last of course no one can say.[77]

Theodore stayed in Paris another three days in order to arrange Elliott's financial matters and "probation." Katy Mann would be satisfied with an out-of-court settlement; Theodore would withdraw the writ of insanity; a trust fund would be established for Anna and the children; Elliott would spend five weeks drying out with "Dr. Keeley's Bi-Chloride of Gold Cure" in Dwight, Illinois, then live apart from his family for one, or two, or perhaps three years. ("The plea of irresponsibility can never be accepted unless accompanied by willingness to submit to restraint.")[78]

Theodore stayed in Paris another week, then sailed back to New York on the White Star steamer. "Do arrange for me to see everyone," he wrote to Bye, "so that I may go on to Washington forthwith."[79]

Elliott followed the next day, but not before saying good-bye to his mistress. "This morning, with his silk hat, his overcoat, gloves and cigar, E. came to my room to say goodbye," Mrs. Sherman wrote in her journal.

It is all over, only my little black dog [a gift from Elliott], who cries at the door of the empty room and howls in the park, he is all that is left to me. So ends the final and great emotion of my life. "The memory of what has been, and never more shall be" is all the future holds. Even my loss was swallowed up in pity — for he looks so bruised so beaten down by the past week with his brother. How could they treat so generous and noble a man as they have. He is more noble a figure in my eyes, with all his confessed faults, than either his wife or brother. She is more to be despised, in her virtuous pride, her absolutely selfish position than the most miserable woman I know. But she is the result of our unintelligent, petty, conventional social life. And why is it that the gentle, strong men always marry women who are weak & selfish. If she were only large-souled enough to appreciate him. ...[80]

Years later, when Eleanor Roosevelt read these words, she did not entirely disagree.[81]

≼15≽

THE END OF ANNA

E lliott sailed back to New York in February 1892 after six months at Chateau Suresnes, where he was "temporarily cured"[1] in Theodore's estimation. He then traveled to Dwight, Illinois, near Chicago, in order to undergo "the Keeley Cure."

Dr. Leslie E. Keeley was a pioneer in the treatment of alcoholism. "Drunkenness is a disease and I can cure it," he claimed. His remedy became widely known between 1890 and 1893, thanks to a challenge Keeley issued to *Chicago Tribune* publisher Joseph Medill. "Send me six of the worst drunkards you can find and in three days I will sober them up and in four weeks I will send them back to Chicago sober men." A steady supply of inebriates was sent to Dwight, and Medill admitted that "they went away sots and returned gentlemen."

His "Keeley Leagues" fellowships of "graduates" of his treatment, a precursor of the Alcoholics Anonymous meetings of a later generation, featured a banner that read:

MEDICAL NOT PENAL TREATMENT

REFORMS THE DRUNKARD

By the end of the 1890s, the Keeley Center had branches all over the country, but the flagship institution opened in 1879 in Dwight, seventy miles south of Chicago. The cornerstone of the treatment was four daily injections of "bichloride" or "double chloride of gold." No one is quite sure of what this formula consisted, but among its ingredients were gold, alcohol, and strychnine, and it was known as the "Gold Cure." In addition, patients were required to take a tonic medicine every two hours during their waking hours. Group therapy and mutual support were also stressed. Alfred Calhoun, a Keeley graduate, authored a book titled *Is It A Modern Miracle?* And since Dr. Keeley could boast a 50 percent success rate, it was indeed miraculous.

Although Dr. Keeley's patients included everyone from business tycoons and judges to clerks and housewives, the Gold Cure became so common among the wealthy and fashionable that talk of "taking the Keeley Cure" or "going to Dwight" would be analogous to "rehab" or the Betty Ford Clinic a hundred years later. Over one hundred of the physicians employed by Dr. Keeley had themselves been cured by his method.

Unlike most institutions of that day, there were no bars on the windows or physical restraints at the Keeley Institute, and the atmosphere was sociable and friendly, reinforced by the town itself.

"The whole town got to know the patients," remembered Mrs. Anne Withrow, in the employ of the Keeley Institute for nearly fifty years. "The town lodged the patients, fed the patients, and watched out for them. Even tavern owners would call the Institute to report a patient who had tried to purchase alcohol. There would be patients and townspeople at the train station every day to greet new Keeley arrivals."

Elliott, like all patients, was assigned a personal attendant who was a recovered alcoholic. The treatment lasted four weeks, during which Elliott stayed in the Livingston Hotel, the name of which may have caused a pang with its reminder of Anna and her relations. Whatever torture this

Elliott, circa 1892, around the time he took the "Keeley Cure." Courtesy of The Franklin D. Roosevelt Presidential Library.

drying-out involved for Elliott, there was no confinement; patients just needed to be in line at "the shot tower" for the daily injections.[2]

Characteristically, Elliott made friends of the people around him, telling his sister about what wonderful chaps his fellow sufferers were. "I am on the third stage of the thing ... and it combines all the troubles flesh is heir to ... All together I am about as uncomfortable as I well can be — But it means freedom and success at last Bye ..."[3]

Upon leaving Dwight, Elliott was given a certificate reading:

To the Keeley Graduate:

You are now numbered among thousands of men and women who have broken the shackles of alcohol and drug addiction by the Keeley method of treatment. Your cure will be as permanent as your life, you will never have any craving for alcohol or other sedative drugs as long as you live, unless you create it by returning to their use, thus re-poisoning your nerve cells.

Prescribed for the future were "regular and balanced meals, regular consumption of water, abstinence from alcohol and caffeinated drinks, and care in the selection of personal associates." He was also advised to write regularly to the Keeley Institute and to one or two fellow patients.[4]

Elliott was deeply upset by the prolonged separation from his family, which he had understood to be for three months. He wanted desperately to see Anna, but she insisted on an entire year, at least, of exile. "I do want her to see me as I *am*. Not as she last saw me, flushed with wine, reckless and unworthy, but an earnest, repentant, self-respecting gentle-man. This is all I wish except for love's sake to see once more my wife and children after these long weary months. Then I shall go on perfectly quietly and without complaint doing what may please her. ..."[5]

Up to this point Anna had believed that Elliott could be cured, that he would one day come to his senses and be a stable husband. By 1892 her faith was shaken but had not crumbled entirely. Theodore convinced her that she had two options — divorce Elliott, or see if he could manage to lead a sober life for an extended period away from her. She still loved Elliott enough to choose the latter course.

Elliott was granted his wish to visit his wife just once. The meeting was eerily serene. Corinne wrote that Elliott and Anna were "so sweet together, so deeply content and so buoyantly happy that I cannot but feel satisfied about him."[6] However, once Anna got used to being away from

Elliott, she could not bring herself to face the stress of being in his presence. Indeed, she never saw him again.

Elliott wanted to be reunited with his wife and children and maintain sanity and sobriety "in my family with the aid and strengthening influence of Home,"[7] but Theodore, and now Anna, would not hear of it.

Corinne always defended Elliott, and now Corinne's husband, the kind-hearted Douglas Robinson, came up with a plan. Elliott would settle in Abingdon, Virginia, near where Douglas owned a huge amount of uncultivated land and where Douglas and Corinne built a cottage at the foot of White Top Mountain and spent the month of May. Douglas hired Elliott as supervisor of the Douglas Land Company, owned by William P. Douglas, whose Manhattan offices were located at 71 Broadway and at 234 Broadway, not far from where Douglas Robinson and Elliott had been partners in the real estate business. Elliott would survey and develop the property, consisting of forest and a wilderness of wildflowers and streams. In the first job he had held in years, Elliott settled boundary disputes, sold property to homesteaders, maintained mountain roads, introduced railroads, and generally made the wilderness habitable.

During Eleanor Roosevelt's early days as First Lady, Goodridge Wilson wrote in a feature for the *Richmond Times-Dispatch*:

> The Roosevelts and Robinsons by their personal contacts and through the choice of wise agents won the confidence of the truculent mountain squatters and changed these formidable antagonists, who were at first disposed to greet them over rifle sights, into warm and loyal friends. Mr. and Mrs. Robinson, Elliott Roosevelt, and John Elliott felt a personal responsibility towards these people. ... They could and did deal with them on the basis of neighbors and friends, and ... avoided any implication of patronizing superiority, so deeply hateful to the free born soul of your

mountaineer. They expended money, time and energy in making effective plans for the permanent well-being of the people whose living conditions they were so radically changing. The mountain folk appreciated this. They uniformly speak of the Robinsons and Roosevelts with respectful and real affection.[8]

One last time, Elliott proceeded to make himself a favorite among those who knew him. Abingdon was a small town with a population of 1,500, but it was the county seat and the center of commerce and social life. The farmers and shopkeepers there at first expected to be snubbed by this upper-class New Yorker, but as William Youngs has observed, "Elliott's flaws did not include condescension."[9]

Elliott rented an apartment above a store and proceeded to charm everyone in town. He inherited both his mother's Southern graciousness and his father's expansive heart, and his neighbors met him with answering warmth. He was cheered and comforted by their support, and put his heart into his work. Whether because he wanted so much to prove himself to his absent wife, or because he was touched by the hospitality and kindness of his Virginia neighbors, Elliott approached his task with a seriousness and devotion that he never showed in his half-hearted attempts at brokerage and real estate in New York. Perhaps, as Joseph Lash has suggested, "he functioned best away from his strong-minded wife and very successful brother, but does not seem to have realized this."[10] Elliott had no past to live down for these Virginians; they saw only his friendliness and genuine concern for their welfare. He showed an instinct for dealing with people, whether coal miners, squatters, or bankers. Indeed, he collaborated with the latter to form a new bank. True to form, he joined the local Episcopal Church, sang in the choir, and in due course was made a vestryman.

February 24, 1935, the *Richmond Times-Dispatch* carried this reminiscence of Elliott's Abingdon days: "By meeting the mountaineers upon their own grounds … [Elliott became] a friend. … Children loved him; negroes sang for him; the poor, the needy and the unfortunate had reason to bless him; the young girls and the old ladies 'fell' for him; and men became his intimate friends. … He dropped into homes and fitted into every family circle, eating apples by the open fire, reading poetry, talking of local things or about his own wife and children."[11]

> Abingdon in the "Nineties" was a rather staid old Virginia village … It was, and is, a fine old town with cultural associations and pioneer background. There were the plain farmers of large and small acreage, the professional men, the merchants, the craftsmen, the tenants, all the usual types, and many poor folks living in little houses, generally log cabins, in the town or on the farms, back in the hills, hollows, and mountain coves. Small colleges of long and honorable career were in or near the town. Old families of the Virginia aristocracy type lived in mellowed houses within the corporate limits and on outlying plantations, or farms, as they are called in this part of Virginia. Ex-army officers, congressmen, state governors and Supreme Court judges, an occasional United States Senator, and men of their ilk, had always been among the leaders of the community. There was sporting blood among the gentry of town and country. These elements gave a certain tone to a social life that was developed on underlying foundation of solid Presbyterianism and devout Methodism.[12]

In this rustic atmosphere Elliott indulged his love for horses and dogs, gathering "a stable of choice mounts" and "a rare assortment of canines, including terriers, setters, pointers, 'coon' dogs, hounds," and of course the mountains of southwest Virginia provided the perfect setting for hunting everything "from snakes to bears."[13]

Elliott in Abingdon, Virginia, circa 1892, with some of his "rare assortment of canines." Courtesy of The Franklin D. Roosevelt Presidential Library.

Six months after his arrival in Virginia, Elliott accomplished more in his work and showed more stability than ever before. He hoped for Anna to visit him, meet his new friends, and see the miraculous improvement in his mental and physical health, but she was afraid: fearful of Elliott himself — the memory of his erratic behavior was too vivid, and she never knew what to expect of him — and afraid that to see him at all would upset what equilibrium she could maintain.

"Anna had come to dread his company," writes Blanche Cook. "Their marriage had been a terrible ordeal for her, and her sympathies were threadbare. She was exhausted, fragile, and unwell. She now wanted Elliott to leave her alone."[14]

Elliott showed only a cheerful face to the people of Abingdon, but he felt, in his words, "homeless and heartsick and lonely."[15] "You who know no sin which compares with mine," he wrote Anna, "can hardly know the agony of shame and repentance I endure and the self condemnation I have to face. I need indeed be brave to make my fight. ... "[16]

Anna was a faithful correspondent, but at this point she dared not make a move without consulting Bye and Theodore. Elliott's letters distressed her. "This letter from Elliott worries me so that I send it to you," she wrote to Bye. "I am so awfully sorry for him. My heart simply aches and I would do anything I could that could really help him. ... It seems to be dawning on him for the first time that he is not coming home this Autumn."[17]

In November, Elliott wrote to Anna's mother, "If you put yourself in communication with those who have been my daily associates for the past ten months, I think you would only hear good of me."[18] He was going along with his wife's harsh demands to show her that he was capable of "the very powers of self-control and purpose she wishes me to have."[19]

As sobriety took hold and Elliott gained a clearer sense of the anguish he had caused his family, he tried desperately to redeem himself in their estimation. He finally repaid Bye the money he owed her. When she sent him books and a loving note for his birthday, he responded: "As I regain my moral and mental balance I am able to appreciate more fully the hideousness of my past actions and I grow stronger daily in my determination to live rightly and do anything required of me by my loved ones ... Try and think lovingly and forgivingly of me. ..."[20]

Even so, Elliott could not understand why Anna could not bring herself to end his exile, at least long enough to allow a brief visit with her and their children. He wrote to Bye that Anna's fears were "groundless." "I signed a deed securing her and the children. ... If I had been a bad man does she think this would have been my line of action[?]" Elliott wanted credit for not having abandoned his family, as he could have "thrown off all obligations," run away and started over "in the west, or in some other country."[21]

"My Dear Anna's Mother," Elliott wrote May 19, 1892, "Do not think because I have not answered your letter of the 5th before that I did not appreciate it, sweet, gentle and kind as you always are Mrs. Hall."

I am sorry my last letter grieved you. But I am so sensitive, so morbidly I fear open to finding an implied reproach or condemnation. And indeed I have told myself enough harsh and bitter, even if terribly true, things dear Mother. I do not need any more — I am so fearfully unhappy and filled with regret as it is — It is just because I do believe in Him and have "put my faith" there that I feel what I do. It is a great heavy burden of sorrow … and it is not wrong to feel it. It does not interfere with my working hard in my business here or striving ever more earnestly day after day to regain the peace and joy only my dear wife's forgiveness and restored confidence, and the right to my home and children can bring. But it is fearfully, awfully sad. If it were not for God's terrible restraint put upon me in this same power of feeling the sorrow I would do anything to escape from the regret of it all. Please Mother dearest I am doing all I can now. I know it seems very little but if you only knew the agony of shame, repentance and the love hunger you would pity. Bear with me for it is a hard fight to make alone. Even with God's promise of help to cheer one. Remember I know I was wrong and you, all of you in the Right, but that only makes it doubly hard. I am very humble and I pray for forgiveness. I am so sorry to hear that you have been ill — I hope you are better now. With best love I am ever your affectionate Son, Elliott[22]

Banishment was terribly hard on Elliott. "At times his homesickness nearly overwhelmed him," in the perceptive observation of William Youngs, "but instead of giving in to despair, he did a remarkable thing: he treated the whole people of Abingdon as a kind of adopted family."[23]

Perhaps the realization that he could do this occurred the day he came back to Abingdon after a sojourn to New York, during which Anna had refused to receive him. Theodore may have met Elliott in Washington and accompanied him part of the way to Abingdon, for Theodore wrote Bye: "Elliott had already written me of his proposed visit here. ... I leave on a trip to the south Wednesday; I have asked him to go with me. He has one or two wild — very wild — plans on hand. These be happy days."[24] To Elliott's surprise, upon his arrival back in Abingdon he was met at the train by Miriam Trigg, who was the same age as Eleanor. When he asked how she knew what train he was on, she told him that she didn't know; she had shown up for the past couple of days for the arrival of *every* train. Miriam was the daughter of Daniel Trigg, who owned a farm near Abingdon. Elliott had asked them to look after his dogs while he was away, and Miriam brought them with her, holding his fox terriers and a puppy he named "Little Nell Dog" after his much-missed Little Nell.[25]

Since Elliott could not visit his own children, he befriended all of the children in Abingdon. They came to his rooms when his dogs had puppies and cheered him when he was ill. (The "old Indian fever" still came and went.) He took them for rides through the country in his bright yellow carriage. "We rarely fail to secure some kind of game," he wrote to Eleanor in a letter that must have been a sword through her heart, "and never return without roses in the cheeks of all those I call now, my children."[26] "I envied [Miriam Trigg] very much, because he was so fond of her," wrote Eleanor years later.[27] Elliott finally realized this, and he wrote to assure Eleanor, "No other little girl can ever take your place in my heart."[28]

Elliott spoke so often to the children of Abingdon about the children he had to leave behind in New York that at least two of the Virginia youngsters wrote letters to Eleanor. Miriam Trigg's letter told Eleanor how fond she was of Elliott and how Elliott talked about his daughter all the time, and included a wish that Eleanor might be allowed to visit soon. The other was from Lillian Lloyd, daughter of the Reverend Lloyd, rector of the local Episcopal Church.

> Dear Eleanor,
>
> I want to write so badly that Mother is holding my hand. Your nice letter came today. I wish I could play with you. Wont you come down and play with my pretty doll and my brother Hubard and spend a week? I named my pretty doll ELEANOR ROOS-EVELT LLOYD. … I love your papa dearly, better than any man but Father. He has my picture with my Maltese cats in it. They are dead.
>
> Send me your picture, Eleanor, if you can't come soon …[29]

The parents of these children loved Elliott as well. He must have found it difficult to explain why his own children were not allowed to visit him, for in a note to the Reverend Lloyd's wife he tells her that there is some question at home as to whether he can lead "a correct life."[30]

"Small town and country folk are keen appraisers of character," wrote Goodridge Wilson for the *Richmond Times-Dispatch* in 1935. "They are apt to remember long and well people who touch their lives. Elliott Roosevelt lives in affectionate memory among small town, rural and mountain dwellers of southwestern Virginia. … One of those great old mountain women … of very little book knowledge but of fine native intelligence, great strength of character and tenderness of heart," when told that Theodore Roosevelt was running for vice president in 1900, "inquired if this Roosevelt was any relation of Elliott's. When told that he was Elliott's brother, she expressed the positive conviction that in that case he ought to be elected. Clearly to her mind it would be no great honor for Elliott to have a brother elected President of the United States, but the fact that Theodore was Elliott's brother eminently qualified him for the position."[31]

Elliott was true to his father's social conscience and became known in Abingdon for distributing clothes to the poor and giving turkeys to needy families at Christmas. When winter came he organized sledding parties and other outings. He prevailed upon Douglas Robinson to send funds to missions among the coal miners whose camps Elliott visited.

> "Mr. Roosevelt was a powerful fine man. He was awful good to poor people," would be the typical characterization from a cabin dweller. In the course of interviewing such of his old acquaintances as have survived the ravages of two score years, the interviewer was struck with this significant fact: the face of every person questioned would light up with pleasure and with the smile that goes with fond memory of a beloved friend. One lady, who forty years ago was a member of Abingdon's younger social set, said, "He was so good to people! He would do so many things for us in such a nice way, and he always seemed to feel that he was receiving the favor. I have known a great many people in my life, but Elliott Roosevelt had more of what is called personal charm than any other human being I have ever seen."[32]

While Elliott established himself in Virginia, Anna struggled to chart her own course in New York. Only in her late twenties, she had trouble with her vision and was often afflicted with what are now called migraine headaches. The one recorded instance of closeness between Eleanor and her mother was when Eleanor spent hours in the darkened bedroom stroking her mother's head.

> My mother suffered from very bad headaches, and I know now that life must have been hard and bitter and a very great strain on her. I would often sit at the head of her bed and stroke her head. People have since told me that I have good hands for rubbing, and perhaps even as a child there was something soothing in my touch, for she was willing to let me sit there for hours on end.
>
> As with all children, the feeling that I was useful was perhaps the greatest joy I experienced.[33]

Anna saw to her children's education by using the third floor of her house at 54 East 61st Street as a classroom for Eleanor and the daughters of several of Anna's closest friends. She hired Frederic Roser, the preferred teacher among fashionable families, to supervise the curriculum, which consisted primarily of *McGuffey's Readers*. Eleanor would always remember her self-consciousness as her mother sat in on her lessons. When Eleanor was asked to spell simple words she knew perfectly well how to spell, she would draw a blank and become even more disoriented upon seeing the distressed look on her mother's face. Mr. Roser was a pompous man lacking a sense of humor, and of course this was no help in putting Eleanor at ease.

"My mother took me aside afterwards and told me seriously that she wondered what would happen if I did not mend my ways! She knew that I knew them all and was too shy to open my mouth."[34]

Eleanor spent a great deal of time with her Auntie Bye, "happy rainy afternoons in the maid's sewing room … where I was allowed to have cambric tea and cookies and no one bothered me." No one, that is, except her cousin Alice, who also visited Bye often. "Already she seemed much older and cleverer, and while I always admired her I was always a little afraid of her."[35]

Above all Eleanor missed Elliott. The adults in her family tried not to discuss his case in front of Eleanor, but of course she heard stray bits of conversation. "Something was wrong with my father and from my point of view nothing could be wrong with him."[36] She witnessed her mother's anguish, for young, beautiful Anna was in a painful state of limbo, in the midst of "the season" with its cotillions, operas, amateur theatricals, polo matches and sets of tennis, horse and dog shows, charity balls and afternoon teas, which she still attended — but as neither "maiden lady," widow, nor even divorcee. She was haunted by the man to whom she was still legally tethered but who was no longer at her side — in a marriage that was now reduced to a poignant correspondence.

Anna regularly consulted Bye as to how she should conduct herself in society. She wanted to avoid further scandal and gossip, but she had many male admirers and enjoyed their attention. Was it all right to accept invitations to go for carriage rides, as long as one did not go too often with the same man? She wrote to Bye from Bar Harbor, where some of her cousins and siblings were enjoying life, that it was

> … an awful temptation when one feels desperately lonely and wildly furious with the world at large, not to make up one's mind to pay no attention to criticism so long as one does no wrong and to try to get some fun out of the few years of our youth. I hate everything and everyone so and am most of the time so miserable that I feel anything one could do would be a comfort to forget for one moment.[37]

Anna moved to 61st Street and Madison Avenue to be near Bye and Theodore, both of whom lived in the neighborhood. In this new house she presided over afternoon tea for the friends she continued to make, and she devoted one hour each day, from six to seven in the evening, exclusively to her children.

> If anyone comes to see me during that hour, they must understand they are welcome, but the children are of the first importance then, and my attention must be given to them. I play with them any way they may want. I get down on the floor and we play horse or we play tag, or I read for them — anything that they may remember the hour happily as "mother's hour," and feel assured that nothing whatever is to interfere with it.[38]

Eleanor did indeed remember these sessions. "Little Ellie was so good he never had to be reproved, the baby Hall ... was too small to do anything but sit upon her lap contentedly. I felt a curious barrier between myself and these three. My mother made a great effort for me ..."[39]

Perhaps compartmentalizing her children was the best Anna could do for them at this point. "Mother's hour" was part of a regimen — the children were brought in punctually at six and dismissed at seven — and sometimes even that was more than she had the strength for. A friend witnessed one of these sessions: "She took the baby in her lap, kissed 'Josh,' and moved the footstool for Eleanor to sit upon. A bit of biscuit was given to each, and then they were kissed goodnight 'as tonight Mamma is very tired' and waved to bed, only little Eleanor remaining at her mother's feet."[40]

This friend provides a touching vignette — our last glimpse of Anna, just two months before her death. Anna serves tea in a comfortable room upstairs. It is October, and outside it is pleasantly chilly, with the woodsy smell that permeates certain New York neighborhoods in autumn. Anna has a fire on the hearth, the gas lamps are lighted, and she is wearing a pink silk wrapper trimmed with white lace. She has been ill and has "a tender, even pathetic" look in her eyes. "A sense of rest, of womanly refinement, of sympathetic intelligence, pervaded the room, and the heart-to-heart talk that followed," remembered the friend.

Anna realizes now that life might require something more than beauty and breeding in a woman, and so the two friends discuss what they plan to study during the winter. Anna wants to learn in order to assist Eleanor with her own education. There is a lecture on astronomy scheduled at Carnegie Hall in the coming week, and the two ladies plan to attend. "Why, we must know about the moon, and all the recent discoveries in the planets! I *must* know this for my children's sake, at least."[41]

Anna is especially concerned not to neglect her children's religious training. Each day before breakfast, Anna tells her friend, Eleanor and her brothers are brought into their mother's room for daily prayers. She hopes above all things that this will keep them from following their father in his errant ways. "Is there anything else in life that can so anchor them to the right?" she asks.

Eleanor listens while her mother tells her friend that it is never too early to "awaken" a love for Sunday and for the church. Then the conversation turns once again to academics, this time to the history of France, which Mr. Roser and his assistant Miss Tomes have included in Eleanor's course of study. The ladies lightheartedly test each other's knowledge. From time to time Anna will "spring lightly up" and get a book to check the answers.

Tonight Anna is "sweet and loving and playful." As Anna's guest leaves, she turns to wave good-bye. There Anna stands at the top of the steps, with Eleanor standing furtively behind her, illumined gently by the soft gaslight. "It was a home picture, with an earnest, sweet mother, rarely to be equaled, never to be excelled."[42]

This friend made a present to Anna of the widely read volume *Christian Nurture* by Horace Bushnell, to help her with raising her children. Bushnell wrote that "A smile wakens a smile, irritation irritates, a frown

withers, love expands a look congenial to itself, and why not holy love? …
The Christian life and spirit of the parents, which are in and by the spirit
of God, shall flow into the mind of the child. … The wickedness of the
parents propagates itself in the character and condition of the children."

What could she do but keep Elliott away?

Anna read late into the night. Before going to sleep she sent her friend
a note thanking her for "that blessed book. … It has helped me to better
resolutions, which only God will know how I keep. …"[43]

Around the time of Eleanor's eighth birthday, Anna had surgery, the
details of which are lost to history. Mrs. Hall came down from Tivoli to
nurse her daughter. Eleanor stayed with the Gracies, with whom she cel-
ebrated her eighth birthday, and Elliott Jr. and Hall stayed with cousin
Susie Parish's mother, Great Aunt Elizabeth Ludlow. "Mother wishes
she could be with you," Eleanor's mother wrote. "I enclose a letter from
Father to you."[44]

> My darling little Daughter,
>
> Many happy returns of this birthday little Nell. I am thinking of
> you always and I wish for my Baby Girl the greatest of joy and the
> most perfect happiness in her sweet young life. Because Father
> is not with you is not because he doesn't love you. For I love you
> tenderly and dearly. And maybe soon I'll come back all well and
> strong and we will have such good times together, like we used
> to have. I have to tell all the little children here often about you
> and all that I remember of you when you were a little bit of a girl
> and you used to call yourself Father's little "Golden Hair" — and
> how you used to come into my dressing room and dress me in the
> morning and frighten me by saying I'd be late for breakfast.
>
> I gave a Doll to the little girl you sent the doll's jewelry to,
> small Lillian Lloyd and she has called it Eleanor and another

little friend of mine the daughter of my good and dear friend Mr. Blair of Chicago has named her most precious doll Eleanor too; after you they are both named. Some day you must meet little Lillian and little Emily and they will be glad to know you in person; they say they know your photograph so well.

Now I must stop writing dearest Little Nell, do take care of yourself and little Brothers, Ellie and Brudie [Hall], and kiss them for me. Love dear Mother for me and be very gentle and good to her 'specially now while she is not well. Goodbye my own little Daughter. God bless you.

Give my best to Aunt Gracie and Uncle.

> Your devoted Father
> Elliott Roosevelt

Eleanor answered her father's letter after arriving at the home of her Grandmother Hall.

Oak Terrace
Tivoli-on-Hudson

My dear Father: —

Your present which you and Mamma sent me was lovely. It is just what I want for washing the doly's clothes which Aunt Pussie and Auntie Maud gave me. I got a ball, walking doll, violin, music boxes, and a bell to draw around the piaza. The candy Auntie Tissie brought up looks lovely, And I have not tasted it as I do not eat between meals, but will have some after dinner. Elsie, Susie and Kittie Hall are coming to dinner and Auntie Maud is going to have Punch and Judy after dinner which I think will be great fun don't you. I was very glad to get your letter and please thank the clerk for the picture. I thank you again for the present you sent me. I hope you are all well and now I must close dear Father from your little daughter, Baby.[45]

Anna's operation precipitated the final tragic act in the long, painful drama of Anna and Elliott. Anna was given ether, and under its effect she finally lost her composure — the eventuality that all her life she had most dreaded and sought to avoid. Her mother and sisters heard her cry out that Elliott had ruined her life, made her miserable, and that now her only desire was to die.

When Elliott heard that Anna was to undergo an operation, he wanted to come to New York immediately, but he was told to stay away from her. Elliott was stunned, and when he insisted on coming north, Corinne — of all people — was delegated to land a devastating blow by informing him that the order to stay away from Anna came from Anna herself. He wrote to his mother-in-law every day of Anna's final week, desperately worried, overwhelmed with remorse, and dumbfounded at being forbidden to see his wife.

It is too awful for me to feel that I have forfeited the right to be in my proper place. … Oh the misery of my Sin! … I am so relieved though to know that you are in charge. … Is my wife very ill Mrs. Hall? *Two* trained nurses has such a terrifying sound. … If I should be wanted, in mercy forgive and remember that I am a husband and a Father and your son by adoption — though I have failed in many things. … I have a right in the sight of God to be at my wife's side in case she should wish me. … Do please *trust* me. …

Three days later he wrote:

Of course I trust you entirely and your words in the telegram "do not come" — I take as Anna's command. ... Did she say she wanted to die, that I had made her so utterly miserable that she did not care to live any more — And did you say that was what your poor child had been suffering in silence all these past killing months? How terribly sad. ...[46]

On December 6 he declared:

I have pledged it to my wife never to force myself upon her. ... You need not fear that even if called to my wife's deathbed that if not at her request I would present myself there. ... I ought to be with her unless my presence is *actually distasteful* to her.[47]

For a few days Anna seemed to recover, but then she caught diphtheria. During Anna's last hours, Elliott was finally sent for — but the family had waited too late. On December 7, 1892, Anna Rebecca Hall Roosevelt died. She was twenty-nine years old.

Eleanor would never forget that day. She was looking out a window when Susie Parish came into the room and told her. "My mother was dead. She was very sweet to me, and I must have known something terrible had happened. Death meant nothing to me, and one fact wiped out everything else — my father was back and I would see him soon."[48]

In a letter written the day Anna died, Elliott could not accept the thought that Anna really did not want to see him.

I cannot understand what influence can have been brought to bear upon her to make her feel the way she evidently does to me. I have before me two letters she wrote me the day before she had me kidnapped in Paris ... and no woman using the terms of endearment she does in them and giving promises of faithful love as she does there could possibly have changed without *outside* influence being brought to bear. ... It is most *horrible* and full of *awe* to me that my *wife* not only does not want me near her but *fears* me. ... [49] And before God I say it, I am honestly worthy of her trust and Love. ...[50]

Even at the end, Elliott was mystified as to why his marriage had been a calamity. Incredibly, he protested to his mother-in-law that "even in my drinking I never did a dishonorable thing, or *one cruel act* towards my wife or children. If Anna cares for it give her my love. ..."[51]

And so Anna was gone, only two months before Elliott's exile was supposed to end. It should be remembered that in one crucial respect Anna put her cultivated self-control in the service of love: she never turned Eleanor against her father, although the temptation to do so must have been overpowering at times. Eleanor never credited her with this, however.

As an elderly woman, Eleanor told an interviewer, "I adored my mother, but rather like a distant and beautiful thing that I couldn't possibly get close to." But to a clergyman friend, during a late-night conversation, she was more candid. "It is a terrible thing to say," she confided, "but I hated my mother."[52]

⚜16⚜

"SOMEHOW IT WAS ALWAYS HE AND I"

The Rev. Henry Yates Satterlee, who had performed Anna's wedding, also conducted her funeral, not at Calvary Church but at Anna's last home, 52 East 61st Street. "Her death Wednesday was entirely unexpected and was a decided shock to her family and friends," read one death notice. "After the confinement of her husband, Elliott Roosevelt, in the private retreat for the insane at Suresnes, France, Mrs. Roosevelt withdrew herself to a great extent from society. ... Mrs. Roosevelt had long been a reigning belle in society circles in this vicinity, and her fame as a beauty was widespread."

"LAST YEARS SADDENED BY HER HUSBAND'S INSANITY" was the subhead in yet another of New York's thirty-six dailies, the masthead of which disintegrated long ago. "Last September, at Bar Harbor, she was regarded as the belle of the 'beauty dinner' given by the Turkish Minister at Washington."[1]

One week after Anna died, however, the society page of *The New York Times* carried this item about the Patriarchs' Ball:

It had been thought that the sad death of young Mrs. Elliott Roosevelt, whom, had she lived, would have been one of the patronesses, would have greatly dimmed the brilliancy of the ball, but New York is a large town, and "we are soon forgot" so that the absence of the few who stayed away … was hardly noticed. …[2]

New York society, where Anna Hall Roosevelt had laid up much of her treasure and heart, was managing nicely without her. Her estranged husband, however, was devastated. Eleanor wrote later that she did not realize at the time what a "tragedy of utter defeat" this was for him. "He had no hope now of ever wiping out the sorrowful years he had wrought upon my mother — and she had left her mother as guardian for her children. My grandmother did not feel she could trust my father to take care of us. He had no wife, no children, no hope!"[3]

Elliott was admired and respected in Abingdon in a way he had never been in New York. He established himself there and was looked up to as a solid citizen. He had dozens of friends who would come to his aid. He had shown — miraculously — that he could remain sober for extended periods. He had finally realized (for the most part) the suffering caused by his self-destructiveness. He had been punished both *for* his sins and *by* his sins. If only he could take his children and start a new life — a completely different life from the routine they had in New York!

One can imagine Elliott arriving in Virginia with his children, and the sympathetic interest the young widower and the motherless little ones would have excited in the kindhearted people there — a most appealing possibility that never was allowed to be realized.

The family of Elliott's rector in Abingdon was looking forward to the prospect, but Elliott explained the situation in a letter to Mrs. Lloyd:

Good as I firmly believe your advice to have been, and sorely as I think myself I need my little ones with me, I will return without them. I have not found one person in either my wife's or my connection who encourages me in the slightest degree when I propose that the children join their Father. If I have a comfortable home they might come down and visit me for awhile during the summer. But all seem to think that the proper place for them now is with their grandmother and surrounded by everything in the way of luxury and all the advantages, both educational and otherwise to which they have been accustomed.[4]

Not even Corinne questioned the wisdom of Anna's decree. Elliott continued:

There seems also to be still a strong feeling of suspicion as to my desire to lead a correct life — which is not even to me unnatural as they have not known me or seen me really for all these months. They have all told me that they would like to see proofs given for another year of my capability to live rightly and of the earnestness of my desire to do so — I have promised nothing but I have told my Mother-in-law that she shall have the children until I feel I <u>must</u> have them and when that time comes she has promised to give them up to me — No matter if I am living alone on White Top [Abingdon] or in Ceylon — There they are to come and join me. I am honestly only anxious to convince them for my dear Wife's sake of my sorrow for sin and to prove beyond doubt my worthiness to possess my Babies.[5]

Elliott didn't want to leave his daughter, but he had to. Their good-bye was the most significant episode in Eleanor Roosevelt's early life.

My father came to see me, and I remember going down into the high-ceilinged, dim library on the first floor of the house in West 37th Street. He sat in a big chair. He was dressed all in black, looking very sad. He held out his arms and gathered me to him. In a little while he began to talk, to explain to me that my mother was gone, that she had been all the world to him, and now he only had my brothers and myself, that my brothers were very young, and that he and I must keep close together. Some day I would make a home for him again, we would travel together and do many things which he painted as interesting and pleasant, to be looked forward to in the future together.

Somehow it was always he and I. I did not understand whether my brothers were to be our children or whether he felt that they would be at school and college and later independent.

There started that day a feeling which never left me — that he and I were very close together, and some day would have a life of our own together. He told me to write to him often, to be a good girl, to study hard, to grow up into a woman he could be proud of, and he would come to me whenever it was possible.

When he left, I was all alone to keep our secret of mutual understanding and to adjust myself to my new existence.[6]

That existence would be no more than a backdrop for Eleanor's real life, the inner world in which she and her father shared adventures within a framework of total acceptance, mutual admiration and companionship — a world they constructed together as a way of escape from emotional abuse and loneliness.

Mary Hall's heart went out to Elliott. She wrote him regularly, keeping him informed of what his children were doing and sending him small gifts and baskets of fruit.

The first Christmas without Anna, Mrs. Hall invited Elliott to visit her and the children. Eleanor would never forget Christmas Eve, 1892, when the Hall family, including Anna's two brothers and three sisters, and Elliott gathered at the house on West 37th Street. Elliott must have remembered with pain how beautifully festive the house was the night of his wedding reception, when it was filled with lilies and roses. Now the house was again magical, this time with Christmas decorations.

The Halls welcomed Elliott to their dinner of roast turkey and then they sang carols around the piano. "I would have given anything to be a singer, because my father loved to sing," wrote Eleanor, "and when he came to the 37th Street house he would sing with Maude and Pussie."[7] Now as Pussie played, Eleanor listened to her father's memorable voice as he sang "Silent Night." Elliott carried his daughter upstairs to her bedroom, where in the morning she found two stockings, one from her grandmother filled with practical things — pencils, a pencil sharpener, soap, a washcloth, a toothbrush. In contrast to these "utilitarian gifts," there was a stocking from her father, who had "put in little things a girl could wear — a pair of white gloves, a pretty handkerchief, several hair ribbons, and a little gold pin." Eleanor's presents for her father were homemade: a tobacco pouch — he still loved his pipe — and a case for his handkerchiefs. The most exciting present was a new puppy, a fox terrier Elliott bred in Virginia and managed to keep quiet under the Christmas tree long enough for Eleanor to be surprised.

Christmas morning everyone went to Calvary Church, surely evoking another poignant memory for Elliott. He must have remembered how holy Anna had looked as she walked majestically up the aisle and took his hand at the altar. His one comfort now was their daughter, as she cuddled beside him while they shared the Prayer Book.[8] Later, he would write his aunt Ella Bulloch how much it meant to have his daughter in church with him and "nestling close to Father."[9] He wrote his aunt Anna Gracie that the children "had a sweet bright Christmas and every body was so kind, so particularly lovely to me and to my precious little babies. They are too young to appreciate the extent of their terrible loss but I am heart sick and oh! so sorrowful, when I look at the poor motherless little ones. ... I do love you and dear old Uncle so very, very much Auntie dear."[10]

One month later Elliott was back in Abingdon, feeling unwell. He thanked his mother-in-law for the fruit she sent him, although it had not yet arrived. "I expect to be called away on business tomorrow for several days. I have arranged that the sick in town shall get them so that they shall not be wasted nor their dear Savior less blest. ... The clothes you send me for the poor will be very acceptable, and Mother they are poor and many of them most worthy — it shall be my first practical use as a Vestry man to see that they are properly distributed."[11]

Elliott with his three children and holding Eleanor's hand, circa 1893. Courtesy of The Franklin D. Roosevelt Presidential Library.

As was often the case with Elliott, churchgoing provided respite. "My day has been very quiet and content — we had a beautiful, peaceful little service at the small Episcopal church here in town where I feel every body is a friend. This afternoon I had a really touching meeting with my class of boys at the mission chapel. ..."[12]

In addition to serving on the vestry and teaching his "class of boys," he became close to the rector and his family, who were deeply interested in his predicament.

It is very kind of you to write to me in such a delightfully old friend spirit — indeed I feel too dearest Lady that you and your husband and in fact all of the family are of those truly nearest and dearest to me — For through all the time of my greatest loneliness and greatest trial you have been to me precious com-forters, and I have felt your sympathy — The strength your hus-band was able to give me was more than any thing else I believe, what enabled me to win what has been, at least to me, a very severe struggle over selfishness and false pride — I do remember as you ask me to the conversation we had at tea that evening.[13]

He was conscientious about the financial needs of his children: "We will leave all business later until I get north. ... So long as you have as much money as you need for the children's support and they are no drain upon your purse at present. In the future when we meet we can plan together what is best. Your scheme and arrangement seem to me very good — even for a future plan — a certain sum regularly from me monthly for their support paid to you ..."[14] He wrote more specifically later of "the money Anna left in trust and the ample monetary trust I established in their favor. At $2500 a year a piece which is the amount they derive from those combined trusts you would have $7500 which is $635 per month.

Then what over and above that you require from time to time I will give you out of what is my share, as it were, of the Estate (my Estate I mean). ... I will not be niggardly with you dear Mother, you need not fear. I want my little children to have everything that I can afford possibly. But I must insist that they do not receive — charity is the only word I can think of — from you. You, not I, are the generous one. ..."[15]

Elliott took a deep interest in Eleanor's progress at school. "I enclose you the only letter I have from Anna that contained any record of her plan in regard to Eleanor's Education — thinking it may help you in knowing what the dear Mother's arrangements for her little daughter's schooling were. Above all if she has any musical bent, let us cultivate it. The bill I sent you should be given to Anna's executors for payment out of the Estate."[16] A note to Eleanor's grandmother from Professor Roser, Eleanor's teacher, gratified Elliott: "The tone of his note is very nice, did you not think so? Our little girl is a good little girl and conscientious. ..."[17]

Elliott was unsure of what to do with himself following the death of Anna, but wished to honor his commitments in Abingdon: "My plans are not entirely settled but tomorrow I will have to spend here on business for the Land Company," he wrote his mother-in-law. "Tuesday and Wednesday I will make an inspection of the property improvements and latest developments. ..."[18]

Theodore, meanwhile, was taking enormous pleasure in fatherhood. "Edith has been including Ted in Alice's little lessons," he wrote Bye, "and he has been pondering over what he has heard. The other evening when I went to kiss him in his little crib, he suddenly asked, 'Papa, is God a fairy?' I said no, to which he responded, 'Then why does he live in Heaven?' and after a pause 'Well, can God fight?'"[19]

Theodore was following in his father's footsteps in pursuing "righteous enthusiasms," currently in an attempt to clean up the Civil Service Commission. "... I have had rather a lull in my warfare with the ungodly lately," he wrote Bye, "but I guess it will soon break out again with two-fold greater virulence." After his wife took the children to Oyster Bay, he told his sister, "I am frightfully homesick for Edith and my own blessed small ones; as I walk through the park I find myself involuntarily looking round for the little merry things."[20]

Theodore, at least, knew the date when he would be reunited with his children. Elliott's separation from *his* children, however, was indefinite. Once again the people of Abingdon were his consolation. "The little people are so sweet and loving to me," he wrote to Mrs. Lloyd. "I spend <u>all</u> my spare time with them and they seem very fond of me and really to want me."[21]

Years later, when she was a student in England, Eleanor Roosevelt visited her great aunt Ella Bulloch in Liverpool, wife of Mittie's brother, Confederate naval officer and expatriate Irvine Stephens Bulloch. Although Elliott was not related to his "Aunt Ella" except by marriage, he was always close to her and corresponded regularly. A letter to Eleanor from her Aunt Ella was filled with reminiscences of Elliott's "many sweet and loving ways":

One [memory] — when he was away from home and longing for you — as he always did. He was spending the evening — he wrote — with some friends and a little fair-haired girl climbed up into his lap, and nestled close in his tender clasp and fell asleep there. They wanted to take her from him then, but he begged she might stay: <u>they</u> did not know, he added, "that to me it was <u>another fair little head</u> I held against my breast, as my thoughts wandered far away, and it comforted me to feel her in my arms." Another time just after your mother's death, when he was in such sorrow, he wrote of "his little Nell" being the greatest help and comfort to him. ...[22]

Elliott reassured Eleanor of their future companionship, writing that he had "found a lot of books we must some day read together."

"My darling little Nell: What can you think of your Father, neglecting to write you for so long. Though you are the naughty pretty little recreant as you owe me one or two I think. … How are your little brothers? Give them my dearest love. … Keep a great deal for yourself my little little Nell. …"[23]

⊰17⊱

"NEVER FORGET I LOVE YOU"

Elliott went back to Abingdon and took up his position in Douglas Robinson's business. He refused to let go of the slender hope that he could one day make a home with his children, an expectation not shared by his family, excepting Eleanor. ("I do not think he is drinking," Edith Roosevelt wrote her mother, "but I do not believe his mind will ever be quite right.")[1] He wrote Eleanor loving, tender letters that would be her prized possessions for the rest of her life. There were recurring episodes of his "old Indian fever," and at one point he suffered severe burns when he knocked over a lamp.[2] However, his first letter after his return to Virginia was chatty and cheerful, full of news about his puppies. "They are both in the armchair beside me and the old Dog is curled up at my feet on the rug dreaming. I suppose of all the rabbits he did <u>not</u> catch today!"[3]

Elliott enchanted his daughter with his rhapsodic compositions.

Shall I tell you of the wonderful long rides, of days through the grand snowclad forests, over the white hills, under the blue skies as blue as those in Italy which you and I and little Ellie, though he was so little he cannot remember it, used to sail over Naples Bay to beautiful Capri. I am afraid in these young "Nell days" you were a little seasick and did not enjoy it as much as you will in the day that is coming when you have worked hard at your lessons and gotten that curious thing they call "education."[4]

Elliott encouraged Eleanor to apply herself to disciplines that did not come easily to her:

I know division, especially long division, seemed to me at your age a very tiresome and uninteresting study. I too longed to be in fractions — or *infractious* but I found afterwards that it had been better, — as it turns out nine times out of ten — that I stood out against my own impatience and lack of desire to become informed, and devoted myself — howbeit against the grain — to the study of the life and the interests of those of God's creation, whom He calls not His own.[5]

In his unique style, Elliott made sure that Eleanor would never forget the priority he wished her to give to learning:

The next time you go walking get your maid to take you where they are building a house and watch the workmen bring one stone after another and place it on top of the one gone before or along side, and then think that there are a lot of funny little workmen running about in your small Head called "Ideas" which are carrying a lot of stones like small bodies called "Facts," and these little "Ideas" are being directed by your teachers in various ways, by "Persuasion," "Instruction," "Love," and "Truth" to place all these "Fact Stones" on top of and alongside of each other in your dear Golden Head until they build a beautiful house called "Education" — Then! Oh, my pretty companionable Little

Daughter, you will come to Father and what jolly games we will have together to be sure — And in your beautiful house "Education," Father wishes you such a happy life — but those little fact stones are a queer lot, and you have to ask your teachers to look well after the Idea workmen that they don't put some in crooked in the walls of your pretty House. Sometimes you'll find a rough hard fact that you must ask your teacher to smooth down and polish and set straight by persuasion, love and truth. Then you'll find a rebellious little factstone that won't fit where it ought to, though it is intended to go just there like the little factstone "music" — may be you will have to get your teachers to use instruction, maybe a great deal of it to get that small stone to fit, but it must go there and it will, if the little Idea workmen stick with it long enough. Then there are what seem to be stupid, wearisome, trying factstones that you can't see the use of in your dear house, that the Ideas are building! Like — "Going to bed regularly and early fact stones," "*Not eating candy* fact stones," "Not telling always exactly the Truth fact stones," "Not being a teasing little girl fact stones" instead of a precious gentle Self amusing and satisfied one.

There are lots of others like those I have mentioned and to have them put in order you must beg your teachers to use all four powers of Persuasion, Instruction, Love, Truth and another force too, *Discipline!* Of all the forces your Teachers use, Father and you too, Little Witch, probably like Love best, but we must remember the little fact stones as I said at first are such a queer lot, that we have to trust to your Teachers, who know by Experience in building other Education houses in little brains, how much the Idea workmen can do and how also the character of the fact stones, what forces to apply. Think of your brain as an Education House: you must always wish to live in a beautiful house and not an ugly one, and get Auntie Maude darling to explain what Father means by this letter tale. Little Terrier says I must go to bed. Goodnight my darling little Daughter, my *"Little Nell."*[6]

Shortly before Easter, Eleanor sent books to her father, who replied, "I thank you for the wonderful books — if I can read through that collection I will be an educated man. I wish that I could be with you this happy Eastertide. In a month or six weeks I will be back with you and so pleased. I enclose a few white violets which you can put up in your Prayer book at the XXIII Psalm and you must know they were Grandmother Roosevelt's favorite flower." Eleanor wore them to church. As for his own holiday, "I thought of *you all day long* and blessed you and prayed for your happiness and that of your precious small brothers."[7]

But the thought that meant the most to her was, "Maybe soon I'll come back well and strong and we'll have such good times together, like we used to have."[8]

The sudden illness and death of his father had been the first devastating knock of Elliott's life; the final unraveling came with the death of his son. In May 1893 both of Elliott's sons contracted scarlet fever. Eleanor was sent out of harm's way to her Ludlow relatives. Hall recovered, but Elliott wrote his daughter "to let you know that dear little Ellie is very, very ill and may go to join dear Mother in Heaven. There is just a little chance that he may not die but the doctors all fear that he will."[9]

Eleanor Roosevelt could never believe "that death was an irreversible deprivation,"[10] in the words of one biographer. This conviction began in childhood. She hastened to comfort her father:

I write to thank you for your kind note and to tell you how sorry I am to hear Ellie is so sick, but we must remember Ellie is going to be safe in heaven and to be with Mother who is waiting there and our Lord wants Ellie boy with him now, we must be happy and do God's will and we must cheer others who feel it to. You are alright I hope. ...[11]

Elliott informed Eleanor that Ellie was indeed "happy in Heaven" with his mother. "My own Little Nell — We bury little Ellie up at Tivoli tomorrow by Mother's side. He is happy in Heaven with her now so you must not grieve or sorrow. And you will have to be doubly a good daughter to your Father and a good sister to our own little Brudie boy who is left to us. I know you will my own little Heart." At this point sadness overwhelmed him. "I cannot write more because I am not feeling very well and my heart is too full. ... I put some flowers close by Ellie in your name as I know you would like me to do."[12]

(For Eleanor Roosevelt, who read her father's letters regularly throughout her life, the exhortation to be "doubly a good daughter and sister" went very deep. When one of her own granddaughters died at age fourteen, Eleanor in a heart-to-heart talk with the surviving sister, advised her that now, more than ever, was the time to be courageous. They talked for a long time about the meaning of courage, and Eleanor made it clear that her granddaughter must get past her own grief and concentrate on being a loving, sensitive daughter to her parents.)[13]

The loss of his and Anna's beloved "Baby Joss" made Elliott cling even more tenderly to Eleanor. "Dear little daughter," he wrote, "you are your father's love and joy."[14] "I wished you to know that you were never out of my thoughts and prayers for one instant all the time." "With abiding and most tender devotion and Love," he signed his letters, "I am always, your affectionate Father. ..."[15]

Elliott's friends and family were stunned by the death of this child while Elliott was still reeling from the loss of Anna. His continued sorrows brought forth a torrent of affection and sympathy. "Your sweet strong helpfulness for me, while in such deep sorrow, has touched me more than I can tell you," wrote Margaret Wilmer, a member of Elliott's church in Abingdon. "As life is made up of our feelings and wishes for each other, think how much you have added to my happiness."[16]

"Oh! My dear Mr. Roosevelt, What can I say to you now? <u>Nothing</u> but that you have all the love and sympathy that my poor old heart can give," wrote Mary Campbell, his elderly landlady in Abingdon. "Come <u>home</u>, just as soon as you can and you will find a host of sympathizing friends to welcome you."[17] Two weeks later she wrote him another letter: "I am so sorry for you. You have such a gentle loving heart and trouble <u>troubles</u> you so much. I do hope you are getting homesick for your mountain home, and the cool, refreshing nights. We miss you & want you back so come at once. Miriam & I will do all we can to comfort you, for we both love you dearly."[18]

The letters Elliott received at this time are a testimony both to the love that he inspired and to the eloquence of literate people in the late nineteenth century. "My dear Roosevelt," (the salutation of several of his male friends), "You will, I know, pardon my intruding on your grief, when I say that the loss of my eldest child and only boy — three years and four months old from scarlet fever some years hence — is brought back to me most vividly by your present great sorrow," wrote W.W. Lane, one of Elliott's "sporting friends." "I feel therefore that I can especially sympathize with you in your bereavement and, although our paths in life have separated since the happy days in the old company, such trials seem to bring us again together, in spirit at least, and make us realize that we still have some bonds in common which time and separation cannot sever."[19]

"One sufferer can always feel for another," wrote one Willoughby Reade of Abingdon, "and I who have lost nearly all that were dear to me on earth and am but a wanderer today upon its face, know the pain of grief that is in your heart and can give you my deepest sympathy, which, believe me, I do."[20]

"Sometimes it helps me to think of those who are waiting beyond as the ministering spirits — watching for the best in our own lives," offered Frank Leffingwell, another of Elliott's Virginia neighbors.[21]

"I have no thought of offering you consolation, I would not know how to go about it, but I do want to let you know, I feel with you very deeply," wrote Elliott's Wall Street friend J. Coleman Drayton. "If there is a heaven as I hope, the little ones must go there, for they save us older ones from many a sin, and I know for me, do more to make me lead at any rate the semblance of a decent and clean life than religion or worldly wealth or honor would, or could. So I say God bless the little ones, and God pity the parents who lose them."[22]

"All your friends here have spoken so affectionately of you, and I have never realized what a strong hold you have on the hearts of people of all classes in this community," wrote Arthur Wilmer of Abingdon. "Trouble seems to have fallen upon you with no light hand during the past year, but I think God is just trying you, and I feel confident that you, dear strong brave fellow that you are, will come out of the cleansing fires a better, stronger man than ever. God bless you always and remember you have the love of so many of us down here. Tears have been shed in sympathy for you. ..."[23] When a letter from Elliott arrived the next day, Mr. Wilmer wrote again: "Your very kind letter of the 26th reached me this morning, and I do appreciate most heartily the fact that you should find time to think of me and my affairs, when you are in such trouble yourself. Dear unselfish fellow it is just like you to do such a thing. ... I have ten of a dozen inquiries made of me after you by people interested in you, and whom you know but slightly."[24]

Even Elliott's sister-in-law Edith Roosevelt, never long on sympathy for Elliott, wrote:

My dear Elliott,

When you are broken with sorrow for the loss of your beautiful boy, there can be no words of consolation. It gives me a heart pang to look at my Kermit and think of his dear little twin cousin. The death of a pure, innocent child should bring sorrow with no sting, but with even a certain joy, but we who love the little ones so tenderly cannot feel this at once and can but hope to in time. Affectionately yours, Edith K. Roosevelt[25]

Theodore sent "heartfelt sympathy," by way of Western Union. "Coming in tonight. Fear public business renders it absolutely necessary to return tomorrow."[26] Corinne, unlikely to be distracted by other considerations, cabled, "My thoughts and sympathy are with you constantly."[27] In addition she sent Elliott a letter filled with emotion, seconded by Douglas Robinson. "To one of your nature, there is an aching void made that cannot be filled by any human consolation," wrote Corinne's husband. "My dear Elliott, such trials as you have been called upon to bear are great tests of faith ... hold fast to Him Who said Suffer little children to come unto me and forbid them not for such is the Kingdom of Heaven. The sure hope of reunion then fills the void. ..."[28]

"... Just now my one greatest longing is to know if you can bear this last most crushing agony," wrote Elliott's aunt Ella Bulloch in Liverpool. "I know how far from well you have been — this added needs superhuman strength indeed!"[29] Superhuman strength, however, was never one of Elliott's qualities, in even his healthiest periods.

"Aunt Annie is heartbroken," Corinne had written of their aunt's response to the news of the death of little Ellie, "is irrepressibly sad that she is so ill at a time when you needed her care & love. She is perfectly helpless at present & until she gets a competent nurse I cannot leave her. … dear Elliott what can I say — I feel perfectly at a loss. … Aunt Annie is grieving as only she can. … Your deeply sorrowing Corinne."[30]

Anna Gracie, sixty years old and suffering with "kidney trouble," had taken a fall that left her with internal injuries. "… She arrived at O[yster] B[ay] and by some mistake her carriage did not meet her," Elliott's cousin Maud Elliott wrote her sister-in-law Helena, wife of Maud's brother John Stewart Elliott. "She took a light wagon and a boy driver, somehow was upset, dragged, and fearfully bruised. Corinne, Edith and two nurses have done everything that could be done. … Corinne speaks of Elliott as being 'far from well' and 'in great distress over the loss of his boy.' Dr. Satterlee [the clergyman who conducted the wedding of Anna and Elliott, later Dean of the National Cathedral in Washington, D.C.] spoke so kindly of him to me, but came out in no measured terms as to his opinion of Anna and her effect on Elliott. He said this to me, so mums the word."[31]

Two nights later, Maud resumed her letter: "Aunt Anna died early this morning, and is to be buried from the Church of the Holy Communion on Monday morning." Annie's husband had been aware for "some time" that his wife had "a mortal illness. … This fact, together with her extreme deafness, which made her unhappy, reconcile them all to her death. Elliott looks remarkably well, Mamma says. He sends word he is coming to see me, and I shall be glad to see him, poor fellow."[32] Elliott had been Anna's favorite nephew, perhaps because she felt he was most like his mother.[33]

"My darling little Nell," Elliott wrote,

I am so glad you wrote Father such a sweet note on Saturday. I received it today and it has comforted me a great deal to know my little daughter was well and happy. … What a sad day today was for all of us. I do not want to write it to you though I would tell you if your dear golden head was on my breast; my dear, *loved* little Nell. But do not be sad my Pretty, remember Mother is with Ellie and Aunt Gracie now.

I sent Morris, my groom, on with your pony and cart tomorrow afternoon's boat so that he will deliver him to you Wednesday morning with Father's tender love to his sweet Daughter. ... He is perfectly gentle and only needs reasonable handling for you to drive him alone. ... I wish I could be with you to teach you how to drive myself but that can not be. ...

With a heart full of love,

ever fondly, your Father.[34]

The children of Abingdon continued to be a source of comfort. "The little children here treat my rooms as if they owned them for a nursery," Elliott wrote to Eleanor. "There are two little twin brothers, sons of Mr. Trigg, just the age of Brudie, who call your old Father 'oosevelt'!!, and are on most intimate terms with my horses and dogs. ... I thank you for your sweet note. I gave the messages to Lillian & Miriam. You write so well my little sweet Heart. ..."[35]

As though his burden of grief weren't onerous enough, the financial foothold Elliott established in Abingdon began to slide out from under him. Through judicious investments and his management of the Douglas Land Company, Elliott became a respected businessman in Virginia. Of course he didn't need the money, but he did need the good opinion of his neighbors and the self-respect that came from diligent gainful employment.

However, in 1893 a severe depression brought financial reversals for many Americans, Elliott included. Seventy-five percent of the workers in Douglas Robinson's mines were fired, and the bank Elliott assisted in establishing closed its doors, although he lost over $30,000 in an effort to keep it afloat. He traversed three states trying "to protect my interests." All of western Virginia went under, including the coal fields.[36] "I have lost heavily, dear lady," Elliott wrote to Mrs. Hall, "and am in great distress and sorrow, for I was doing so well. I hope to pull out all right."

Part of his "distress and sorrow" was for the plight of the miners, as he wrote to Eleanor: "I have had a very trying time of it down here and am now trying to quiet the poor miners in the coal field who will listen to no one but me, and who are absolutely, for lack of employment, starv-ing. There is great distress all through this country and I too have suffered much. I like to think of you as happy and would like to hear the same from your dear sweet lips or read the words from your pen."[37]

This was Elliott's most poignant calamity, for it was not brought on by self-destructiveness. Throughout his life so much about his circumstances could have been helped through changes made by himself in his patterns and thinking. Now he *had* changed, yet all was undone through misfortune over which he had no control.

"Fifteen years before, when Elliott's father had fallen to cancer, he had embraced Elliott, as if to pass his life on to his son," writes William Youngs. "Now Elliott, beset with problems he could not conquer, reached out to Eleanor. He reached into himself for what was best and sought to pass it on distilled and purified for Eleanor. Elliott was a gentle man. He hoped his daughter would be tender, too."[38] "Of all the forces your Teachers use, Father and you too ... probably like Love best."[39]

What could Elliott give Eleanor? As he felt his own life and strength ebbing away, he could exhort her to be the sort of person he knew he should have been. In the late 1920s, Eleanor Roosevelt wrote:

I knew a child once who adored her father. She was an ugly lit-tle thing, keenly conscious of her deficiencies, and her father, the only person who really cared for her, was away much of the time; but he never criticized her or blamed her, instead he wrote her letters and stories, telling how he dreamed of her growing up and what they would do together in the future, but she must be truthful, loyal, brave, well-educated, or the woman he dreamed of would not be there when the wonderful day came for them to fare forth together. The child was full of fears and because of them lying was easy; she had no intellectual stimulus at that time and yet she made herself as the years went on into a fairly good copy of the picture he had painted.[40]

He continued to write cheerful letters to his daughter — although still on black-bordered stationery — asking about the horse and cart he gave her:

Darling little Daughter
I must write you a line just to ask how you and Brudie are. Do you drive your little cart, and do you ride your pony yet? Would you like a saddle for your birthday present? I have thought of you often during these beautiful days. I have been way up in the North woods and way off in Pennsylvania [blotted] (My, but Father can not spell such a long word!) Write me about your self my "Little Nell." Don't forget that I love you dearly even if I have not time to write often. Give my love to Grandma and all & kiss Brudie for me & remember me to Madeleine.[41]

(Elliott was still the only member of his family to greet the servants in his letters. Madeleine, his daughter's governess, would blight Eleanor Roosevelt's childhood with her cruelty, but this was not known until some years after Elliott's death, when Eleanor blurted it out to her grandmother. Madeleine was immediately discharged.)[42]

For Eleanor, no place could be home without her father. "I cannot tell you dear little girl, when you are coming home until I have seen Grandma and consulted her," he informed Eleanor. That consultation yielded disappointing results, however, for no one in the family thought Elliott could be trusted to care for his children. Mary Hall thought it better for Elliott to stay away from Tivoli that summer and to send Eleanor to Newport. Elliott begged her to let him come to Newport, "where I can see them and enjoy a little love which my heart craves and for lack of which it has broken. Oh, Mrs. Hall, I have tried and it has been so lonely & weary and the break down seems to me natural in my strained condition. Above all believe me it was not drunkenness. Let me see you soon please Mother. ..."[43]

Mrs. Hall pitied Elliott and turned to Bamie for counsel. Bamie replied that she was at a loss because Elliott had turned against her. Any chance of Elliott ever becoming stable enough to do his children no harm "lay in the management being purely between you and himself."[44]

In the autumn of 1893, Elliott left Abingdon and wandered in and out of New York. During the week of Eleanor's ninth birthday, Corinne was dumbfounded when Eleanor spotted Elliott in New York; he had returned to the city without telling anyone.

> Eleanor saw him driving in a Hansom the other day and waved at him (this is what the governess says) & he stopped & took her with him to her sewing class. Mrs. Hall was naturally much worried. I told her she ought to tell the governess that when Eleanor is under her care she should not allow her to go *with any one*, not even her father. It is so strange & sad that he should not be able to see his children & yet there seems to be *no other* course. Poor, poor Elliott. If I don't hear from him soon I shall take some means of seeing him. ...[45]

No one in his family ever seemed to know exactly where he was staying. He told Corinne he was going back to Virginia, but ten days later she encountered him in New York. Afterward, Corinne and Douglas attempted to look in on him every day at his hotel, but he never was available. At this time he began a pattern of writing notes to them or to Theodore or to his uncle James Gracie, asking them to meet him at various locations. They would show up, but Elliott would not. Nor was Eleanor exempt from his erratic behavior; he would send her a note that he was coming to take her for a drive, only to stand her up.

The family could not find Elliott at any of his old haunts; later it turned out that, although he gave his address as the Knickerbocker Club, in fact he was living as "Maxwell Eliot" at 313 West 102nd Street with a "Mrs. Evans." "I do wish Corinne would get a little of my hard heart about Elliott," Theodore wrote to Bamie. "She can do, and ought to do nothing for him. He can't be helped and he simply must be let go his own gait. He is now laid up from a serious fall; while drunk he drove into a lamp post and went out on his head. Poor fellow! If only he could have died instead of Anna!"[46]

Elliott's daughter, however, did not see it this way, and she never would develop a "hard heart" toward her father or his memory. She lived for his visits; occasionally he would show up at 11 West 37th Street, sweep Eleanor off her feet, then disappear again.

These reunions were among the happiest moments of her life. She never forgot the thrill of recognizing her father's voice at the door and the way her heart would pound with joy as she slid down the banister into his arms. He would take her walking or driving and tell her about the plans he was making for the home they would have together; but in the meantime she must be his angelic little girl, not give her grandmother any trouble, and grow up into a fine woman of whom he would be proud.

These visits were not without their harrowing moments; there were times when Elliott's recklessness filled her with "abject terror." Once on their way to Central Park in a high, two-wheeled carriage with no top, called a "dog cart," Elliott's horse Mohawk was startled by a streetcar. Elliott lost his hat in the scuffle; after a policeman retrieved it and they calmed the horse, Elliott gave Eleanor a thoughtful look, asking, "You weren't afraid, were you, little Nell?" "No," she answered — remembering his disappointment with her in Italy — and tried to stop trembling. Elliott must have known that her bravery was an act to please him, for when they joined the line of carriages in the park, he teased her. "If I were to say 'hoop-la' to Mohawk, he would try to jump them all." "I hope you won't say it," she admitted, barely above a whisper. "I won't," he assured her.[47]

Eleanor credited her father with being "a fine horseman" with one wild horse that he decided to break and drive in New York City in a two-wheeled cart. "… We would go on rather mad chases. … My father enjoyed every minute of the excitement as he tried to control the spirited horse." This is hardly the way the "excitement" affected Eleanor; even so, "these drives were the high point of my existence," she later wrote.[48]

With great tenderness Elliott would help his daughter into her seat and carefully tuck the woolen lap robe over her legs. She put her arm around him while he held the reins. He told her about his adventures in "the wild west" and in India and of how the two of them would visit all of those places "someday." He would teach her how to shoot so that she could hunt tigers with him while they both rode elephants, side by side. He told her about the beauty of the Taj Mahal in the moonlight, and of how he looked forward to showing it to her. He made it sound as though the Taj Mahal was something he had invented and that he was keeping as a gift that he would present to her one day.

As soon as her father left, Eleanor would go back into her dream world, the only world that mattered to her, in which the two of them were always together. He had described what he called his "favorite drink," a concoction he remembered from his Indian days consisting of milk, rose water left out all night with the morning dew topping it off, whipped up with "a silver leaf." Eleanor was not sure where to find a silver leaf, but she knew that one day, when she kept house for her father, she would bring him this drink and he would enjoy it while they sat together in the evening.[49]

One day during this period Elliott took his children to a photographer's studio. In the resulting portrait, Elliott sits with Hall on his knee and Eleanor in a sailor suit next to him. Elliott is looking his best — hair meticulously parted in the middle, moustache carefully waxed at the ends, tie knotted around a wing collar, white carnation in his jacket buttonhole — but it is his expression as he gazes down at Eleanor, her hand held in his, that makes the picture memorable.

"Elliott is up and about again; and I hear is drinking heavily; if so he must break down soon," Theodore wrote August 12th to Bamie. "It has been as hideous a tragedy all through as one often sees."[50] During this period Elliott took Eleanor for a walk that neither she, nor anyone else in the family, ever forgot. "My father had several fox terriers that he seemed to carry everywhere with him," she remembered. "One day he took me and three of his fox terriers and left us with the doorman at the Knickerbocker Club. When he failed to return after six hours, the doorman took me home."[51] She confided to trusted friends in later years that she had actually seen her father carried out. "He disappointed her in almost everything," wrote her friend and biographer Joseph Lash, "yet her love never faltered, her trust never weakened."[52]

When that last summer was underway, Mary Hall took Elliott's children out of the Manhattan heat to her Hudson River mansion at Tivoli, where Eleanor kept their father informed of their doings: riding her pony with her uncles ("I wish you were up here to ride with me"); setting out for Boston ("we are in a great flurry and hurry"); from there to Bar Harbor ("I went to the Indian encampment to see some pretty things I have to find the paths all alone I walked up to the top of Kebo mountain this morning and I walk three hours every afternoon"); eating unfamiliar dishes ("We eat our meals at the hotel and the names of the things we get to eat are so funny Washington pie and blanket of Veal are mild to some other things we get"); studying French with her grand-mother; going fishing for the first time.[53]

Elliott replied from the Knickerbocker Club:

When you go to the Indian encampment you must say "How" to them for your old Father's sake, who used to fight them in the old claims in the West, many years before you opened those little blue eyes and looked at them making birch bark canoes for Brudie and Madeleine to go paddling in and upset in the shallow water, where both might be drowned if they had not laughed so much.

Give my love to all the dear home people and all of my good friends who have not forgotten me.

Would you like a little cat, very much like the one you used to have at Hempstead and called an "Angostura" kitten instead of what was his correct name, "Angora?" If so, I have a dear friend who wants to make you a present of one. Let me know after you have asked grandma.

Please do not eat all the things with the funny names you tell me you have, — that is, if they taste like their names, — for a Wash-ington pie with a blanket of veal, and Lafayette left out, would be enough to spoil your French-American history of the latter part of the last century, for some time to come, possibly for so long that I might not be able to correct your superstition. The blanket was what Washington needed and the pie should have been laid out of veal and the neglected Lafayette should have eaten it.[54]

In the last month of his life, Elliott went to Annisquam, Massachusetts, to visit Florence Bagley Sherman, the woman with whom he had lived in Paris, and her children. While there he collapsed. Mrs. Sherman called a doctor, who informed her that Elliott needed rest, quiet, and the attention of people he loved. At times he was delirious and called out for Corinne, who "alone had given him the love he needed."[55] Over the next few days he rallied enough to sail with Mrs. Sherman and her children, Mary and Harold. He asked them to write greetings to Eleanor, explaining that they were "the children of my dear Friend, Mrs. F. B. Sherman of Detroit. These little children I saw a great deal of in Paris when we were there — I gave them my handsome old black poodle — 'Dick'... You must know these two dear little friends of mine some day."[56]

Already in a state of alcoholic confusion, Elliott began his last despairing slide almost as soon as he set foot in New York. After the incident at the Knickerbocker Club, Eleanor's grandmother was deeply apprehensive about allowing Elliott to spend time with his children, and by this time even he was inclined to agree. "I have a desolate feeling that I cannot overcome," he wrote her, "but I do not care to see anyone."[57]

He continued to send loving notes to Eleanor, still on black-bordered stationery, topped with a silhouette of a plumed knight above his initials:

My dearest little Nell,

Father will not call for you this afternoon to drive. Will you thank Cousin Susie for the very sweet note she wrote to me and say how pleased I was to know that the flowers I sent had given her enjoyment. With Father's dearest and tenderest wishes for your happiness.

Ever devotedly yours,

Elliott Roosevelt

He worried that his children would forget him. "I love them with all my heart," he told his mother-in-law. "Try and make them love my *name* at least as '*father*'. ..."[58] While at Tivoli, Eleanor spent many hours riding the pony Elliott had given her, overcoming her fear long enough for her Uncle Vallie to teach her how to jump. Her goal was to please Elliott when next she saw him.

What she could not know was that Elliott spent most of his days that last summer drinking until he fell unconscious. His sisters and even Theodore attempted to find him, but he would sleep in sordid corners of the city they could know nothing about. Theodore "wanted to reach out for him, but he was repelled by the degeneracy," writes one biographer. "Elliott wanted to reach out too but could not stand to be near the brother he could never hope to match."[59] Elliott mailed two or three notes a day to Theodore's office at the Civil Service Commission, but would not let his brother see him.

Edith wrote her sister Emily Carow that she felt Aunt Anna "was taken from evil to come. Elliott has sunk to the lowest depths. Consorts with the vilest women, and Theodore, Bamie and Douglas receive horrid anonymous letters about his life. I live in constant dread of some scandal of his attaching itself to Theodore."[60] Elliott now drank six or seven bottles of champagne and brandy every morning, and his valet wrote Corinne that many of Elliott's waking moments were spent hallucinating: once he thought he was showing Elliott Jr. his dogs; on other occasions he would ring the doorbells of strangers, ask, "Is Miss Eleanor Roosevelt at home?" and then stumble away in bewilderment when they did not recognize the name.[61] After one such incident he said, "'tell her her father is so sorry not to see her,' and soon became excited and ran violently up and down stairs,'" wrote Corinne to Bamie.[62]

For a while on August 13, Elliott was lucid enough to compose and mail a letter to Eleanor. Shortly afterward he either jumped or fell out of

One of Elliott's last photographs, circa 1894. "He was like some stricken, hunted creature …" Courtesy of The Franklin D. Roosevelt Presidential Library.

a parlor window. Mrs. Evans, with whom Elliott was still living from time to time, called a policeman, Douglas Robinson, and Uncle James Gracie, all of whom tried to soothe and restrain Elliott, but he suffered "fearful nausea"[63] and "one of those convulsive attacks." Finally, he fell asleep. The next morning, August 15, Douglas sent a telegram to Corinne: "Elliott died suddenly last night."[64]

"Theodore came to me at once," from Washington, wrote Corinne to Bye, who was in England, "and we did together the things always so hard to do connected with the death of those we love."[65] Together, they went to Elliott. Upon seeing him, Theodore "was more overcome than I have ever seen him — cried like a little child for a long time."[66]

"For the last few days he had dumbly felt the awful night closing in on him," Theodore wrote in his own letter to Bye. But Elliott would not allow anyone who loved him "to come to his house, nor part with the woman, nor cease drinking for a moment, but he wandered ceaselessly. … wrote again and again to us all. … He was like some stricken, hunted creature. …"[67]

The day of Elliott's funeral, which it was thought better for Eleanor not to attend, she received this letter:

> What must you think of your Father who has not written in so long. … I have after all been very busy, quite ill, at intervals not able to move from my bed for days. … Give my love to Grandma and Brudie and all. … I hope my little girl is well.
>
> … Kiss Baby Brudie for me and *never forget* I love you. …[68]

⊰18⊱

"Utterly Impossible
to Explain"

Elliott's death never seemed real to Eleanor. "He was her life," wrote her first biographer. "Nothing else mattered except him."[1] "The poor child has had so much sorrow crowded into her short life she now takes everything very quietly," wrote Mary Hall to Corinne. "The only remark she made was, 'I did want to see father once more.' I think since last winter she felt there was something not right, but I don't believe she realized what it was."[2]

Theodore was shattered. "I have never seen him so overcome in my life. He sobbed so bitterly and so long, that it frightened me."[3]

Corinne wrote to her aunt Susan Elliott:

We both felt that it could not be true that our darling playmate had gone in such a way. It was all like a frightful and incongruous dream — the house furnished with the old 57th Street, familiar furniture — the woman living in the midst — very gentle, she seemed to have really loved E. and she went through much that was really awful.[4]

"The terrible bloated swelled look was gone & the sweet expression around his forehead and eyes made me weep very bitter tears," wrote Corinne.[5]

"There he lay, peaceful at last, with the same old look of his innocent childhood — all the terrible traces of dissipation had vanished — the expression around his forehead and eyes was particularly lovely. I am sure, dear Aunt Susie, he was possessed of an evil spirit, like the poor man in the Bible, and like him the evil spirit had now been exorcised."[6]

Several months earlier, while feeling particularly unwell, Elliott had asked Corinne, "Will you promise to come to see me, when I am dying?" She answered, "Elliott, I would come from the end of the world."[7] When Corinne arrived, she was told that Elliott had been unconscious for several hours before expiring and would not have known her.

The New York World reported Aug. 16, 1894:[8]

The curtains of No. 313 West 102nd Street are drawn. There is a piece of black crepe on the door-knob. Few are seen to pass in and out of the house, except an undertaker and his assistants. The little boys and girls who romp up and down the sidewalks will tell you in a whisper: "Mr. Elliott is dead," and if you ask, "Who is Mr. Elliott?" "We don't know, nobody knows," they will answer.

At the door a sad-faced man will meet you. "Mr. Roosevelt died at 10 o'clock Tuesday evening," he will say. In a darkened parlor all day yesterday lay a plain black casket. Few mourners sat about it. Beneath its lid lay the body of Elliott Roosevelt. Few words will tell about his last days. ...

The physician and a valet were the only watchers at the end. The first of the family notified was James K. Gracie of Oyster Bay, an uncle of Elliott Roosevelt. To him was left the duty of breaking the news to the others. Many of them did not know that Elliott Roosevelt was in New York. Few of them had seen him for a year. At the clubs no one knew his address. Even the landlord from whom he rented his house knew him only as Mr. Elliott. Under that name he has lived there with his valet for over ten months. He sought absolute seclusion.

Many people will be pained by this news. There was a time when there were not many more popular young persons in society than Mr. and Mrs. Elliott Roosevelt.[9]

When it was suggested to Theodore — by whom it is difficult to ascertain from the family correspondence at this period — that Elliott be interred next to Anna, "I promptly vetoed this hideous plan, Corinne, who has acted better than I can possibly say throughout, cordially backing me up." Elliott was buried at Green-Wood Cemetery, close to "those who are associated only with his sweet innocent youth, when no more loyal, generous, disinterested fellow lived."[10]

Vallie was the only one of the Halls able to attend Elliott's funeral. Mrs. Hall sent a note to Elliott's uncle James Gracie "asking him to order flowers for the children and myself," but this arrived too late, to her sorrow. "Elliott loved flowers and always brought them to us, and to think not one from us or his dear ones went to the grave with him grieves me deeply."[11]

It seemed to Theodore that Elliott's funeral was typically Elliott, with "the usual touch of the grotesque and terrible, for in one of the four carriages that followed to the grave, went the woman, Mrs. Evans, and two of her and his friends, the host and hostess of the Woodbine Inn. They behaved perfectly well, and their grief seemed entirely sincere. ..."[12]

Shortly afterward, Corinne received a letter from Mrs. Sherman, the Paris mistress at whose home in Massachusetts Elliott had spent part of his last summer.

I do not know if you know that not quite a month ago, your brother Elliott came to me for a few days' visit. He seemed to take comfort and delight in being with the children and me, in our quiet country home, but he was a very ill man, and the physician I called the day after his arrival, begged me to do all I could to keep him quietly here, or see to it when he returned to New York that he was with some one who would love and care for him. I wanted to write you, for he seemed so sure of your love, and was so grateful to you for your manifestation of it, but I delayed doing so, and now it is perhaps useless to say any thing. But unless it is too hard for you — Will you not tell me how he died? He seemed so much stronger when he left, that even the physician was astonished at his vitality, and I hoped for his children, he would try to take care of himself.

He was so strong, and had such a gay, sweet nature, that I could not realize seeing him with my children, so interested in their work and play, that he was mentally and physically so worn out.

I do beg of you to have his children's memory of him a beautiful one; his tender courtesy, his big, generous heart and his wonderfully charming sweet nature, ought to be kept before them. If in saying this, I am overstepping the line of discretion or courtesy, I beg you to forgive me.

Believe me, dear Mrs. Robinson, your brother suffered greatly, as only a big tender man like him could suffer — and while he was here, and I watched him sick and half wandering in his mind while he slept, he spoke constantly of you, how you had held to him and alone had given him the love he needed. Of course you do not need for a stranger to tell you this, but I know what a grief your brother's death must be to you, and it may be a little consolation to you to hear this.

I cannot forgive myself for not keeping him here, where he was loved and guarded, and where he might have regained some strength so as to have gone back a little more able to meet his lonely fight there — but it is too late to even regret. One thing you can do for him — see to it that he does not lose the place he deserves in his children's lives. He loved them, and ought to have been with them.[13]

Corinne lamented Elliott's "incongruous" life, "its beautiful & its evil influences."[14] "A sharp pain runs through me constantly when I think of the darling Elliott of my girlhood, the lovely, generous unselfish brother who shielded me from any shadow of impurity and guided me in my way," she wrote to the wife of John E. Roosevelt, "Jack" of Elliott's Texas adventures. "It seems impossible that that adored Elliott could have died as he did, that I was not even at his deathbed as I promised so solemnly to be, a few short weeks ago, but being so far away I did not get the news in time."[15]

Like Elliott, Corinne had an understanding heart. A year later, Mrs. Sherman wrote to her: "I've been sadly wondering about his children, if they are well and strong — and inherit anything of his charms."[16] Even the boatman who had taken Elliott and Mrs. Sherman for a sail had inquired after Elliott; when told that he had died, the boatman could not believe it. "That's wrong," he said.[17]

From Bar Harbor, Mary Hall wrote: "No one can feel more deeply for you than I do. ... You certainly did everything a sister could do, and it must be a great consolation to you now. ..." She bore no "ill feelings" for Elliott, and thought only of the time before "this trouble came [when] he was the dearest man I ever knew, so gentle and kind-hearted." He was "not accountable for his words, or deeds," and "it was with deep regret that I tried to keep him from his children, but truly *I was afraid of him*, for I never knew what he would do."[18]

Mary Hall had promised Elliott that he could be buried next to his lost wife and son. He "took such interest in the vault we were going to build, and I planned the vault so that he and his family should be all together. In October we are going to move Anna, Ellie, and my immediate family from the present vault to the new one, and I wish you would then allow Elliott to be taken there. Will you please consult Bamie and Theodore, and if possible comply with Elliott's wish and ours." (At the top of the letter, in different handwriting, reads, "Elliott was laid by Anna.")[19]

"I want to write you a few lines to thank you for having let me know that all was safely accomplished and that Elliott now lies by Anna and his boy," wrote Corinne two years later.[20] "I cannot help but feel glad that it is so, and I must tell you once more how deeply I appreciate the feeling which led you to wish him brought to Tivoli, a feeling which I dared not think could be there, or I should never have laid him at Greenwood. I often wonder how much I respect and admire your attitude about every thing that has happened dear Mrs. Hall. It is a lesson and an example which I hope never to forget. With love to dear little Eleanor and cunning Brudie. ..."[21]

Mary Hall wrote to Corinne, "I hope you and Bamie will always advise me about the children, for I want them influenced by their father's family as well as by their dear Mother's."[22]

⎯⎯⎯⎯

Even after Elliott died, Theodore still wrote to Bye about avoiding "scandal":

> Freddy Weeks has been in charge of Mrs. Evans and poor Elliott's affairs generally; and he has now closed them all out, without a scandal. We narrowly missed one, too; for Mr. Evans arrived on the scene and threatened both his wife and Fred with a loaded revolver! But finally left, pacified. Freddy has behaved like a

trump, as he always does in such emergencies! Emlen [Roosevelt] and Harry Weeks, the executors, have not behaved at all well, wishing to refuse to pay Mrs. Evans her claim of $1250.00, writing Corinne to pay it! They say they do not see that the interests of the children are concerned! She has a fair claim to it, and it is not our affair, but the children's; and I have written them very sharply that they ought to pay at once.[23]

Corinne arranged Elliott's funeral. "I remained late the night I arrived, arranging clothes, papers, etc. I then went to 689 Madison Avenue to spend the night. The funeral took place at the Holy Communion. The coffin was covered with flowers.[24] The first hymn was 'Just as I Am.' I felt as if God would surely hear and accept our poor Elliott that way, and then I had 'Jesus, Saviour of My Soul,' and 'Rock of Ages,' those hymns we sang so often with Aunt & Mother."[25]

Theodore's hard feelings about Elliott diffused in his heartbreak.

There is one great comfort I already feel; I only need to have pleasant thoughts of Elliott now. He is just the gallant, generous, manly boy and young man whom everyone loved. I can think of him now ... the time we were first in Europe ... and then in the days of the dancing class, when he was distinctly the polished man-of-the-world from outside, and all the girls, from Helen White to Fanny Dana to May Wigham used to be so flattered by any attentions from him. Or when we were off on his little sailing boat for a two or three days trip on the Sound; or when we first hunted; and when he visited me at Harvard. ...[26]

Corinne shared this conclusion. "I cannot but feel that the real Ellie was the lovely, unselfish, considerate brother of my girlhood — I think he has never been himself through these last dark years," she wrote her aunt Susan Elliott. "We took him out to Greenwood, and laid him by mother and father, and he is at rest at least, my poor dear one."[27]

Corinne went back to Henderson Home, the Robinsons' country house in Herkimer County, September 11th. Bamie, who had been living in England as secretary to "Rosy" Roosevelt at the American embassy, arrived in New York the next day.

"Poor Elliott R! Of course you have heard of his death in N.Y.," wrote "Johnnie" Elliott, companion of Elliott's childhood and youth, to his sister Helena. "I saw an account of his funeral in a N.Y. paper. Have not yet heard from Theodore or anyone, but I write them all today, and shall not wait for letters. What a dismal ending to a life that at the onset seemed so full of promise. The news gave me a great shock as you may well imagine, although I foresaw such an end for the poor fellow."[28]

"I mailed you two letters last Thursday, including a letter to me from Aunt Susan relating to poor Elliott's end. Did you not get a splendid idea of Corinne's character from the 'extracts' enclosed to you, last Monday? She is a noble woman," John Elliott observed. "Theodore must have felt very badly — Elliott and he never having been reconciled. Poor Elliott. His was a sad ending, and yet he was not so much to blame. All the Roosevelt children must lead exciting, active lives, and this same force in him came in contact with an intellectual makeup, where something had been left out. Not his fault!"[29]

"I know it is best," Corinne wrote. "I know it had to come sooner or later. I know it makes his memory possible to his children. I know all, and yet my heart feels desperately sad for the brother I knew, the Elliott I have loved and known, which all that has passed cannot efface."[30]

Elliott "would have been in a straightjacket had he lived forty-eight hours longer. It was his fall, aggravated by frightful drinking, that was the immediate cause," wrote Theodore in his last missive to Bamie in their long, anguished correspondence over their brother.

He had been drinking whole bottles of anisette and green mint, — besides whole bottles of raw brandy and of champagne, sometimes half a dozen a morning. But when dead the poor fellow looked very peaceful, and so like his old, generous, gallant self of fifteen years ago. The horror, and the terrible mixture of grotesque, grim evil continued to the very end; and the dreadful flashes of his old sweetness, which made it all even more hopeless. I suppose he has been doomed from the beginning; the absolute contradiction of all his actions, and of all his moral even more than his mental qualities, is utterly impossible to explain.

His house was so neat, and well-kept, with his Bible and religious books, and Anna's pictures everywhere, even in the room of himself and his mistress. Poor woman, she had taken the utmost care of him, and was broken down at his death. Her relations with him have been just as strange as everything else. ... He was hunted by the most terrible demons that ever entered into man's body and soul. Well, it is over now; it is fortunate it is over; and we need only think of his bright youth. ... Poor Anna, and poor Elliott.[31]

⚜ CONCLUSION ⚜

A biographer attempts to understand a subject's goals, influences, values, and turning points. Elliott Roosevelt's goals, values, and influences were essentially the same as those of Theodore Roosevelt. Elliott's ambitions were less clearly defined — he wanted in some unspecified way "to do good" and to enjoy himself. These vague objectives dissolved gradually in the mist of addiction. His influences — his philanthropist father, his southern belle mother and colorful uncles, the high-minded literature of the day — were beneficent and sometimes demanding. As alcoholism and drug usage increasingly demoralized Elliott, the role models of his boyhood became nothing more than a reproach to him. As Blanche Cook writes, "his disease ... challenged love, mocked adventure, destroyed hope."[1]

Elliott's values, like those of all Roosevelts, were fundamental — loyalty, patriotism, the serious practice of religion, "the joy of living," kindness to the poor, cleanliness of mind and body. Elliott's abuse of his body trapped him in a nightmare that undermined these values, yet for all his confusion he never discarded belief in his ideals. Ultimately he discarded himself for what he perceived to be his inability to live up to them.

In a biography of Theodore Roosevelt, or Eleanor, or Franklin, turning points mark occasions at which the subject was, in Hemingway's phrase, "made stronger at the broken places." By contrast, Elliott's life had four turning points, all of which were catastrophically wounding: the death of Theodore Sr.; the death of Mittie; the misdiagnosed broken ankle, which led to drug dependence; and the deaths of his wife and son. It was not until this last that Elliott was discouraged beyond help.

Without alcoholism Elliott's life would have been much like that of his friend Winthrop Astor Chanler (1863–1927), who, like Elliott, did not quite qualify as a "dude," in the parlance of the day, but was rather a "B.Y.M." ("Beautiful Young Man"). An Etonian and Harvard man, Chanler was intelligent and brave, but unfocused. According to Maude Howe Elliott, cousin to both Chanler's wife and Elliott Roosevelt, "Wherever thrills were to be had, there was Wintie in the thick of them." In the mid-1890s, when Theodore Roosevelt was New York City Police Commissioner, Chanler accompanied him on his "night rounds" in which Theodore would uncover both unsuspecting criminals and policemen who slept on the job. (Since both Theodore and Chanler were devoted hunters, it has been speculated that they thought of law-breakers as "big game.") Like Elliott, Chanler admired Theodore's seriousness and "foolish grit," without sharing it. "Roosevelt may perhaps have been ready to help Chanler harness his alert and restless mind to some sustained occupation," wrote their mutual friend Owen Wister. "That was never to be."[2]

Chanler's one moment of gravity came in Cuba when, as one of Theodore's "Rough Riders," he took a bullet in his right arm. He was a dilettante who briefly speculated in oil, "although his qualifications as an oil geologist were not obvious," notes an observer of the era.[3] Essentially he devoted himself to the innocent enjoyment of his comfortable life.

Elliott, like Theodore, loved to write; unlike Theodore, Elliott enjoyed writing light verse and fiction. One of his surviving stories is a strange, infuriating tale called "Was Miss Vedder an Adventuress?" It is the story of a woman who has wasted her life on "pleasure" and does not wish to "burden" others. It is a chilling window into Elliott's state of mind; although the story is undated, a safe assumption is that it was written during his last five years. That this man, who hobnobbed with the author of *Tom Brown's School Days* and whose brother was writing books with titles like *Hunting Trips of a Ranchman*, dedicated to "that keenest of sportsmen and truest of friends, my brother Elliott Roosevelt," would write a defense of frivolity and despair, is staggering. And why would he choose a female character as his alter ego?

If Elliott's efforts are less than great literature, are they not at least as well written as much of what was published at that time? Had Elliott "harnessed his mind to some sustained occupation," might he have been a popular novelist or magazine writer? James Oliver Curwood, Harold Bell Wright, Olive Higgins Prouty, Faith Baldwin ... Elliott Roosevelt?

If Elliott had lived to an advanced age and been sober and healthy, one can imagine him making his family proud by joining his brother and friends in their grand military exploit as they drove the Spanish from Cuba, then enjoying the social whirl in Manhattan, Hempstead, Europe, and Newport, freed by wealth to pursue adventure anywhere on the globe and living a long life as "a perfect sporting gentleman." But if this had been the case, what sort of person would Eleanor Roosevelt have become? And would it have made a difference to the shape of liberal thought in the twentieth century?

"Studying the lives of women whose voices have transformed our own, one comes time and again to the influence of an absent father and a nearly conscious search for his approval," writes one psychologist. "When considering the lives of women — great or merely good, troubled or serene — it behooves us to understand that a missed relationship with father is at least as affecting as one that is still going on; that in impact and influence, in fact and in essence, the imperceptible relationship with father never ceases to go on. ... Behind every great man, there is a woman, we are told. Behind many of these women, there is a man that got away."[4]

It was as an inheritor of his father's legacy that Elliott taught his daughter to be mindful of the needs of others, but Eleanor Roosevelt's compassion was deepened by the remembrance of her own father's suffering and vulnerability. Throughout her life she made excuses for him. Could this have led her to sympathy for the "underdog" that became automatic, irrespective of the parties or the issues involved? Did the example set by Eleanor Roosevelt, having as its foundation her desperate love for her father, give rise to a liberalism that, abetted by a culture increasingly in thrall to therapeutic psychology, soured into a "victimology"? By its normalization of self-pity, has contemporary liberalism, ironically, made Rooseveltian values — stoicism, joyfulness in the face of overwhelming adversity — unfashionable?

In a stunning instance of the law of unintended consequences, once the "sin" of drunkenness was redefined as the "disease" of alcoholism, there began a trend that ultimately de-stigmatized nearly all forms of immoral behavior.[5] Eleanor Roosevelt, exemplar of the deeply moral Roosevelt tradition, would be given pause, as she might have said. As she often *did* say, "You must do the thing you think you cannot do." No self-pity here. No special pleading. No preferential option. Just do it. We may safely assume that she would challenge what columnist George F. Will calls "the culture of complaint that produced the politics of victimhood that resulted in government by grievance groups."[6]

And yet ... Eleanor Roosevelt could not bear the thought of anyone falling through the cracks as her father had. Never, ever, would she have agreed with her aunt Edith Carow Roosevelt, who said of her servants, "If they had our brains, they would have our place."[7] Eleanor knew something about extenuating circumstances and about people whose gifts are not necessarily those best expressed in competition. Elliott was certainly competitive with his brother and with his friends at the Meadowbrook Country Club, but his real talents were his extraordinary charm, his light-heartedness, his ability to make people laugh, his kindness, his understanding heart.

One nineteenth-century figure who felt deep compassion for alcoholics was Abraham Lincoln. His feeling was that those who had never known the temptation of alcohol had no business feeling superior to those under its spell.

"In my judgment, such of us as have never fallen victims, have been spared more from the absence of appetite, than from any mental or moral superiority over those who have," Lincoln wrote in the 1840s. "Indeed, I believe, if we take habitual drunkards as a class, their heads and their hearts will bear an advantageous comparison with those of any other class."

There seems ever to have been a proneness in the brilliant and the warm-blooded to fall into this vice. The demon of intemperance ever seems to have delighted in sucking the blood of genius and of generosity. What one of us can but call to mind some dear relative, more promising in youth than all his fellows, who has fallen a sacrifice to his rapacity? He ever seems to have gone forth, like the Egyptian angel of death, commissioned to slay if not the first, the fairest born of every family.

Lincoln saw alcoholics as trapped, taken as prisoners by a demon that held them "prostrate in the chains of moral death." On their behalf, he invoked Scripture: "Come from the four winds, O breath! and breathe upon these slain, that they may live."[8]

Elliott's instability and early death tempted Eleanor to expect desertion from those she loved, and yet the loving heart she inherited from Elliott enabled her to sustain many friendships, in particular with her biographer Lorena Hickok and her bodyguard Earl Miller, both of whom were perceptive enough to discern what she needed in a friend. As Blanche Cook writes:

> The wonder of her life is that despite all limitations, all childhood hurt and adult complexity, ER protected herself from further pain as best she could, while indulging her habit of emotional curiosity and commitment. The barriers she created to protect herself were not barriers to loving. She cherished Hick, and also Earl, because they determinedly crashed through her protective barriers. Her aloof, seemingly cold demeanor, so forbidding to some, had represented a challenge to them. ER, in turn, responded to their persistence, trusted and felt secure with them. She felt needed by them, depended on their love, and intended to preserve it.[9]

Eleanor Roosevelt attempted to bring an understanding heart to politics. If she was sometimes misguided, this is because, like Elliott, "with [her] the heart always dominated." People — all people — counted with Eleanor; this she absorbed from Elliott. Her father was never dismissive, and Eleanor almost never. If her own children felt neglected at times, this had more to do with their relationship with Franklin's mother — but that is the subject of another book (and a good one at that — see *Sara and Eleanor* by Jan Pottker). "I do not feel that I am a natural born mother," Eleanor reflected. "If I ever wanted to mother anyone, it was my father."[10]

"Many people whom I have mentioned will be described far better and more fully by other people, except in the case of my father, whose short and happy early life was so tragically ended," wrote Eleanor in her memoir. "With him I have a curious feeling that as long as he remains to me the vivid, living person that he is, he will, after the manner of the people in the 'Blue Bird,' be alive and continue to exert his influence which was always a very gentle, kindly one."[11]

In Dickens's *The Old Curiosity Shop*, Eleanor and Elliott's favorite book, Eleanor's namesake Little Nell worries "that those who die about us, are so soon forgotten." It is likely that "Little Nell" Roosevelt took comfort throughout her life in the reply given the original Little Nell:

... Do you think ... that an unvisited grave, a withered tree, a faded flower or two, are tokens of forgetfulness or cold neglect? Do you think there are no deeds, far away from here, in which these dead may be best remembered? Nell, there may be people busy in the world, at this instant, in whose good actions and good thoughts these very graves — neglected as they look to us — are the chief instruments. ... There is nothing ... innocent or good, that dies, and is forgotten. Let us hold to that faith, or none. [Even] an infant ... will live again in the better thoughts of those who loved it, and will play its part, through them, in the redeeming actions of the world. ... There is not an angel added to the Host of Heaven but does its blessed work on earth in those that loved it here. ... If the good deeds of human creatures could be traced to their source, how beautiful would even death appear; for how much charity, mercy, and purified affection, would be seen to have their growth in dusty graves![12]

As this has been a nineteenth-century tragedy, let us end on that Victorian note.

⚜ AFTERWORD ⚜

THEODORE ROOSEVELT was never tempted by alcohol. "I have never taken a highball or a cocktail in my life,"[1] he wrote when he was in his fifties. At formal dinners it was unusual for him to have more than two glasses of champagne, and even this was usually in response to toasts.

Theodore had a sort of chemical reaction to hard liquor. On a hunting trip to Africa, he became ill and was ordered to take a dose of brandy. "It was measured out like medicine, perhaps two ounces or three in water," remembered a friend. "He drank it and at once spat it out. He explained that as soon as spirits entered his throat, his muscles always automatically contracted and rejected them."[2]

As president of the United States, Theodore Roosevelt attempted to keep even the military free from alcohol. The temperance movement had succeeded in persuading government officials to ban the sale of alcohol on military bases, and this action had Roosevelt's full support. "The removal of the drink from the army was a most fortunate thing for the men themselves and the nation they represent, and I promise you that so long as I am President, or so long as I shall have any influence whatever in the Republican party or in American politics, intoxicants shall never come back into the canteen."[3] Throughout his career he would rail against "the hideous evil wrought by the liquor traffic."[4]

"The liquor business does not stand on the same footing with other occupations. It always tends to produce criminality in the population at large and law breaking among the saloonkeepers themselves."[5] Roosevelt believed that because so much of the business of local New York politics was conducted in saloons, it left "small ground for wonder at the low average grade of the nominees."[6]

Theodore was in all likelihood thinking of Elliott when he lent his support to the Prohibition movement toward the end of his life. "The American saloon has been one of the most mischievous elements in American social, political, and industrial life,"[7] he wrote. He never publicly mentioned Elliott.

GRACIE HALL ROOSEVELT, the baby brother of Eleanor's anguished childhood, carried the names of three distinguished New York families. His first name was given in honor of Elliott's aunt Annie, Mrs. James King Gracie,[8] but like Eleanor, he never was called by his first name. Like his uncle Theodore, Hall was a brilliant student and a well-intentioned, vivacious man. "Even if he had not belonged to the nation's first family, he could have been justly proud of his career as an electrical engineer, World War flier, banker, financier and municipal official," wrote *The New York Times* at the time of his death. "Mr. Roosevelt possessed the full share of the family charm."[9] Unfortunately, like his father, he developed a drinking problem early in life. Hall "was a superior scholar and seemed to be on the road to great things," wrote his nephew James. "Then he lost his way."[10]

"I became more or less responsible for my brother when I was eighteen and he was twelve," Eleanor wrote in her column the day following Hall's death. "But I remember him very vividly as a very small boy with round curls and a round roly face; whom my young aunts made much of and called the 'cherub,' thereby creating much jealousy in me because I could not aspire to any such name."[11]

Hall's childhood was even lonelier than Eleanor's, for he had no memory of either of his parents and did not know the companionship of children his own age until he attended school in Manhattan. Eleanor had been exhorted by Elliott to take care of "Brudie," and this was to her a sacred trust. She became mother as well as doting sister to Hall, and the devotion was mutual. At every stage of his life, he wrote her lengthy, affectionate letters, usually addressing her as "Dearest Eleanor," or "Dearest Sister." As children, he called Eleanor "Totty," as did all of their Hall relatives. While their cousin Franklin courted Eleanor, he befriended Hall, calling him "Kid," and this is the way Hall signed his notes to Franklin, at least while following in his footsteps at Groton. Eleanor wrote to Hall every day. "I want him to feel he belongs to somebody," she explained to her friend Helen Cutting.[12] When he entered Groton, she came for all functions to which parents were invited, standing in for them. Once Franklin and Eleanor were married, they considered Hall as one of their children[13] and told him that he was always welcome to live with them.[14]

The Rev. Endicott Peabody, Groton's famous headmaster, was impressed with Hall and wrote laudatory comments on his report cards ("Excellent"; "Very good"; "He has done us most valuable service."), all of which were carefully saved by Eleanor. Hall followed family tradition and worked at the "'Groton School Summer Camp' for boys from the slums of Boston and New York."[15] As a student he depended on Eleanor for practical help, and she made certain he had what he needed in order to be a success, socially and athletically. "Thank you very much for the tennis racket," begins a typical letter from Hall to Eleanor.[16] "Thank you very much for the clothes and tennis balls. ..."[17]

Hall enjoyed making his sister laugh with his ebullient chatter and his arch, breezy writing style. "There is absolutely no news," he informed her from Groton, "except that I took off a pound just sitting in Chapel this morning."[18] A letter from Uncle Theodore contained ideas that were "an offense against human nature as now moulded."[19]

"By the time my brother was eighteen, he was an entirely independent person, and from that time on, the only way that anyone could hold him, was to let him go," Eleanor informed her public. "He loved life, he could enjoy things more than almost anyone I have ever known. He had fine qualities, generosity, a warmth of heart which brought him an endless number of friends, courage, which amounted almost to foolhardiness, a brilliant mind, and a capacity for work which made him able to perform prodigious tasks physically and mentally. …"[20] "By the time he realized that he could not stop drinking whenever he wanted to," she said later, "he had been through so much that he no longer wanted to stop."[21]

Hall graduated from Harvard in three years with a Phi Beta Kappa key, followed by a master's degree in engineering. He married Margaret Richardson of Boston in 1912 at Boston's King's Chapel while still a Harvard undergraduate, with Franklin as his best man.[22] In the early years of his marriage, Hall worked for the Canadian Klondike Company as an electrical engineer, running a "sub-station" in the Yukon Territory.[23] Hall was "a veritable giant"[24] with blond hair, standing six feet three inches and weighing 240 pounds.[25] During the First World War, Hall and his cousin Quentin joined the Army Air Service together in Mineola, Long Island.[26] Quentin was killed in action, but Hall was an instructor in the "Ground School" at Cornell[27] before serving as a "pursuit plane" flying instructor in Florida, where he designed a pursuit plane that was used successfully.[28] Following the war, most of his working life was spent in the employ of General Electric, at its headquarters in Schenectady, New York, as well as in Tacoma, Washington, Montana, and Chicago.

FDR valued Hall's opinion concerning business and the stock market, and asked his advice on investments ranging from rice plantations in Louisiana to Shell-Union Oil to the Hudson Valley Aviation Company. "Tell me what you know about the prospects of the Radio Corporation of America," Franklin requested, foreshadowing the historic use he would make of radio. "People down here seem to feel that they paid an unconscionable price for the Marconi, and have a very big load to carry even if they make good on their communications. Are they putting up any more Radio Stations either in the United States or elsewhere?"[29] Prefiguring the Tennessee Valley Authority, Franklin shared with Hall his ideas about utilizing the tidal power of "Passamaquoddi Bay" for hydroelectric development.

> As you know, I have absolutely no knowledge of hydro-electrics except the conviction that electrical development has advanced sufficiently far to take an intelligent interest in the use of tidal power. Therefore, it is natural that I should think of the General Electric Company as the logical developers of such a problem if it is to be developed in the near future. It would interest me intensely, and it might be a very far-sighted effort. ...[30]

After Franklin became ill with polio, Hall attempted to distract him with correspondence about promising investments and business opportunities. When Eleanor kept the Roosevelt name alive in Democratic circles, Hall was proud of the political savvy his sister showed in her early forays on behalf of candidates in whom she and her husband believed.

"Many, many congratulations on your very effective work in NY. I hope [Governor Alfred] Smith gets a chance to put something across tho' I despair of our usual assemblies. Also, it has always seemed as though the Democratic hangers-on were a terrible thorn in the flesh for any officer anxious to make a record."[31]

When Hall and Margaret had three children — Henry, Daniel, and Eleanor — Hall's sister was delighted, hoping that a family would compensate for the absence of his parents in his earliest years. However, on July 1, 1922, Hall deserted his wife and children in Schenectady, and two years later Margaret's lawyer contacted FDR looking for Hall in order to serve him with "a writ of libel in divorce."[32] Franklin took care of many of the legal details involved in the divorce and acted as a father figure to Hall.[33]

In 1925 Hall moved to Detroit with his second wife, Dorothy Grant Kemp, a concert pianist. This marriage, too, produced three children — Amelia, Diana, and Janet. In 1929 Hall was made vice president of Detroit United Railways. In addition he was vice president of American State Bank in Detroit. He was appointed city controller by Detroit Mayor Frank Murphy, obtaining credit from banks in various parts of the country, and during the Depression of the 1930s he also served as chairman of the Detroit Unemployment Bureau.

"Some of the things which he did, such as living himself for weeks on the same amount of money which he was distributing to relief clients in Detroit, in order to be sure that they could live on it, probably benefited many people," wrote Eleanor. "There was a Quixotic side to him that made him not want to subject other people to anything he could not stand himself."[34]

Hall was greatly respected in these positions for his intelligence and energy, and he kept close watch on the political scene in Michigan. "Father Coughlin [the controversial "radio priest"] with his forty-two secretaries working daily has the largest following of any man in the United States," he wrote Eleanor in the heat of the 1932 campaign, before the presidential nomination was secured. "He has offered to come out over the radio for Franklin at a propitious time. This would lay 'the Smith Ghost for Good.' It would also lay the groundwork for the election. I can't urge it too strongly."[35]

Hall was uninterested in political office himself, rejecting the entreaties of a group of Michigan Democrats that he run for governor, but FDR often asked Hall to test the local political waters. "Do not breathe this thought to a soul," wrote the president in a November 15, 1935, memorandum marked "Very Confidential." "What would you think of my offering a place on the Securities and Exchange Commission to Senator Couzins [Couzens]?"[36] Mayor Murphy, however, found Hall's ideas too socialistic and his style lacking in diplomacy, and he was eventually dismissed.

A recommendation Hall made to FDR provides a window into his personality and sense of humor: "You met Edward T. Gushee in Albany. ... He is inclined to worship, an idealist, but none the less hard-boiled. ... He has tact and a tactful wife. ... He was gassed in the trenches which interferes with too great exertion on the squash court. ... There is no stigma of wealth but he has a small competence. His father, a campaigner for you, is a padre of the High Church!"[37]

After FDR's first 100 days in office, he took a vacation aboard his yacht with *USS Indianapolis* as escort. Stephen Early sent a radiogram to Marvin McIntyre, who was aboard *Indianapolis*: "G. Hall Roosevelt telephoned from Michigan yesterday and again today declaring bank situation there in critical condition and requires quick action. He insisted that I radio you report that [Reconstruction Finance Chairman] Jesse Jones has cold feet and refuses to act. Mr. Roosevelt anxious that you telegraph Jones to give report immediately on Michigan situation."[38]

Hall was a loyal and enthusiastic New Dealer. "Hall, what should I do about this?" was Eleanor's handwritten notation on a memorandum concerning housing projects and slum clearance.[39] Hall was protective of Franklin and Eleanor, and the president trusted Hall's instincts when it came to looking out for the administration. "Hall Roosevelt reports that he has information from Copeland's office that Senator Copeland, on September 10th, will come to Washington and renew the investigation of the

Bureau of Aeronautics, Department of Commerce," wrote FDR's press secretary Stephen Early in a 1936 memorandum for the president. "Hall thinks that this investigation should not be permitted as it is, he believes, designed to produce adverse political repercussions. Hall says further that [Postmaster General] Jim Farley will not ask Copeland anything; that he doubts if you want to take a hand in this. Hall thinks that he himself can handle the situation if you care to have him do so. Please advise." At the bottom of the note is written in pencil: "Yes, do his best. FDR."[40]

Mayor Murphy may have been correct about Hall having socialist tendencies, for Hall corresponded regularly with the president regarding Federal Reserve loans to industry.[41] However, Hall once served (in Michigan) as go-between for FDR and Henry Ford.[42]

Hall couldn't seem to establish a foothold in his personal life, and by 1930 he was separated from his second wife, much to his sister's distress. "Dearest Dorothy," wrote Eleanor from the Governor's Mansion in Albany:

I think you are a marvelous person. Hall is thoroughly blind I fear — I've written him now & hope to hear soon but there seems to be nothing one can do. I hope he will do all he can financially at least and remember that we want you to feel that from our point of view you have been most understanding & patient & kind beyond words — I hope you will bring the little girls to us when you can & feel always our deep interest & gratitude to you. Perhaps Hall is one of those people who must always "walk by his lone,"[43] but they are never very happy people I fear. Please write me if I can help in any way. ...[44] It's a tragedy my dear, but the little girls are busy and have you and in time I hope even you will be happier. ... Hall I fear will never be happy. ... I do want to watch the little girls grow and will take every chance when I do get near you to see you.[45]

"I have thought much about your suggestion that Franklin or Cousin Henry [Parish] should talk to Hall but I think this useless," wrote Eleanor the following spring, finding herself ironically in a position similar to that of her uncle Theodore and "Auntie Bye" as they dealt with her father.[46]

All he inherited he put in a trust for his first wife and their children, and that is now beyond his control. He has no prospect of any inheritance. ... My only suggestion is that you put a clause in your agreement that anything above $10,000 a year which he may earn in the future shall be equally divided between him and your children up to a certain amount. ... I am deeply sorry for you and the little girls for I know how you have suffered. Hall has suffered too.[47]

By the time FDR was president, Dorothy was still trying to decide what to do about her troubled marriage and asking Eleanor for advice. "As to any publicity that may come, I have absolutely no feeling about it. What one feels is right to do, one must do and I for one should not for a moment suggest that you change anything which you feel you are right in doing."[48]

As Hall was like a son to Eleanor, she kept in touch with his ex-wives, just as she maintained cordial relations with most of the ex-spouses of her sons and daughter. "It is hard for you and the children and making life over again is a dreary task but I know you will dear and I can only hope that in one way or another some day you will be repaid," she wrote Dorothy. "I am enclosing a small check for the little girls' birthdays which I have sadly neglected. May the coming year bring some happiness and peace and health and joy to the little ones. ..."[49]

Dorothy ran for Congress from her district in Michigan in 1942, but lost the election. "I was sorry to learn that you had been defeated,"

Eleanor wrote. "It is always difficult for a woman to be elected to office, and doubly so in a year when the swing is away from one's party."[50]

Hall and Dorothy did not legally divorce until 1937. At that time Hall, whose drinking had increased in severity, returned to New York. He tried to work as a banker and consulting engineer, but seemed unable to hold a job. "Whenever his responsibilities became irksome he tended to thrust them aside," said Eleanor.[51] With the discipline provided by Eleanor's steady encouragement, he managed to complete a history of the earliest Roosevelts in America entitled *Odyssey of an American Family*. Like his father, Hall occasionally wrote short stories, historical fiction based on the swashbuckling sea captains of the Delano family.[52]

Hall's "Quixotic side" did not always extend to his wives and children. Hall was closest to his son Danny, despite the fact that during a drunken episode at Val-Kill, Eleanor's cottage, he became violent with the boy and, throwing him to the floor, broke his collarbone. Hall attempted to drive Danny to the hospital, but drove into a ditch instead. "A state trooper took over," Eleanor's son James remembered. "Mother, thinking her friend, Marion Dickerman, had been driving, telephoned Marion in a fury. Mother would blame anyone but Hall. Father apologized to Marion for mother."[53]

In December 1939, reporter Edwin Cox of *The Washington Post* sent a telegram to secretary Howell G. Crim at the White House, asking for permission to include a story about Hall in his "Private Lives" column, having heard that Hall resembled Eleanor "in briskness and energy. Have read that he often enters White House door in such a hurry that attendants there fail to catch his hat as he goes by." Crim responded with a terse, "Regret inability to comply with your request."[54]

"With him life was unusually gay," wrote Eleanor.[55] Hall loved to take Eleanor's sons "on the town" with him in New York City. "We were at the age where we thought it was fun," remembered Eleanor's son James. "He was past it, but never grew up."[56]

Hall embarrassed FDR on several occasions, such as the time he attempted to instigate a movement not approved by the administration to oppose his former mentor Frank Murphy, who had been elected governor. When a concerned citizen wrote to the president complaining about this, Marvin McIntyre's note to the president read, "I think that probably the best thing to do with this is just forget it."[57] During the Spanish Civil War, Hall became involved in an abortive attempt to procure aircraft for the Spanish Republican forces in a blatant circumvention of embargo measures in place at that time.[58]

Hall made an unfortunate habit of using White House telephones to request "work loans" from Reconstruction Finance Corporation Chairman Jesse Jones. On one such occasion Hall asked for $1,250,000 for a "pan-mining" operation in Alaska, looking for gold in creek beds. Jones approved a loan for half that amount, and two days later he received a call from Tom Corcoran, one of FDR's assistants. "The President is very anxious for you to make this loan," said Corcoran. "Because if you do it, Hall will get a job with the company as chief engineer, and FDR wants Hall as far as possible from the White House." Hall did indeed take the job in Alaska, but soon he was back in Washington, using White House phones to pester Jones about other projects.[59]

Hall's grasp of technology was useful during the period leading up to American involvement in World War II, particularly in the development of landing beams "for the safety of trans-oceanic air lines" and the "safety of landing of airplanes on land in fog."[60]

Toward the end of his life, Hall bought property in Hyde Park and began a low-income housing project in which the average monthly rent would be $15.00.[61] Eleanor informed Hall that she did not believe in "rural slums," and FDR, who designed his own cottage, offered suggestions. "I think you should consider some kind of porch because it really is used in hot weather," he wrote to Hall with a blueprint for the Federal

Housing Authority "standard house." "I wish also you would try your hand at a sketch of a one-story house with all four rooms on a straight line — same number of square feet. It would look much more impressive than those square houses and would, therefore, rent more easily."[62]

Occasionally, the father of whom Hall had no recollection would be remembered to him. In the spring of 1939, one H.R. Forbes, who had known Elliott in Virginia, wrote to say that he was writing his memoirs for his family and wondered if Hall would be willing to share any photos of Douglas Robinson or Elliott, whom he characterized as "a gallant chap — they never made any better." He requested also "a moment or two confab over the gentleman — the lovely gentleman — who — alas — disappeared all too early." Hall was touched by the request, which he forwarded to Eleanor.[63]

In an uncanny echo of Elliott's sorrow, the beginning of the end for Hall was the loss of a son. Intelligent and deeply engaged, it seemed as though Daniel Stewart Roosevelt might turn out to be the sort of man that Hall — and Elliott — should have been. Danny traveled extensively throughout Spain during the heaviest fighting of the Spanish Civil War and wrote detailed letters indicating his anti-fascist sentiments, which Hall published in *Odyssey of an American Family*. However, during his Easter vacation in 1939, Danny was killed when the airplane he was piloting crashed near Canoitas, Mexico.

Hall spent his last two years "mourning his lost son, dabbling in new consulting and investment ventures, sitting in lonesome rooms and offices, and nursing his chronic liver ailment."[64]

On the day of her mother-in-law's funeral, Hall asked Eleanor to take him from Vassar Hospital in Poughkeepsie to Walter Reed Hospital in Washington.[65] "I went to Walter Reed Hospital yesterday morning to arrange for the admission of Hall Roosevelt," Stephen Early wrote Eleanor's secretary, Malvina Thompson. "The hospital had an old telephone bill for expenses incurred by Hall when he was in the hospital some time ago. I paid it, since the hospital did not know what to do with it. Attached is the receipted bill."[66] A handwritten notation at the top reads, "Has been paid to S.T.E. by Mrs. R."

Despite the delinquent bill, Hall was loved and treated well by the staff at Walter Reed. Colonel Corbett, the executive officer of the hospital, offered to cancel an engagement at the War Department in order to receive Hall in person upon his arrival. "I told him that would not be necessary," telegraphed Early to FDR. "Patient will have the same room and same facilities as when he was last here. Colonel Corbett will give him personal attention."[67]

On September 21, 1941, President Franklin D. Roosevelt received this message from Bill Hassett, his appointments secretary:

MEMORANDUM FOR THE PRESIDENT:
At 2:35 p.m., Admiral McIntire [FDR's doctor] telephoned that Mr. Hall Roosevelt had suddenly gone very bad.

Admiral McIntire said he may not last throughout the afternoon. While Admiral McIntire was phoning, Mrs. Roosevelt was on the way to the hospital.

Admiral McIntire thought it best to get this word to you, in order that you might know that Mr. Roosevelt's end is very near.[68]

Eleanor left her work as head of the Office of Civilian Defense to be at Hall's bedside as he struggled in the final stages of cirrhosis of the liver. Like his father during his last years, Hall was watched over by a devoted mistress. This was Zena Rasset,[69] who now kept the vigil with the First Lady. Eleanor was reminded of William Ernest Henley's verse, "Out of the night that covers me, / Black as the pit from pole to pole / I thank whatever gods may be / For my unconquerable soul."[70]

My idea of hell, if I believed in it, would be to stand & watch someone breathing hard, struggling for words when a gleam of consciousness returns & thinking, "this was once the little boy I played with & scolded, he could have been so much & this is what he is." It is a bitter thing & in spite of everything I've loved Hall, perhaps somewhat remissibly of late, but he is part of me. I do have a quieting effect on him & so I stood by his bed & held his hand & stroked his forehead & Zena stood by me for hours. She won't give up hope of his recovery & keeps asking me if I don't think he's strong enough to pull through 'til I could weep.[71]

With reluctant compassion during Hall's last two weeks in the hospital, Eleanor brought him his daily ration of gin.

Hall died at 5 a.m., E.S.T. "Will you please tell the children their father died peacefully this morning."[72] That day, FDR canceled all of his appointments, including his regular Friday morning press conference and a meeting with the Duke and Duchess of Windsor. Hall lay in state in the East Room at the White House, where his funeral was held. The flag over the White House flew at half-staff during the service.[73] Belle Willard Roosevelt, wife of his cousin Kermit, was the only one of his Oyster Bay relatives in attendance.

Hall was placed "in his family's weather-beaten brick vault,"[74] "a sort of dungeon-like filing place for deceased members of a family," in the words of Ellie, Hall's eldest daughter. At the churchyard of St. Paul's Episcopal Church (now Trinity/St. Paul's) at Tivoli, twenty-six miles up the Hudson River from Hyde Park, "The grounds around the old church support lofty trees. ... The wild grasses are mowed into the semblance of a lawn. ..."[75] At the interment, President Roosevelt, leaning on the arm of his son Jimmy, now a Marine Corps captain, wore a black suit, with a black armband in memory of his mother, who had died less than three weeks previously. Eleanor, "attired in black with a string of pearls about her throat, was pale but composed."[76]

After dinner that evening at Val-Kill, Eleanor sipped her coffee with her secretary Malvina Thompson (called "Tommy") and Ellie. The First Lady excused herself and went to her bedroom. "She returned with a shoebox full of her brother's letters, sat on the couch by the fire and took her glasses out of her purse. One by one, she took his letters out of the box and read them through quietly to herself. Tommy and I sat in silence, watching her, until Tommy finally said, 'Mrs. Roosevelt, you must not be too hard on yourself.' Only then did Aunt Eleanor look up, her eyes glistening. 'I'm trying to find where I failed him, Tommy.'

"… An era ended for my aunt that night. Her impossible struggle to help her brother had failed. But she would carry on now, more than ever inspired by the desire to help people everywhere."[77]

"He was capable of great loyalty to the people for whom he really cared deeply," wrote Eleanor,[78] and by all accounts he cared deeply about her. "If he ever loved anyone, it was ER," wrote Hall's daughter. "He knew he could count on her support, and he respected her."[79]

Eleanor had brought about reconciliation between Hall and Ellie, the daughter from his first failed marriage, arranging for them to meet for the first time in twelve years. "Our times together had been sad celebrations for me," Ellie remembered after Hall died. "A birthday party, an evening at a night club, a Thanksgiving Day with his friends." Never was it just the two of them. Eleanor had even arranged for Ellie to have her "coming out" at the White House in 1938, during which both Hall and Eleanor impressed everyone with what graceful dancers they were, and after which Hall took everyone "on the town." "It was as if he couldn't let anyone see him quietly," Ellie wrote. "And alcohol was his protection."[80]

"The loss of a brother is a sad breaking of a family tie, but in the case of my brother it was like losing a child."[81] Hall died prematurely "in spite of her enduring love and hope for him," wrote Ellie,[82] but Eleanor never regretted her devotion. "In the end it boils down to how much we can love others and forget ourselves, doesn't it?"[83]

Hall's personal belongings were sold at auction. Among Hall's private items were his beloved Phi Beta Kappa key and several pocket watches, including one that the auctioneer claimed had belonged to the father of Hall and Eleanor Roosevelt. May Gibbens, a family friend, purchased several of Hall's effects on behalf of Eleanor, who gave the key to her nephew Henry, Hall's eldest son. Eleanor was relieved to find that the watch had not in fact belonged to Elliott.[84]

Eleanor did indeed love Hall, whose face was to her a haunting reminder of both of their parents.[85] Her son James remembered:

Eleanor and Hall, circa 1933. Courtesy of The Franklin D. Roosevelt Presidential Library.

When ... Mother's brother, Hall, died and Mother needed Father, he did not fail her. She slept in her clothes in the hospital for ten days while her brother was dying, and I remember clearly the day she went to Father and said simply, "Hall has died." Father struggled to her side and put his arm around her. "Sit down," he said, so tenderly I can still hear it. And he sank down beside her and hugged her and kissed her and held her head on his chest.

I do not think she cried. I think Mother had forgotten how to cry. But there were times when she needed to be held, and that certainly was one. Hall had been a trial to her. His life had been a disappointment to her and to him, too. When it was over, I think it was the waste of it that hurt her. And she spent her hurt in Father's embrace. It is too bad they were together like that so seldom.[86]

ELLIOTT ROOSEVELT MANN, son of Katy Mann, whom the "expert in likenesses" felt had "decidedly Rooseveltian features," was born in New York City March 11, 1891, three months before Hall, his "legitimate" half-brother. He was known for most of his adult life as Elliott Robert Mann.[87] He married Lena Prigge of Brooklyn in 1921 and had two daughters, Mildred and Eleanor.

November 26, 1932, Elliott Mann and his mother wrote congratulating Eleanor Roosevelt on her new position as First Lady of the United States. "I was very interested to receive your letter and to learn that you were named after my father," Eleanor responded. "I shall hope sometime to see both you and your mother."[88] Eleanor Mann Biles, daughter of Elliott Mann, told TR biographer Edmund Morris that the Manns were never invited to the White House, nor were any subsequent letters answered,[89] and that any money the Roosevelts may have put in trust for the Manns was presumed stolen.[90]

Apparently Hall was in touch with the Manns during the last year of his life, for in January 1941 the First Lady received an unexpected request. "We have received a note from a Mr. Ben Mann, 227 East 57th Street, New York, saying that at your suggestion he is 'taking the liberty of asking for an invitation to the inauguration.'" Eleanor's secretary wrote to Hall, "Do you know who he is and do you think we should send him an invitation?"[91] "[I] hope you will honor me by favorably granting my request,"[92] Ben Mann had written, but there is no record that it was granted.

MARY LIVINGSTON LUDLOW HALL, responsible for the upbringing of Eleanor and her brothers after the death of their mother, provided a home for her grandchildren invariably described as "gloomy"; but while it was not without its austere aspect, it was in fact a healing refuge in many ways. Eleanor's young aunts and uncles, whose lives sometimes seemed a series of misadventures, were kind and sympathetic to their orphaned niece, paying her much attention, although in later years alcoholism rendered her uncles — Vallie in particular — unstable and dangerous.

Married at eighteen, Mrs. Hall, although only nine years younger than her husband, was treated as a "child bride." Subsequently, she felt that she had failed miserably in the upbringing of her own children and was therefore strict with Eleanor and Hall. Eleanor, however, was grateful in later years both for the structure provided during her adolescence and also for the considerable freedom she was given to explore the woods around Tivoli, to enjoy nature and to spend hours perched in a comfortable cherry tree, reading her favorite books. Eleanor also appreciated that it was her grandmother who sent her to study in England, a period Eleanor regarded as the happiest of her life.

Mary Hall lived to see her granddaughter the wife of the Assistant Secretary of the Navy and the mother of four sons and a daughter of her own. Mrs. Hall died at Oak Terrace, her home in Tivoli, August 14, 1919, at the age of seventy-nine, exactly twenty-five years after Elliott.

"Her life was a sad one in many ways, and yet those who were closest to her mourned her deeply and sincerely," wrote Eleanor, who felt that her grandmother's life had been marred by the fear of venturing beyond the confines of the narrow world she knew. As a young woman her grandmother had "painted rather well. Could she have developed that talent? I know that when she was young she might have had friends of her own, might even have married again. Would she have been happier, and would her children have been better off? She was not the kind of person who would have made a career independently; she was the kind of woman who needed a man's protection. Her willingness to be subservient to her children isolated her, … and it might have been far better, for her boys at least, had she insisted on bringing more discipline into their lives simply by having a life of her own." Eleanor decided to try the opposite approach: "I determined that I would never be dependent on my children by allowing all my interests to center in them."[93]

This doesn't seem to have worked, either; the five children of Franklin and Eleanor Roosevelt were restless in their professional and personal lives, with nineteen marriages between them.

Eleanor never wrote or spoke of her grandmother other than in terms of the deepest affection and gratitude. "It is only after all these years," she wrote in 1919, "that I have realized what it meant for her to take Hall, Ellie and me into her home as she did."[94]

EDITH HALL MORGAN, "Aunt Pussie" of Eleanor's youth and the least stable and most self-dramatizing of the exquisite Hall sisters, went through a series of romantic attachments before marrying, at age thirty-two, William Forbes Morgan, nephew of financier J.P. Morgan. Pussie spent many hours reading poetry to Eleanor and playing the piano for her, and was greatly loved by her. It was she, however, who felt the need to disabuse Eleanor of the notion that her father had been anything other than the perfect gentle knight his daughter imagined him to be.

This information was blurted in anger to Eleanor when the latter suggested gently the possibility that Pussie's distress over the breakup of her latest love affair would soon pass. Pussie told Eleanor that she couldn't possibly understand — being the "ugly duckling," after all, with the "Roosevelt mouth," she would in all likelihood never have the numbers of suitors enjoyed by the Hall women. As for Eleanor's father, "You're so innocent, you don't know anything about him," she taunted. She then proceeded to inform Eleanor, in lurid detail, of Elliott's disgrace. "That's the kind of father you had," she sneered.[95] When Eleanor begged her grandmother to deny Pussie's account, Mary Hall could not. "But it's true," she replied. "It ruined your mother's life."[96]

This attack, although devastating, lessened neither Eleanor's devotion to her mercurial aunt nor to her father's memory. March 17, 1905, the day Eleanor married Franklin Roosevelt, it was Aunt Pussie who kissed Eleanor three times: "For Father & Mother & Ellie."[97]

Pussie's marriage, although it produced three children, ended in divorce, and shortly afterward, in the midst of a blizzard February 4, 1920, she died as a result of smoke inhalation along with her two daughters, aged fourteen and ten, when a sudden fire consumed their Greenwich Village apartment.

"Given greater discipline, the drive of necessity and wider opportunities, I believe that Pussie might have been an artist of real quality," wrote Eleanor in her autobiography,[98] echoing her *post mortem* for her grandmother. To family friend Isabella Ferguson, Eleanor wrote, "If it were not for the horror, I would feel sure that Pussie was happier than she's ever been here. She could not meet an everyday existence, [although] she had some lovely qualities and was always groping for spiritual thoughts. Forbes ...

had a deep affection for her and loved the children and often went to see them but no one could live with her. Isn't it a strange world, tragedies on every side in life and death and yet so much kindness, goodness and helpfulness that one knows it must all be for some worthwhile end."[99]

It has been speculated that Pussie was the model for Lily Bart, protagonist of Edith Wharton's novel *The House of Mirth*. Unlike Lily, however, Pussie had no need to hunt a fortune. She fell in and out of love, "not always wisely, but deeply," Eleanor believed.[100]

Eleanor would always cherish the memory of getting up early with her aunt on warm mornings to row their little boat into Tivoli to get the mail and the newspapers, and of family gatherings in the parlor on West 37th Street, listening to Pussie play the piano while Elliott sang.

ANNA ROOSEVELT COWLES, Elliott's sister "Bamie" and Eleanor's "Auntie Bye," always seemed more mature than everyone else in the family. In Theodore's childhood journals he explained that when he referred to "the big people," he meant his parents and Bamie.

It was she to whom Elliott's distraught wife turned for advice; it was she who accompanied Elliott and Anna to Europe in an attempt to keep Elliott on the straight and narrow. A family friend wrote of her capacity for "cheerful independent thinking based on brains, goodness and kindness."[101] She was the "Dearest Bye" and "Darling Bysie" of Theodore's frantic correspondence over the best way to deal with Elliott.

In 1893 Bamie accepted an invitation to live in England as assistant to James Roosevelt, known as "Rosy," Franklin Roosevelt's half-brother and first secretary to the United States Embassy in London. While there, she met and married naval officer William Sheffield Cowles, who retired with the rank of rear admiral. All her life Bamie suffered from a slightly misshapen appearance because of curvature of the spine and later crippling arthritis. She had never expected to marry, although many men admired her; she possessed a superior intelligence that rivaled that of Theodore. (The Roosevelts referred to Bamie's gentleman friends as her "Joe-Bobs," for they included Joseph Alsop, Sr., and future Rough Rider Robert Munro Ferguson.) FDR's father James Roosevelt had also been a suitor; Bamie did not return his interest, but made a major contribution to history by introducing him to her friend Sara Delano.

Admiral Cowles, according to a family friend, had the "sense" to see the *real* Bamie.[102] At her insistence he was the only one to call her by her Christian name, Anna, rather than the nicknames given her by her father and brothers.[103] At the age of forty-two she had a son, named for his father and called "Shef."

Bamie proved indispensable to Theodore's career. During his tenure as Civil Service Commissioner, at regular dinner parties in her Washington, D.C. home they entertained artists, intellectuals, and prominent men of the day. He would tell her who he wanted to be there, for he knew they would come if she invited them; they all found her invigorating intellectually, for she had the Roosevelt charisma and a nuanced understanding of international and domestic policy.

Eleanor wrote that her Auntie Bye "had remarkable judgment. She was interested in public affairs and in history. I used to think she might have governed an empire, either in her own right, or through her influence over a king or an emperor. She was subtle, interesting, tactful, and had the great gift of being able to listen to others, as well as to talk delightfully herself.

"I am sure that all my generation would have taken any amount of trouble to spend an hour with Mrs. Cowles, even in the days when she could no longer move from her wheelchair and her body was wracked with pain. Only a little black box on the table made it possible for her to hear us, and yet her spirit rose above all physical trials and shone out of the most beautiful eyes I have ever seen."[104]

In her teens, Bye was a student at Les Ruches, in Fontainebleau, France, where she met educator Marie Souvestre. When Eleanor was fifteen and her grandmother decided it was time for her to study abroad, it was Bye who suggested Allenswood, the boarding school in England of which Mlle. Souvestre was now the head.

When Franklin D. Roosevelt was appointed Assistant Secretary of the Navy, it was Auntie Bye who tutored Eleanor in the fine points of naval customs and courtesies, as well as Washington protocol and the art of "paying calls."

In later life Bye and the retired admiral lived at Oldgate, his family home near Farmington, Connecticut. She lived to see Elliott's daughter First Lady of New York; she was pleased with Eleanor's idealism and tireless energy, although she didn't always approve of the directions these took, especially when Eleanor fractured family solidarity by campaigning in 1924 on behalf of Al Smith and against Teddy Roosevelt, Jr. in the New York gubernatorial race. Eleanor's more bohemian friends were not to her liking, either.

"I just hate to see Eleanor let herself look as she does," Bye wrote to her niece Corinne Robinson Alsop. "Though never handsome, she always had to me a charming effect, but alas and lackaday! Since politics have become her choicest interest, all her charm has disappeared, and the fact is emphasized by the companions she chooses to bring with her."[105]

Even so, during this period Bamie's son witnessed a scene redolent of the true Rooseveltian ethos, when Franklin paid a visit to the Cowles family.

Bamie was bent almost in half now, immobilized by her arthritis, and so deaf that people had to shout into the boxlike hearing device called an accousticon she kept beside her chair. Franklin maneuvered his wheelchair next to hers, and shouted jokes into her primitive listening device to make her and the Admiral laugh. Sheffield Jr. was struck by the quiet courage with which these afflicted Roosevelts went about dealing with their ailments.[106]

"You felt such gallantry in all of them," remarked a family friend who was there also. "Such humor, such complete elimination of any problem about bodies."[107]

Eleanor loved and appreciated "Auntie Bye" — friend, comforter, and confidante of her adolescence, mentor of her early womanhood, and indispensable support for all Roosevelts. She agreed with Alice that if Bye had been a man, she would have been president. She is in fact the subject of her own biography: Lillian Rixey's *Bamie: Theodore Roosevelt's Remarkable Sister*. In the family drama she was the mirror image of Elliott, as steadfast and disciplined as he was erratic and dissolute.

CORINNE ROOSEVELT ROBINSON, who never gave up on Elliott and was the one sibling he still trusted at the end of his life, spent thirty-six years as the wife of Douglas Robinson, who died in 1918. They had four children, and through her daughter Corinne Robinson Alsop, Corinne became the grandmother of columnists Stewart and Joseph Alsop. She wrote a memoir, *My Brother Theodore Roosevelt*, a loving account of their early life.

Corinne was active behind the scenes in Republican politics and occasionally played a more visible role. At the 1920 G.O.P. Convention in Chicago, Corinne became the first woman to give a speech at a major party convention when she seconded the nomination of Leonard Wood (who ultimately lost the nomination). She enjoyed making speeches and thereafter was in great demand as a speaker.

Corinne was also a poet, with four published volumes of poetry to her credit. One of these, *One Woman to Another and Other Poems*

(1914), contained verse dedicated to Mrs. Evans, Elliott's last mistress, with whom Corinne had spent considerable time in the days immediately following Elliott's death. Speaking from the point of view of Mrs. Evans, Corinne wrote:

Often he told me that you never failed,
And that when others with averted gaze,
Would have him know his own unworthiness,
Your eyes held only memories of the past. …

I was of that strange world you cannot know,
The "half-world" with its glamour and its glare,
Its sin and shame. …

Mrs. Evans told Corinne that she had been in a "vagrant and despairing" state when she met Elliott, and that his love and companionship had "saved" her. In his last days she devoted herself to his care, and told Corinne that "he was so very good to me."

How can you judge of him, and how could she
Whose fair white bosom was a thought too chaste
To pillow a repentant weary head?
But I who know the evil of the world
Could never shrink before so sad a thing, …
Only, when in his eyes I read the look
That longed for her, my swift resentment rose; …
Then, sometimes, friends of his would come and speak
Of that fair world of yours, unknown to me,
And afterward he would be lost in gloom. …

Corinne, grateful to this woman who had shown her brother compassion in his last desperate days, kissed Mrs. Evans at the end of their visit. "You would kiss me?" Corinne has Mrs. Evans ask. "*Yes, I take your kiss; / We are both women, and we both have loved!*"

Eleanor valued this poem and remained close to her Aunt Corinne,[108] who gave her Mrs. Sherman's letters.[109]

"Corinne impresses me more and more each time I am with her; such strength and tenderness of both mind and heart, a truly wonderful and most attractive woman," wrote Maud Elliott to John Elliott. "She sorrows so over Elliott and his life."[110]

Corinne "was entirely different" than Bamie, who was in England when Elliott died and had given up on him. "Greater charm perhaps, greater gentleness, a more easily loveable quality and feeling for the arts. She had a gift for writing poetry, but her appreciation of others' talents illuminated their work for those of us with duller perception. ... She could join with youth in joy or sorrow as though she was of their generation. Time with her was a precious gift granted to all of us — not only appreciated by my generation, but by those even younger." Eleanor remembered Corinne "with a tender gaiety and all of us are grateful for the windows of her soul which she opened to us."[111]

Corinne was a lifelong stalwart of the G.O.P., but in 1928 and 1930 she voted for Franklin D. Roosevelt for governor, and again in 1932, this time for president, because "Eleanor was her niece, after all."[112] A grateful Sara Delano Roosevelt, her contemporary, wrote, "There is no one on earth like [you]. ... Some people have fine *minds*, others have warm *hearts*, but you have both."[113] Both Theodore and Elliott — indeed all who knew Corinne — would have agreed.

On the night of January 17, 1933, a party was given at the Waldorf Astoria Hotel in honor of First Lady–elect Eleanor Roosevelt. Corinne had been feeling unwell, but nothing could keep her away on this bitterly cold night "from this celebration for her favorite brother's favorite child."[114] She died exactly one month later, the last of the affectionate family that had lived at 28 East 20th Street.

EDITH CAROW ROOSEVELT, the one person who seemed immune to Elliott's charm, feared that Eleanor may have taken after him. "I never wished Alice to associate with Eleanor so shall not try to keep up any friendship between them."[115] (That friendship was intense, however; at least until 1924. See Linda Donn, *The Roosevelt Cousins*.) Edith outlived her husband by nearly thirty years, and bore the sorrow of outliving three of her sons.

For many years Edith was markedly condescending regarding Eleanor. "I got Alice a beautiful dress at Thorn's, dark large plaid with navy blue and how much do you think it cost?" Edith wrote her sister Emily. "Forty-two dollars, and her coat rough blue cloth lined throughout with plaid silk, will be $45 — Mrs. Lee [Alice's grandmother] makes it and I am glad as Alice is a child who needs good clothes, and would look quite as forlorn as Eleanor in makeshift. ..."[116]

Edith and Theodore offered to host a White House wedding for Eleanor, but she declined.[117] Eleanor was married at the Manhattan townhouse of Cousin Susie Parrish, who had broken the news to Eleanor of Anna's death twelve years before. The wedding took place March 17, 1905, and would have been Anna's forty-second birthday. The president of the United States, standing in for Elliott, gave the bride away.

Edith was a loyal Republican but, unlike Corinne, never allowed family ties to compel her to vote for Franklin D. Roosevelt. Indeed, she campaigned actively for Hoover in 1932. This may have been because she had never forgiven Eleanor's zeal during Al Smith's run for the governorship against Teddy Roosevelt, Jr., Edith's son, when Eleanor's car was fitted with a *papier-mâché* teapot, suggesting that Ted, who had served as Assistant Secretary of the Navy during Warren Harding's administration, was somehow tainted by the Teapot Dome scandal. (Eleanor later claimed to be ashamed of getting "so carried away.")[118]

Even so, upon becoming the thirty-third First Lady of the United States, Eleanor wrote a warm epistle to the twenty-sixth. "Your letter was an answer to prayer," replied Aunt Edith, "full of things which I wanted to know. Much such conditions met me in the White House, and I am quite sure I did not deal with them as efficiently as you have done."[119]

ELEANOR ROOSEVELT. When Elliott died, Eleanor lost "all the realties of companionship which he had suggested for the future, but as I said in the beginning he lived in my dreams and does to this day."[120]

The little girl wanted to be left alone to live in her dreams with her father. Her first compositions are windows into her inner world; the first being the scenario she wished had happened during the painful shipboard catastrophe of her early childhood:

The Tempest

We were all crowded in the cabin, no one had dared to go to bed for it was midnight on the sea, and there was a dreadful storm raging. It is a terrible thing in winter to be tossed about by the wind, and to hear captain calling through the trumpet "Cut away the mast." So we all sat there trembling, and none of us dared to speak, for even the bravest among us held our breath while the sea was foaming and tossing, and the sailors were talking death. And while we sat there in the dark, all of us saying our prayers, suddenly the captain rushed down the stairs. "We are lost!" he shouted. But his little girl took his cold hand and said, "Is not God on the ocean just as well as on the land?" Then we all kissed the little girl, and we spoke more cheerfully, and the next day we anchored safely in the harbor when the sun was shining brightly.[121]

"In those later years her father had been the one who needed help and in reality as well as in fantasy, she had been the one to sustain and comfort him," writes her friend Joseph Lash.[122]

In the three-year interval between Elliott's death and boarding school in England, Eleanor's life revolved around reading, in particular books that reinforced her "dream world in which I was the heroine and my father the hero."[123] Prominent among these was *Peter Ibbetson* by George du Maurier, a unique romance in which an orphan discovers his inner "private oasis" where he learns to "dream true" — to call to mind the people he has loved and lost and so continue his relationships with them. Eleanor took comfort also in lachrymose novels enjoyed by emotional Victorians, such as *Sans Famile* (*Nobody's Boy*) by Hector Mallet, and *Misunderstood* by Florence Montgomery, both of which dealt with orphaned children. The latter particularly resonated with Eleanor, as the story concerns a boy whose mother has died and whose father makes no secret of preferring the other son. The boy looks forward to death, for then he will be reunited with the parent who appreciates him. In her sixties Eleanor wrote that she could still derive pleasure from these stories, but that they were "very sentimental, foolish books to allow a rather lonely child to read."[124] Even so, they gave her a place to go with her sadness. And there was always *The Old Curiosity Shop*.

In a composition book given to Eleanor by her Aunt Pussie, she wrote:

She had waited so long, so long. One night she awoke. Someone was whispering in her ear. Suddenly the room seemed to be filled by millions of shadowy forms who whispered to her, "He has broken his word. He has broken his word." She could stand it no longer & she cried out in the dark "Oh my father come" & a voice answered "I am here" & he stood beside her & his cool hand lay on her hot head. She clasped it in both hers & sighed contentedly. "Oh I knew you must come." But he answered, I have kept my word I have come back but I must go away again, & the child cried out Oh! take me with you I have waited so long & it has been so hard I cannot stay alone. He bent down & kissed her & she fell asleep. The next morning the people who had never understood came in & looked pityingly at her lying cold and dead & they said "poor child to die so young (how sad)" & a few tears were shed & then she like all those who have ceased to move in this earthly sphere sank into oblivion.[125]

Here she is Little Nell, the Little Match Girl, the child in *Misunderstood*, even the dreaming Peter Ibbetson — all the sad children of nineteenth-century literature. Even when Eleanor Roosevelt's picture regularly appeared in newspapers under the headline "America's Most Beloved Woman," on a deep level she would always define herself as Elliott's tragic daughter.

Another composition:

A child stood at a window watching a man walking down the street, the little face was white & set & the big tears stood in the brown eyes but the mouth smiled till the man was out of sight & the sob which was choking her did not break out till he was gone & she could see no more. Her Father [was] the only person in the world she loved, others called her hard & cold but to him she was everything lavishing on him all the quiet love which the others could not understand. And now he had gone she did not know for how long but he had said "what ever happens little girl some day I will come back" & she had smiled. He never knew what the smile cost. His letters came often telling of the life he was leading, his hopes & fears & sometimes there would come a letter without any news, filled with only love for her & these were the letters she loved & kissed before she went to bed. But a time came when there were no more letters & a grown up person told the child that her Father was dead, but the child did not cry. Dead people did not come back & her father had promised to come & he never broke his word. At first she could not bear to hear him spoken of as dead but at last she grew accustomed to it, they were making a mistake but what was the difference? The years went by & she still believed but doubts came sometimes now. ...[126]

Faith, too, sustained Eleanor Roosevelt throughout her life. When Marie Souvestre, headmistress of the Allenswood School and one of the most important influences in Eleanor's life, attempted to talk her out of being a Christian, she made no headway with Eleanor. "Religion and prayer touched mystic chords in Eleanor that bound her to her dead father and to all humanity," writes Joseph Lash.[127] There was no way that she would give up the hope of seeing Elliott again.

Dwelling in what novelist Jack Finney called "the deep peace" of the late nineteenth century, Eleanor Roosevelt's sensibilities took shape. Many years later she wrote that in her youth there was "a quality of tranquility in people, which you rarely meet today."[128] It was a world without traffic, income tax, pollution or the threat of nuclear destruction. There was a minimum of social unrest. It was an environment in which it seemed there was a place for everything and everything was in its place, a world of mannerly, well-ordered people, with rectitude supported by faith. "This religious training was not just an affair of Sundays — there were family prayers every morning, and you grew up with the feeling that you had a share in some great spiritual existence beyond the everyday round of happenings."[129]

Eleanor and Franklin had six children (one died in infancy). There was Anna, named for Eleanor's mother; James, for Franklin's father; and then Elliott. Eleanor doted on him as she had on Hall and on the first Elliott. He was her most troublesome child, yet even with their tempestuous relationship, Eleanor seemed to have a bond with this wayward son that she did not experience with her other children.

First Lady–elect Eleanor Roosevelt attended the Metropolitan Opera one Saturday before Christmas 1932. The performance was Verdi's *Simon Boccanegra*, featuring Lawrence Tibbett, whose career she followed subsequently. Set in Genoa, the story deals with a nobleman much-loved by the people of the city for his generous, forgiving ways — another fellow "with whom the heart always dominated." Simon is "the Good Father," and there is a stirring duet in which he is reunited with his long-lost daughter. ("Daughter! At that name I tremble / as if heaven had opened to me.") This is the reunion for which the daughter has longed throughout her life. ("Father, you shall see your watchful daughter / always near you; / I will wipe away your tears. / We shall taste undiscovered joys, / I will be the dove of peace / of your royal palace.")

During the intermission directly following this sequence, Eleanor Roosevelt, about to take up residence in another "royal palace," decided to claim her mantle as her father's daughter. Spontaneously, she strode upon the stage to the surprise of the audience and made an appeal for the Emergency Unemployment Relief Committee on behalf of the victims of the Depression. "When you come face to face with people in need, you simply have to do something about it." She spoke of her own experience encountering the jobless "face to face," telling of a man who walked into her office saying he could not go home to face his family unless he had a job. "There was no heat at home, no food, and even the gas had been turned off. And there were five children." "After all, this is the richest country in the world," she concluded. "We cannot allow anyone to want for the bare necessities of life."[130]

The first thing Eleanor did upon realizing that she would indeed be First Lady was to bring honor to her father's memory. Elliott had thought about turning his letters from India into a book. Elliott thought about doing a lot of things. Eleanor, however, was determined that her father would not fall through the cracks of history, and so she presented him to the reading public in *Hunting Big Game in the 'Eighties: The Letters of Elliott Roosevelt, Sportsman*, "edited by His Daughter, Anna Eleanor Roosevelt."

"He loved people for the fineness that was in them and his friends might be newsboys or millionaires. Their occupations, their possessions, meant nothing to him, only they themselves counted," wrote Eleanor. "That trait," writes one of Eleanor's biographers, "represented the core of her father's bequest to her."[131]

During her first summer as First Lady, Eleanor took a night train to Abingdon, Virginia, where her father had sobered up for ten months and begun to heal, in order finally to meet the people who had loved and comforted him there. She attended the White Top Mountain Music Festival, where she was serenaded by children and venerable citizens playing banjos, dulcimers, mandolins, and "fiddles," along with much singing of hymns and mountain tunes. It was on this visit that she was introduced to square dancing, which she enjoyed for the rest of her life. "It looked to me far more fun than much of the modern dancing of today."[132]

"Asked during the lull of an hour for luncheon, 'Is there anybody in particular you wish to find and meet?' Mrs. Roosevelt replied, 'Yes, there's an old colored valet of my father's, John Smith, of Bristol, whom I want to see,'" reported the *Herald Courier* of Bristol, Virginia.

The faithful retainer of Elliott Roosevelt was easily located, carefully dressed in a new suit, and Mrs. Roosevelt and he were promptly photographed by the swarm of cameramen present. "John," straight and tall despite his seventy years, posed with the cup and saucer once given him by Elliott Roosevelt, and presented yesterday to his distinguished daughter.[133]

These Virginians were drawn to Eleanor, as they had been drawn to Elliott. It was a highly emotional visit for her, permeated as it was with

In 1933, at White Top Music Festival in Abingdon, Virginia, Elliott's long-ago valet presented First Lady Eleanor Roosevelt with a cup and saucer given to him by her father. Reproduced from the collections of The Franklin D. Roosevelt Presidential Library. Courtesy of Norfolk and Western Magazine, Norfolk Southern Corporation.

memories of Elliott, with scenes and people, some now very old, described with such appreciation in the letters she never ceased to re-read.

Eleanor, like Theodore, once confided "that the very smell of alcoholic beverages was distasteful to her."[134] In an era when the temperance movement was associated with the Republican Party, Eleanor was a strong representative for "dry" Democrats, who were chiefly women.[135] She commended President Hoover's efforts to enforce the law when Prohibition was blatantly flaunted.[136] As time went on, she had reservations about the effectiveness of the law and was attacked by Prohibitionists for refusing to lend wholehearted support.

Describing herself as "personally absolutely dry,"[137] she found herself in the awkward — and, one can safely assume, distasteful — position of serving alcohol in the White House again after fourteen years on the day Prohibition was repealed. "The personal views and tastes of the First Lady ... notwithstanding," reported *The New York Times*, April 4, 1933, beer was served in iced-tea glasses. Each afternoon, the president mixed martinis for a few members of his staff and attempted to forget about politics for a while, but the First Lady disapproved, and on those rare occasions when she was present, demurely sipped a glass of sherry.

Eleanor brought the portrait of her grandfather, Theodore Roosevelt, Sr., the father Elliott had so loved, from her New York townhouse and hung it over the mantle in the Monroe Room at the White House, which had been the Cabinet Room during Teddy Roosevelt's administration.

Eleanor's "reconnection with her father and her childhood helped her to reach beyond fear," writes Blanche Cook. "As she reconstituted her father's life, she embraced a powerful source of courage and vision that was her mysterious treasure."[138]

"Mrs. Roosevelt, you must visit India as my guest," Prime Minister Jawaharlal Nehru invited Eleanor one evening when he visited her at Val-Kill, her cottage in Hyde Park. "Your views on the direction my country should follow would be most welcome."[139] At last Eleanor traveled to the scenes of Elliott's youthful adventure, where he hunted in Ceylon and in the Himalayas, and in the rain forests of Hyderabad. ("I think I know a little about heads and horns," Eleanor wrote in her column.)[140] "This for the mere pleasure of living is the only life," Elliott had written long ago, and Eleanor enjoyed it nearly as much, for the experience brought her father close to her. Like him, she was entertained by maharajahs and by the Nizam of Hyderabad, although in a childlike way she was disappointed when he would not allow her to ride an elephant.[141]

The most important journey for Eleanor, however, was to the Taj Mahal, for Elliott "always said it was the one thing he wanted us to see together."[142] "As we came through the entrance gallery into the walled garden and looked down the long series of oblong pools in which the Taj and the dark cypresses are reflected, I held my breath, unable to speak in the face of so much beauty. ... The others walked on around, but I felt that this first time I wanted to drink in its beauty from a distance. ... Somehow love and beauty seem close together in this creation."[143]

Eleanor Roosevelt was in her late sixties and had been called "First Lady of the World" by this time, but when she returned that evening to gaze by moonlight at this tomb commissioned by a long-ago potentate for his wife, once again she was Little Nell, enjoying a long-awaited moment with her father. "The purity of the white marble makes ... the eternal purity of real love a very living thing. I escaped the guides as much as possible," she attempted to explain, "because I felt that this was perfection that one must feel and let sink in."[144] In fact, Eleanor wanted to be alone with Elliott.

His namesake grandson understood this. "She gazed at the Taj and thought of it as a kind of memorial to the other Elliott Roosevelt. 'Little

Eleanor Roosevelt in July 1953, "First Lady of the World," wearing the tiger claw necklace that was Elliott's gift to her grandmother. Courtesy of The Franklin D. Roosevelt Presidential Library.

Nell,' he had told her, 'when you grow up you must go and see the Taj Mahal on a night of the full moon. There is a bench not far away, next to one of the lotus-leaf basins, where you should sit and contemplate.' This was such a night. She waited through the day, then, finding the same place where he had sat before she was born, she recaptured his feeling that this was the one unforgettable sight he had seen in India. 'I will carry in my mind the beauty of it as long as I live,' she said. She had never known greater tranquil joy than this."[145]

When Eleanor Roosevelt died ten years later, even her old political antagonist Herbert Hoover admitted, "Mrs. Roosevelt was a lady of fine courage and great devotion to her country."[146] The tribute she would most have appreciated, however, and that spoke most directly to Elliott's legacy, came from James A. Weschler, editorial page editor of *The New York Post*: "She was a great and good woman, who understood the difficulties all humans traverse in their lives and who was always trying to help them on the long road."[147]

≾ Chronology ≿

1853   December 22. Theodore Roosevelt of New York City marries Martha (Mittie) Bulloch of Roswell, Georgia.

1855   January 18. Their daughter Anna Eleanor (Bamie) Roosevelt is born.

1858   October 27. Son Theodore Roosevelt, Jr. (Teedie), future president of the United States, is born.

1860   February 28. Son Elliott Roosevelt is born.

1861   September 27. Daughter Corinne Roosevelt is born.

1874   Elliott begins to suffer fainting spells, is unable to continue at St. Paul's School.

1876   Elliott is sent to Texas to recuperate. Health improves in the West.

1878   February 9. Elliott's father, Theodore Roosevelt, Sr., dies after a brief foray into politics. Elliott begins drinking heavily.

1880   Elliott embarks upon world tour; hunts big game in India; contracts a form of malaria, a lifelong ailment.

1882   Elliott returns to New York City; is named godfather to Franklin Delano Roosevelt, son of James and Sara Delano Roosevelt of Hyde Park, New York.

1883   December 1. Elliott marries Anna Rebecca Hall of Tivoli, New York, in New York City.

1884   February 14. Elliott's mother Mittie Roosevelt and sister-in-law Alice Hathaway Lee Roosevelt (Theodore, Jr.'s first wife) die within hours of each other.

1884   October 11. Elliott's daughter Anna Eleanor Roosevelt is born.

1887   Elliott resigns from real estate firm and sets sail with his wife and daughter for Europe. After initial shipwreck, Eleanor is left in the care of Elliott's aunt and uncle.

1887   Elliott enters banking and brokerage firm of his uncle James King Gracie and begins construction of home in Hempstead, Long Island.

1889   September 29. Son Elliott Roosevelt, Jr. is born.

1891   Elliott commits himself to a sanitarium in Austria. Son Gracie Hall Roosevelt is born on June 28. Servant Katy Mann simultaneously brings paternity suit against Elliott. Civil Service Commissioner Theodore Roosevelt brings commitment proceedings against Elliott.

1892   Elliott undergoes treatment for alcoholism at Keeley Center in Illinois; subsequently sent to manage brother-in-law's property in Abingdon, Virginia; flourishes among Virginians while enduring forced separation from his family.

1892   December 7. Elliott's wife Anna Hall Roosevelt dies of diphtheria. Anna's will stipulates that her mother, rather than her husband, have custody of their children.

1893   May 25. Elliott Roosevelt, Jr. dies of scarlet fever; Elliott returns to New York City and resumes drinking.

1894   August 14. Elliott Roosevelt dies in New York City. Theodore Roosevelt arranges for Elliott to be buried in Green-Wood Cemetery in Brooklyn, next to his parents.

1896   Elliott's body is moved and interred next to his wife and son in the cemetery of St. Paul's and Trinity Parish in Tivoli, New York.

1901   September 14. Theodore Roosevelt becomes president of the United States upon the death of President William McKinley.

1905   March 17. Elliott's daughter Anna Eleanor Roosevelt marries her distant cousin (and Elliott's godson) Franklin D. Roosevelt in New York City. President Theodore Roosevelt gives away the bride in lieu of his late brother Elliott.

1933   March 4. Eleanor Roosevelt becomes First Lady of the United States.

1962   November 7. Eleanor Roosevelt, often called "First Lady of the World" and one of the world's most beloved women, dies in New York City.

⚔ NOTES ⚔

The two indispensable archives containing primary sources pertaining to the Roosevelt family are the Franklin D. Roosevelt Presidential Library in Hyde Park, New York, and the Theodore Roosevelt Collection in the Houghton Library at Harvard University. In the notes for each chapter, the name of the archive is stated in full at its first reference in that chapter. Thereafter, the former is indicated by the abbreviation FDRL and the latter by T.R. Collection, Harvard.

INTRODUCTION

1. Geoffrey Ward, *Before the Trumpet: Young Franklin Roosevelt 1882–1905* (New York: Harper and Row, 1985), 287.

2. Joseph P. Lash, *Eleanor and Franklin: The Story of Their Relationship* (New York: Norton, 1971), 27.

3. Robert Woodruff Anderson, *I Never Sang for My Father* (New York: Random House, 1968).

4. Ted Morgan, *FDR: A Biography* (New York: Simon and Schuster, 1985), 94.

5. Anna Eleanor Roosevelt, ed., *Hunting Big Game in the 'Eighties: The Letters of Elliott Roosevelt, Sportsman* (New York, Charles Scribner's Sons, 1932), vii.

6. Ibid., viii.

7. Ibid., 181.

8. Michael Teague, *Mrs. L.: Conversations with Alice Roosevelt Longworth* (Garden City, N.Y.: Doubleday and Co., 1981), 153–155.

9. Roosevelt, *Hunting Big Game*, 173–174.

10. Ibid., vii.

11. Ibid., x.

12. Ibid., 19.

13. Anna Eleanor Roosevelt, *This Is My Story* (New York: Harper and Brothers, 1937), 9.

14. Roosevelt, *Hunting Big Game*, 157.

15. Ibid, 167.

16. Ernest Hemingway, *A Farewell to Arms* (New York: Scribners, 1929), 34.

17. Morgan, 92.

18. Peter Collier with David Horowitz, *The Roosevelts: An American Saga* (New York: Simon and Schuster, 1994), 254.

CHAPTER 1

1. *New York Tribune*, February 18, 1878.

2. Joseph Bucklin Bishop, *Theodore Roosevelt and His Time, Shown in His Own Letters* (New York: Charles Scribner's Sons, 1920), 3–4.

3. Ibid.

4. David McCullough, *Mornings on Horseback* (New York: Simon and Schuster, 1981), 186.

5. Corinne Roosevelt Robinson, *My Brother Theodore Roosevelt* (New York: Charles Scribner's Sons, 1921), 3.

6. Ibid., 8.

7. Joseph Lash, *Eleanor and Franklin: The Story of Their Relationship* (New York: Norton, 1971), 28.

8. Letter from Sylvia Jukes Morris to the author, August 2003.

9. Franklin D. Roosevelt Presidential Library, Roosevelt Family Papers Donated by the Children. Letter to "Mrs. Franklin D. Roosevelt" from "Roosevelt & Son," June 9, 1920.

10. Theodore Roosevelt Collection, Houghton Library, Harvard University.

11. Carlton Putnam, *Theodore Roosevelt: The Formative Years 1858–1886* (New York: Charles Scribner's Sons, 1958), 5.

12. T.R. Collection, Harvard.

13. Geoffrey Ward, *Before the Trumpet: Young Franklin Roosevelt 1882–1905* (New York: Harper & Row), 1985.

14. Putnam, 41.

15. Ibid.

16. Ibid.

17. *New York Evening Post*, February 11, 1878.

18. Putnam, 42.

19. *Frank Lister* [according to Elliott; possibly *Frank Leslie's Illustrated Newspaper*], March 2, 1878. From Elliott Roosevelt's scrapbook, T.R. Collection, Harvard.

20. Putnam, 42.

21. Ibid., 42–43.

22. *The New York Times*, February 17, 1878.

23. Putnam, 158.

24. Ibid., 43.

25. Ibid., 44.

26. *Harper's Weekly*, March 2, 1878.

27. Nathan Miller, *The Roosevelt Chronicles* (Garden City, N.Y.: Doubleday and Co., 1979), 139.

28. Harold I. Gullan, *Faith of Our Mothers: The Story of Presidential Mothers from Mary Washington to Barbara Bush* (Grand Rapids, Mich.: William B. Eerdmans Publishing Co., 2001), 146.

29. Miller, 141.

30. McCullough, 47.

31. Ibid., 30.

32. Gullan, 152

33. Edmund Morris, *The Rise of Theodore Roosevelt* (New York: Random House, 1979).

34. Gullan, 152–153.

35. T.R. Collection, Harvard.

36. Lash, 28.

37. Morris, 6.

38. Gullan, 146.

39. T.R. Collection, Harvard.

40. Collier and Horowitz, 32.

CHAPTER 2

1. David McCullough, *Mornings on Horseback* (New York: Simon and Schuster, 1981), 35.

2. Harold I. Gullan, *Faith of Our Mothers: The Story of Presidential Mothers from Mary Washington to Barbara Bush* (Grand Rapids, Mich.: William B. Eerdmans Publishing Co., 2001), 149.

3. Quoted in Carlton Putnam, *Theodore Roosevelt: The Formative Years 1858–1886* (New York: Charles Scribner's Sons, 1958) 39.

4. McCullough, 49.

5. Ibid., 10.

6. Ibid., 238.

7. Franklin D. Roosevelt Presidential Library, Roosevelt Family Papers Donated by the Children.

8. Putnam, 45.

9. Theodore Roosevelt Collection, Houghton Library, Harvard University.

10. McCullough, 37.

11. Ibid., 23.

12. Joseph Lash, *Eleanor and Franklin: The Story of Their Relationship.* (New York: Norton, 1971), 36.

13. Letter (undated), T.R. Collection, Harvard.

14. Walter E. Wilson, *The Bulloch Belles: Three First Ladies, a Spy, a President's Mother, and Other Women of a 19th Century Georgia Family* (Jefferson, N.C.: McFarland and Company, 2015), 189.

15. McCullough, 57.

16. Ibid.

17. Edmund Morris, *The Rise of Theodore Roosevelt* (New York: Random House, 1979), 35.

18. Putnam, 234.

19. Theodore Roosevelt, *Theodore Roosevelt's Diaries of Boyhood and Youth* (New York: Charles Scribner's Sons, 1928), various entries.

20. McCullough, 15.

21. Geoffrey Ward, *Before the Trumpet: Young Franklin Roosevelt 1882–1905* (New York: Harper and Row, 1985) 261.

22. McCullough, 125.

23. Ibid.

24. Peter Collier and David Horowitz, *The Roosevelts: An American Saga* (New York: Simon and Schuster, 1994).

25. McCullough, 125.

26. T.R. Collection, Harvard.

CHAPTER 3

1. Letter dated June 6, 1873, Roosevelt Family Papers Donated by the Children, Box 5, Folder 4, Franklin D. Roosevelt Presidential Library.
2. Ibid.
3. David McCullough, *Mornings on Horseback.* (New York: Simon and Schuster, 1981), 144.
4. Ibid., 147.
5. Ibid., 146.
6. Ibid., 144.
7. H.W. Brands, *Traitor to His Class: The Privileged Life and Radical Presidency of Franklin D. Roosevelt* (New York: Doubleday, 2008), 34.
8. McCullough, 145.
9. Ibid., 79.
10. McCullough, 145.
11. Ibid.
12. Ibid., 146.
13. Ibid.
14. Peter Collier and David Horowitz, *The Roosevelts: An American Saga* (New York: Simon and Schuster, 1994).
15. Joseph Lash, *Eleanor and Franklin: The Story of Their Relationship* (New York: Norton, 1971), 31–32.
16. Letter dated Sept. 11, 1875, FDRL.
17. Ibid.
18. Letter dated Sept. 23, 1875, Roosevelt Family Papers Donated by the Children, Box 5, Folder 4, FDRL.
19. Ibid.
20. Ibid., letter dated July 19, 1871.
21. Ibid., letter dated Sept. 23, 1875.
22. Anna Eleanor Roosevelt, ed., *Hunting Big Game in the 'Eighties: The Letters of Elliott Roosevelt, Sportsman* (New York: Charles Scribner's Sons, 1932), 10.
23. McCullough, 147.
24. Collier and Horowitz, 43.
25. Letter dated Feb. 27, 1873, FDRL.
26. Roosevelt, *Hunting Big Game,* 3.
27. Letter dated July 18, 1873, FDRL.
28. Ibid., letter dated July 20, 1873.
29. Ibid., letter dated Sept. 15, 1873.
30. Ibid., letter dated June 15, 1873.
31. Ibid., letter dated July 17, 1873.
32. Ibid., letter dated Sept. 15, 1873.
33. Ibid., letter dated June 15, 1873.
34. Ibid., letter dated June 29, 1873.
35. Ibid., letter dated Sept. 28, 1873.
36. Ibid., letter dated June 13, 1873.
37. Ibid., letter dated July 9, 1873.
38. Ibid., letter dated July 1873.
39. Undated letter, FDRL.
40. Letter dated Feb. 1, 1875, FDRL.
41. Letter dated Feb. 14, 1875, FDRL.
42. Ibid.
43. Letter dated Feb. 9, 1875, FDRL.
44. Ibid.
45. Roosevelt, *Hunting Big Game,* 13.
46. Ibid., 16.
47. Ibid.
48. Ibid., 17.
49. Ibid., 17–18.

CHAPTER 4

1. Captain Mayne Reid, *The Rifle Rangers; a Thrilling Story of Daring Adventure and Hairbreadth Escapes during the Mexican War* (New York: Hurst & Company, 1899), title page.
2. Captain Mayne Reid, *The Young Yagers, or a Narrative of Hunting Adventures in Southern Africa* (Boston: Ticknor and Fields, 1857), 190.
3. Anna Eleanor Roosevelt, ed., *Hunting Big Game in the 'Eighties: The Letters of Elliott Roosevelt, Sportsman* (New York: Charles Scribner's Sons, 1932), 11.
4. Ibid., 9.
5. Ibid., 19.
6. Ibid., 20.
7. Ibid., 21.
8. Ibid., 22.
9. Ibid., 24.
10. Ibid.
11. Ibid., 26.
12. Ibid.
13. Ibid.
14. Letter dated Jan. 5, 1876, Franklin D. Roosevelt Presidential Library.
15. Ibid.
16. Ibid., letter dated Jan. 8, 1876.
17. Ibid., letter dated Jan. 12, 1876.
18. Ibid., letter dated Jan. 23, 1876.
19. Ibid.
20. Ibid., letter dated Jan. 20, 1876.
21. Ibid., letter dated Jan. 30, 1876.
22. Roosevelt, *Hunting Big Game.*
23. Letter dated Aug. 24, 1873, FDRL.
24. Ibid., letter dated Feb. 28, 1876.

25. Ibid., letter dated March 18, 1876.
26. Ibid., Undated letter.
27. Ibid.
28. Ibid.
29. Ibid.
30. Ibid., letter dated Feb. 26, 1877.
31. Ibid.
32. Ibid.
33. Ibid.
34. Ibid.
35. Ibid., letter dated March 10, 1877.
36. Ibid., letter dated March 4, 1877.
37. Ibid., "Vox Buffalorum," Jan. 14, 1877.
38. Blanche Wiesen Cook, *Eleanor Roosevelt, Volume 1: 1884–1933* (New York: Penguin, 1993), 35.
39. "Vox Buffalorum," Jan. 14, 1877, FDRL.
40. Ibid.
41. Ibid., "Vox Buffalorum," Jan. 21, 1877.
42. Ibid.
43. Ibid., "Vox Buffalorum," Jan. 28, 1877.
44. Ibid.
45. Ibid.
46. Ibid.
47. Ibid., "Vox Buffalorum," Jan. 21, 1877.
48. Ibid.

CHAPTER 5

1. David McCullough, *Mornings on Horseback* (New York: Simon and Schuster, 1981), 154.
2. Ibid., 153.
3. Ibid., 151.
4. Ibid., 152.
5. *The New York World*, Feb. 13, 1878.
6. *The New York World*, Feb. 15, 1878.
7. McCullough, 182.
8. Ibid., 183.
9. Blanche Wiesen Cook, *Eleanor Roosevelt, Volume 1: 1884–1933* (New York: Penguin, 1993), 36.
10. McCullough, 162–185.
11. Cook, 36.
12. Elliott Roosevelt's scrapbook, Theodore Roosevelt Collection, Houghton Library, Harvard University.
13. *The New York Herald*, Feb. 11, 1878.
14. Ibid., Feb. 11, 1878.
15. Ibid.
16. *The New York Times*, Feb. 13, 1878.
17. Ibid.

18. *The New York World*, Feb. 13, 1878.
19. *The New York Tribune*, Feb. 13, 1878.
20. *The New York Times*, Feb. 13, 1878.
21. *The New York World*, Feb. 13, 1878.
22. *The New York Tribune*, Feb. 13, 1878.
23. Corinne Roosevelt Robinson, *My Brother Theodore Roosevelt* (New York: Charles Scribner's Sons, 1921).
24. Elliott Roosevelt's scrapbook, T.R. Collection, Harvard.
25. *The Nation*, Feb. 14, 1878.

CHAPTER 6

1. *The New York World*, Feb. 15, 1878.
2. *The New York Tribune*, Feb. 18, 1878.
3. Peter Collier and David Horowitz, *The Roosevelts: An American Saga* (New York: Simon and Schuster, 1994), 52.
4. Ibid.
5. Letter dated Aug. 11, 1880, Theodore Roosevelt Collection, Houghton Library, Harvard University.
6. David McCullough, *Mornings on Horseback* (New York: Simon and Schuster, 1981), 228.
7. Ibid., 229.
8. Blanche Wiesen Cook, *Eleanor Roosevelt, Volume 1: 1884–1933* (New York: Penguin, 1993), 40.
9. McCullough, 228.
10. Collier and Horowitz, 25.
11. Quoted in Dale Carnegie, *How to Develop Self-Confidence and Influence People by Public Speaking* (New York: National Board of Young Men's Christian Associations, 1926), 101.
12. Collier and Horowitz, 61.

CHAPTER 7

1. Letter from John C. Newcomer of York Town Auction Inc. to Wallace F. Dailey of Harvard University, March 5, 1998, copied by Mr. Dailey for the author.
2. Anna Eleanor Roosevelt, ed., *Hunting Big Game in the 'Eighties: The Letters of Elliott Roosevelt, Sportsman* (New York: Charles Scribner's Sons, 1932), foreword.
3. Ibid., 33.
4. Elliott Roosevelt, *An Untold Story: The Roosevelts of Hyde Park* (New York: G.P. Putnam's Sons, 1973), 16.
5. Roosevelt, *Hunting Big Game,* 35.
6. Thomas Hughes, *Tom Brown's School Days, by an Old Boy* (Boston: Ginn and Company,

1918), 137. Originally published 1857.

7. Roosevelt. *Hunting Big Game*, 37.

8. Franklin D. Roosevelt Presidential Library.

9. Roosevelt, *Hunting Big Game*, 35.

10. Ibid., 36.

11. Ibid.

12. Anna Eleanor Roosevelt, *This is My Story* (New York: Harper and Brothers, 1937), 71.

13. Roosevelt, *Hunting Big Game*, 40.

14. Ibid., 43.

15. Ibid., 44–45.

16. Ibid., 46.

17. Ibid., 47.

18. Roosevelt, *Hunting Big Game*, 48.

19. Blanche Wiesen Cook, *Eleanor Roosevelt, Volume 1: 1884–1933* (New York: Penguin, 1993), 40.

20. Roosevelt, *Hunting Big Game*, 48.

21. Ibid.

22. Ibid., 48, 49.

23. Ibid., 48.

24. Ibid., 49.

25. Ibid., 50.

26. Ibid., 51.

27. Ibid., 51.

28. Ibid., 53.

29. Ibid., 54.

30. Ibid., 55.

31. Ibid., 56.

32. Ibid., 58.

33. Ibid.

34. David McCullough, *Mornings on Horseback* (New York: Simon and Schuster, 1981), 241.

CHAPTER 8

1. Lorena A. Hickok, *The Story of Eleanor Roosevelt* (New York: Grosset & Dunlap), 1959.

2. Anna Eleanor Roosevelt, ed., *Hunting Big Game in the 'Eighties: The Letters of Elliott Roosevelt, Sportsman* (New York: Charles Scribner's Sons, 1932), 61.

3. Ibid.

4. Blanche Wiesen Cook, *Eleanor Roosevelt, Volume 1: 1884–1933* (New York: Penguin, 1993), 41.

5. Roosevelt, *Hunting Big Game*, 64, 65.

6. Ibid., 65.

7. Ibid., 65.

8. Ibid., 72.

9. Ibid., 72.

10. Ibid., 75.

11. David McCullough, *Mornings on Horseback* (New York: Simon and Schuster, 1981), 240.

12. Letter dated Dec. 7, 1880, Franklin D. Roosevelt Presidential Library.

13. Ibid.

14. McCullough, 240.

15. Ibid., 76.

16. Ibid., 241.

17. Roosevelt, *Hunting Big Game*, 80.

18. Ibid.

19. Ibid., 83.

20. Ibid., 83.

21. Ibid., 85.

22. Undated letter, FDRL.

23. Letter dated Nov. 27, 1880, FDRL.

24. Letter dated Jan. 12, 1881(?), FDRL.

25. Laura Astor Delano, sister of William Backhouse Astor, husband of Caroline Schermerhorn Astor, arbiter of the New York social scene. Franklin D. Roosevelt was named for Laura's husband, his great-uncle Franklin Delano.

26. J. Coleman Drayton, from a distinguished family in South Carolina, married (and divorced) Charlotte Augusta Astor, a daughter of Mr. And Mrs. William Astor. Their divorce proceedings made sensational newspaper reading when Drayton challenged Hallet Alsop Borrowe, his rival for his wife's affections, to a duel. Borrowe fled to England. Charlotte followed him, and Drayton followed her. She divorced Drayton and settled in England, not with Borrowe but with her second husband George Ogilvy Haig, of Haig & Haig whiskey.

27. John Jacob Astor IV (1864–1912) and his first wife, Ava Lowle Willing. John Astor perished on the *Titanic*.

28. Harriette Louise Warren Goelet (d. 1913), sister of architect Whitney Warren.

29. Undated letter, FDRL.

30. Letter dated Thanksgiving Evening, 1880, FDRL.

31. Letter dated Dec. 5, (year?), FDRL.

32. "Robert Grant, novelist, essayist in the lighter vein, and Judge in the Probate Court of Suffolk, is appropriately in the heart of Boston's most cherished residential district, the Back Bay," reported Wilder D. Quint in *The New York Times* "Saturday Review of Books and Art" section, November 27, 1897. Grant, Harvard class of 1873, was "a Bostonian of the typical sort, cultivated, able, and intensely proud of the traditions of his native city."

Author of "The Little Tin God on Wheels," "The Confessions of a Frivolous Girl: A Story of Fashionable Life," and "The Reflections of a Married Man," he was "one of the wits, litterateurs and good fellows of the Hub." A "learned Justice of the Probate Court," his writing "generally includes some keen satire upon the foibles of modern life, sometimes not sparing the most cherished institutions of the city's fashionable set."

33. Undated letter, FDRL.

34. Ibid., letter dated Jan. 2, 1881.

35. William Backhouse Astor (1829–1892) was the grandson of the first John Jacob Astor (1763–1848), a German emigrant and the Astor dynasty patriarch. He was the husband of Caroline Webster Schermerhorn Astor; "the 400" were the members of "Society with a capitol S" who could fit in the Astor ballroom. His daughter Helen married James Roosevelt Roosevelt, half-brother of Franklin D. Roosevelt. William Astor died in England of heart failure while attempting to quell the scandal caused by another of his daughters, Charlotte Drayton.

36. Undated letter, FDRL.

37. Roosevelt, Hunting Big Game, 87.

38. Ibid., 89–94.

39. Ibid., 91.

40. Ibid., 91.

41. Undated letter, FDRL.

42. Ibid.

43. Ibid.

44. Letter dated August 7, 1881, FDRL.

45. Roosevelt, Hunting Big Game, 98.

46. Undated letter, FDRL.

47. Roosevelt, Hunting Big Game, 100.

48. Ibid., 101.

49. McCullough, 238.

50. Roosevelt, Hunting Big Game, 113.

51. Letter dated Dec. 10, 1880, FDRL.

52. McCullough, 243.

53. Ibid., 244.

54. Roosevelt, Hunting Big Game, 68–69.

55. McCullough, 244.

56. Letter dated Sept. 29, 1881, FDRL.

57. McCullough, 238.

58. Undated letter, FDRL.

59. McCullough, 241.

60. Joseph Lash, Eleanor and Franklin: The Story of Their Relationship (New York: Norton, 1971).

61. bms Am 1785.8 (479) *77m–69, Theodore Roosevelt Collection, Houghton Library, Harvard University.

62. McCullough, 242.

63. McCullough, 242–243.

64. McCullough, 241–242.

65. Undated letter, FDRL.

66. Letter dated Dec. 4, 1881, FDRL.

67. Letter dated Dec. 25, 1881, FDRL.

68. Letter dated Sept. 29, 1881, FDRL.

69. Undated letter, FDRL.

70. McCullough, 240.

71. Ibid., 243.

72. Ibid., 242.

73. Ibid., 245–246.

74. Ibid, 246.

CHAPTER 9

1. Peter Collier and David Horowitz, The Roosevelts: An American Saga (New York: Simon and Schuster, 1994), 62.

2. Anna Eleanor Roosevelt, This Is My Story (New York: Harper and Brothers, 1937), 4–5.

3. Elliott Roosevelt's scrapbook, Theodore Roosevelt Collection, Houghton Library, Harvard University.

4. Valentine Hall's Sunday school instruction book and pupil attendance record, courtesy of The Rev. Stephen Garmey, former Vicar of The Parish of Calvary/St. George's in the City of New York.

5. Joseph Lash, Eleanor and Franklin: The Story of Their Relationship (New York: Norton, 1971), 15.

6. To judge from his correspondence, The Rev. Dr. W.C.P. Rhoades was hardly the eccentric "pet clergyman" some historians have implied. He was extremely fond of the Halls and regarded Anna as particularly level-headed. Apparently he spent summers with the Halls, returning in the autumn to his parish in Granville, Ohio. He was idealistic and sincere: "My dear Sir, I have wished more than once that writing letters were your favorite pastime, but I know that it is not. It seems to me I have thought of you and yours more the last winter than ever before — and that is saying a great deal," he wrote to Valentine Hall. "I often wonder how you all are, and the children's letters are always welcome; have been looking for one from Anna for several weeks. It seems to me I would enjoy more than almost anything else tonight one of those long peripatetic conversations or discussions which we used to have at Tivoli. You know Tivoli is the only place where one feels

like a philosopher, especially in those after dinner meditations. My life is a much more unpretending one. I read and study and visit the sick and call on the well and receive calls from them, and I try to teach the wonderful truths of the wonderful Word and to get the people to study it more and follow it better. There are some very, very great pleasures in my life; and, of course, there are hours of dissatisfaction that I cannot do more work and do it better. Life means more to me than it used to, and the privilege of helping anyone to a better life seems more and more precious. ... I have just come from our young people's prayer meeting; about two hundred were there. It does me good every week. ..."
(Letter dated April 27, 1875)
"My dear friend, I have done a large day's work today, and now, at evening time, I wish I could have a walk and a talk with you, for I am lonesome. ... I am always glad to be unusually busy when I first return for it helps to drive away loneliness until I get used to loneliness. Last week I was away from Wednesday afternoon until Friday night at midnight. Our association, twelve or fifteen churches, met at Delaware, about twenty five miles north of Columbus ...there is a fine, cold sulphur spring there from which I drank a silent health to all at Tivoli. My church is the strongest working church in the association and I believe I am the youngest minister. ... I wish at times I could be old for you do not mind an old man's telling you how to do everything; and somehow I feel sure I know how to do many of these things better than they are generally done. We had good business meetings and I trust the missions work will be greatly prospered. There is much of such work indeed for in some country districts people grow up as ignorant of the Bible as the heathen are. Two aged members of my church died while I was away; one of them I had called to see every week for a long time; a mother could not be more solicitous for the health of an only son than she has been for mine; something made her take a special interest in me and I shall miss her hopeful Christian faith and godly conversation; she knew her Bible almost by heart and could recite hymn after hymn; she was as perfectly ready as one can be — so it has seemed to me — to go to the Father's house. I do not believe there is anything that endears people to one another like Christian life and Christian work. I found the tears coming and could scarcely check them several times at the hearty welcome which greeted me. What

pleasure can compare with that of knowing you have helped somebody toward a better life; it would be reward enough for even great sacrifice and continued toil. I want to do much personal work this year in addition to more earnest public teaching. There is so much to be thankful for; I was not at all well when I went away for my vacation. I came back perfectly well; no one ever had kinder, better friends and relatives; no life, it seems to me, could be more full of the tender mercies of God — and I do desire that my thanksgiving may be something more than mere words.

'Give me to walk with girded garments white;*
The understanding heart, to read
 aright
Thy word, Thy law, Thy will, my
 soul's delight, —
That I may be
More like Thyself, Lord Jesus, more
 like Thee!'"

(Letter dated September 11, 1876, Roosevelt Family Papers Donated by the Children, Franklin D. Roosevelt Presidential Library.)

Dr. Rhoades was appointed pastor of the Marcy Avenue Baptist Church in Brooklyn, New York, December 17, 1885 (*The New York Times*, December 18, 1885).

7. Jerry E. Patterson, *The First Four Hundred: Mrs. Astor's New York in the Gilded Age* (New York: Rizzoli International Publications, 2000), 112.

8. Lash, 15.

9. Ibid.

10. Ibid., 15–16.

11. J. William T. Youngs, *Eleanor Roosevelt: A Personal and Public Life* (Boston: Little, Brown and Company, 1985), 14.

12. Lash, 85–86.

13. Kenneth S. Davis, *FDR: The Beckoning of Destiny 1882–1928* (New York: G.P. Putnam's Sons, 1972), 178.

14. Ibid., 179.

15. Lash, 16.

16. Ibid., 17.

17. Louisa May Alcott, *Little Women* (New York: Grossett and Dunlap, 1947), 327. Originally, Boston: Thomas Niles, 1868.

18. Patterson, 39.

19. Lash, 17.

20. In an interview conducted in January 1941, Edith Carow Roosevelt stated, "Elliott's wife

was so pretty and so good and bore him so patiently. Elliott was a lovable person — had a great deal of charm. … He drank like a fish and ran after the ladies — I mean ladies not in his own rank, which was much worse. … Anna was a sincerely religious and good woman, something you don't often see. … I don't know who Eleanor looks like." Theodore Roosevelt Collection, Houghton Library, Harvard University.

21. Curiously, a lone dissenting voice comes from John Ellis Roosevelt, cousin "Jack" referred to in Elliott's adolescent correspondence. These observations were recorded in "short(ish) hand by Jean Schermerhorn Roosevelt, wife of P(hilip) James Roosevelt and daughter of John Ellis Roosevelt, October 13, 1936": "Elliott's wife was ugly, charmless, wondered why he married her. She made him play in with the fast Meadow Brook hunting set. Nannie [Vance Roosevelt, John Ellis's wife] did not like her. A bad likeness of Eleanor, and I'd hardly call that a baby-like countenance, would you? Was a real estate man's daughter in New York. Probably made quite a lot of money. Two or three sisters. Elliott drank too much on occasion, even on our hunting trip. J.E.R. remembers lunching at their house when Eleanor was a little girl in hair ribbons. Remembers thinking Eleanor a plain girl for a Roosevelt. Eleanor awfully sweet, very considerate. N.V.R. and J.E.R. often talked about it and thought Elliott would have been a great deal better man in a different atmosphere. They saw very little of him in the last five or six years of his life. Elliott had lots of falls from horses [while] hunting." T.R. Collection, Harvard.

22. Letter dated June 12, 1883, Eleanor Roosevelt Papers, Box 1, Folder 6, FDRL.

23. Lash, 17.

24. Ibid., 18.

25. Essay entitled "My Love," dated February 1883, Eleanor Roosevelt Papers, FDRL.

26. McCullough, 249.

27. Lash, 18.

28. Ibid.

29. Ibid.

30. Ibid., 18.

31. Letter dated August 22, 1883, E.R. Papers, Box 1, Folder 6, FDRL.

32. Letter dated October 2, 1883, FDRL.

33. Lash, 19.

34. Ibid.

35. Undated letter, Box 1, Folder 6, FDRL.

36. Francis Randall Appleton (1854–1929), Harvard 1875, was an attorney with Robbins and Appleton in New York City and an overseer of Harvard University. (Patterson, 207).

37. Lash, 19.

38. Undated letter, E.R. Papers, Box 1, Folder 6, FDRL.

39. Lash, 19.

40. Youngs, 16.

41. Letter dated October 3, 1883, E.R. Papers, Box 6, Folder 1, FDRL.

42. Lash, 19.

43. Youngs, 16.

44. Letter dated October 7, 1883, E.R. Papers, Box 6, Folder 1, FDRL.

45. Letter dated October 16, 1883, FDRL.

46. Letter dated October 17, 1883, FDRL.

47. Youngs, 17.

48. Ibid.

49. Ibid., 18.

50. Ibid.

51. Lash, 19.

52. Ibid.

53. Ibid., 20.

CHAPTER 10

1. Joseph Lash, *Eleanor and Franklin: The Story of Their Relationship* (New York, Norton, 1971), 20.

2. J. William T. Youngs, *Eleanor Roosevelt: A Personal and Public Life* (Boston, Little, Brown and Company, 1985), 19.

3. Letter dated Dec. 3, 1883, Franklin D. Roosevelt Presidential Library, Roosevelt Family Papers Donated by the Children.

4. David McCullough, *Mornings on Horseback* (New York: Simon and Schuster, 1981), 245.

5. Ibid.

6. Undated letter, Roosevelt Family Papers Donated by the Children, FDRL.

7. Theodore Douglas Robinson (1883–1934), son of Corinne Roosevelt and Douglas Robinson, served as Assistant Secretary of the Navy from November 11, 1924, until March 4, 1929. His marriage to Helen Rebecca Roosevelt (1881–1962), Franklin D. Roosevelt's niece (although they were contemporaries), marked the first wedding linking the Oyster Bay and Hyde Park Roosevelts. He died of pneumonia at the age of fifty-one.

8. Undated letter, Roosevelt Family Papers Donated by the Children, FDRL.

9. Ibid., letter dated Jan. 3, 1884, FDRL.

10. Ibid., letter dated Dec. 21, 1883, FDRL.

11. Ibid., undated letter, FDRL.

12. Ibid., letter dated July 11 1884(?), FDRL.

13. Ibid., letter dated Sept. 2, 1884. (Note: Anna Hall Roosevelt was not given to including the year when dating her correspondence; as in the preceding citation, 1884 is the author's surmise, based on the sequence of events.)

14. Ibid., letter dated Sept. 2, 1884 (?). *Late in life Winthrop Rutherfurd, who had courted Consuelo Vanderbilt before her arranged marriage to the Duke of Marlborough, became the husband of Lucy Mercer, long-time skeleton in the Roosevelt closet. See Arthur T. Vanderbilt II, *Fortune's Children: The Fall of the House of Vanderbilt* (New York: William Morrow and Company, 1989), and Joseph Persico, *Franklin and Lucy: Mrs. Rutherfurd and the Other Remarkable Women in Roosevelt's Life.* (New York: Random House, 2008).

15. Ibid., undated letter, FDRL.

16. Eric Homberger, *Mrs. Astor's New York: Money and Social Power in a Gilded Age* (New Haven, Conn.: Yale University Press, 2002.)

17. Lash, 21–22.

18. Youngs, 25.

19. The Theodore Roosevelt Collection at Houghton Library, Harvard University, contains the following letter by Mrs. James King Gracie (Elliott's Aunt Annie), dated March 25, 1884, and addressed to the infant Alice. It conveys vividly the family's tenderness and grief over the death of Alice and the birth of her daughter:

Alice Lee Roosevelt born Tuesday morning, February 12th, 1884, at half past eight o'clock at 6 West 57th Street. Her mother said when I took her from the doctor, "I love a little girl," because I said to the baby you ought to have been a little boy. I laid her all rolled up in flannel in a large armchair and went back to the bed side. She sneezed. Her mother said, "Dr. don't let my baby take cold." He said she is not taking cold. The little girl sneezed again and her sweet mother said, "Dr. you must attend to my baby." He said I always attend to the mother first. She said, "I suppose you know best." I left the sweet mother after all was settled for the night with the doctor and her own mother and went with the nurse and baby into the nursery to help get the sweet little girl washed and dressed and weighed. She weighed full 8¾ lbs. I made up the little bassinet with all the dainty pretty little things her sweet little mother had laid aside ready for her to sleep in. At eleven o'clock the baby's Grandmother Lee told me "Alice has had her child in her arms and kissed it."

Alice Hathaway Roosevelt died Thursday Feb 14th at 14 of 2 p.m. Her baby was baptized Sunday afternoon at 2:30 p.m. Her dear Father held her. She was baptized from the same silver bowl he and all the young uncles and aunts had been. The nurse who dressed her for the baptism happened to select … the little slip with the five tucks her sweet mother liked more than anything else I had given her.

The service was a beautiful consoling one. She had on a locket of her sweet mother's golden hair.

A sentence in Dr. Hall's prayer was that all her life he prayed God "comfort her as one whom his mother comforteth." This lock of hair and this little paper I wish the little girl to have if I die before she is old enough for me to tell her these few things. She is six weeks old today. I want her to know how her mother loved me, and trusted me. And how I loved her Mother. It is enough to say that from the moment her husband brought her here I never felt that I was childless. I loved her as my own child, and she knew it and loved me in return. Time lets some of these little details pass away from the memory, so I put down one or two only because they are too precious to be lost. I was with her dear Mother nearly all day and some time after the little girl was born, and she said so many lovely motherly things I wish the little girl always to know for it shows that she loved and longed for her sweet little daughter.

I too love you my sweet baby girl.

I am your own

Aunt Anna B. Gracie

20. McCullough, 283.

21. Harold I. Gullan, *First Fathers: The Men Who Inspired Our Presidents* (Hoboken, N.J.: John Wiley and Sons, 2004), 143.

22. Jean Edward Smith, *FDR* (New York: Random House, 2007), 39.

23. Letter dated Aug. 23, 1883, Franklin D. Roosevelt Library, Roosevelt Family Papers Donated by the Children.

24. Ibid., undated letter.

25. Ibid.

26. Ibid.

27. Ibid., letter dated July 7, 1883.

28. Ibid., undated letter.

29. Ibid.

30. Ibid.

31. McCullough, 64–65.

32. Letter dated Sept. 15, 1883, Roosevelt Family Papers Donated by the Children, FDRL.

33. Peter Collier and David Horowitz, *The Roosevelts: An American Saga* (New York: Simon and Schuster, 1994), 64.

34. Ibid., 65.

35. Geoffrey Ward, *A First-Class Temperament: The Emergence of Franklin Roosevelt 1905–1928* (New York: Harper and Row, 1989), 416. The following poem, clipped from a newspaper, is called "Psyche," by Virginia Moore. It was found among Eleanor Roosevelt's papers after she died.

> The soul that has believed
> And is deceived
> Thinks nothing for a while
> All thoughts are vile.
> And then because the sun
> Is mute persuasion,
> And hope in Spring and Fall
> Most natural,
> The soul grows calm and mild
> A little child,
> Finding the pull of breath
> Better than death …
> The soul that had believed
> And was deceived
> Ends by believing more
> Than ever before.

36. Youngs, 25.

CHAPTER 11

1. Jack Finney, *Time and Again* (New York: Simon and Schuster, 1970), 175–176.

2. Jack Finney, *Forgotten News: The Crime of the Century and Other Lost Stories* (New York: Simon and Schuster), 1986.

3. Joseph Lash, *Eleanor and Franklin: The Story of Their Relationship* (New York: Norton, 1971), 25.

4. Anna Eleanor Roosevelt, *This Is My Story* (New York: Harper and Brothers, 1937), 5.

5. Lash, 72.

6. Roosevelt, *This Is My Story*, 6.

7. Youngs, 26.

8. Charles Dickens, *The Old Curiosity Shop* (Mineola, N.Y.: Dover Publications, 2003), 438. (Originally published in 1841, serialized in *Master Humphrey's Clock*.)

9. Eleanor Roosevelt and Allida Black, ed., *What I Hope to Leave Behind: The Essential Essays of Eleanor Roosevelt* (Brooklyn, N.Y.: Carlson Publishing, 1995), 39.

10. Roosevelt, *This Is My Story*, 13.

11. Ibid., 6.

12. Jerry E. Patterson, *The First Four Hundred: Mrs. Astor's New York in the Gilded Age* (New York: Rizzoli International Publications, 2000), 12.

13. Ibid., 117–118.

14. Letter dated August, 8, 1885, Theodore Roosevelt Collection, Houghton Library, Harvard University.

15. Undated letter, Franklin D. Roosevelt Presidential Library, Roosevelt Family Papers Donated by the Children.

16. Roosevelt, *This Is My Story*, 15.

17. J. William T. Youngs, *Eleanor Roosevelt: A Personal and Public Life* (Boston: Little, Brown and Company, 1985), 27.

18. Lash, 28.

19. Roosevelt, *This Is My Story*, 6.

20. Blanche Wiesen Cook, *Eleanor Roosevelt, Volume 1: 1884–1933* (New York: Penguin, 1993), 70.

21. Peter Collier and David Horowitz, *The Roosevelts: An American Saga* (New York: Simon and Schuster, 1994), 81.

22. Ibid.

23. Elliott Roosevelt with James Brough, *An Untold Story: The Roosevelts of Hyde Park* (New York: G.P. Putnam's Sons, 1973), 14.

24. Roosevelt, *This Is My Story*, 5.

25. Letter dated August 8, 1885, Theodore Roosevelt Collection, Houghton Library, Harvard University.

26. Roosevelt and Brough, *An Untold Story*, 15.

27. Roosevelt, *This Is My Story*, 3.

28. Patterson, 221.

29. Roosevelt, *This Is My Story*, 4.

30. Youngs, 27.

31. Patterson, 225.

32. Ibid., 115.

33. Ibid.

34. Patterson, 116

35. Lash, 29–30.

36. Collier and Horowitz, 79.

37. Lash, 29.

38. Ibid., 29–30.

39. Roosevelt. *This Is My Story*, 7.

40. Cook, 49–50.

41. Ibid., 52.

42. David McCullough, *Mornings on Horseback* (New York: Simon and Schuster, 1981), 288.

43. Letter dated April 16, 1887, T.R. Collection, Harvard.

44. Ibid., letter dated September 13, 1887.

CHAPTER 12

1. Letter dated July 1, 1888, Theodore Roosevelt Collection, Houghton Library, Harvard University.

2. Ibid., letter dated June 24, 1888.

3. Ibid., letter dated July 30, 1888.

4. Blanche Wiesen Cook, *Eleanor Roosevelt, Volume 1: 1884–1933* (New York: Penguin, 1993), 51.

5. Letter dated August 5, 1888, T.R. Collection, Harvard.

6. J. William T. Youngs, *Eleanor Roosevelt: A Personal and Public Life* (Boston: Little, Brown and Company, 1985), 32.

7. Cook, 53.

8. Jerry Patterson, *The First Four Hundred: Mrs. Astor's New York in the Gilded Age* (New York: Rizzoli International Publications, 2000), 125.

9. Joseph Lash, *Eleanor and Franklin: The Story of Their Relationship* (New York: Norton, 1971), 32.

10. Cook, 53.

11. Letter dated "Thursday morning," T.R. Collection, Harvard.

12. Ibid., letter dated March 11, 1889.

13. Anna Eleanor Roosevelt, *This Is My Story* (New York: Harper and Brothers, 1937), 8.

14. Youngs, 27.

15. Cook, 46.

16. Letter dated "Saturday," 1889, Franklin D. Roosevelt Presidential Library.

17. Cook, 54.

18. Elliott Roosevelt and James Brough, *An Untold Story: The Roosevelts of Hyde Park* (New York: G. P. Putnam's Sons, 1973).

19. Letter dated June 17, 1888, T.R. Collection, Harvard.

20. Ibid., letter dated July 1, 1888.

21. Cook, 54.

22. Ibid., 55.

23. Letter dated April 24, 1890, T.R. Collection, Harvard.

24. Lash, 34.

25. Letter dated April 30, 1890, T.R. Collection, Harvard.

26. *Frank Leslie's Illustrated Newspaper*, October

12, 1889, Vertical File "Elliott Roosevelt 1860–1894," FDRL.

27. Cook, 57.

CHAPTER 13

1. Joseph Lash, *Eleanor and Franklin: The Story of Their Relationship* (New York: Norton, 1971), 34.

2. Anna Eleanor Roosevelt, *This Is My Story* (New York: Harper and Brothers, 1937), 10.

3. Lash.

4. Roosevelt, *This Is My Story*, 9.

5. Ibid.

6. *Look* magazine, March 1939, cited in Blanche Wiesen Cook, *Eleanor Roosevelt, Volume 1: 1884–1933* (New York: Penguin, 1993), 59.

7. Roosevelt, *This Is My Story*, 9.

8. Lash, 35.

9. Ibid.

10. Ibid.

11. J. William T. Youngs, *Eleanor Roosevelt: A Personal and Public Life* (Boston: Little, Brown and Company, 1985), 35–36.

12. Roosevelt, *This Is My Story*, 9.

13. Lash, 36.

14. Cook, 59.

15. Letter dated February 1, 1891, Theodore Roosevelt Collection, Houghton Library, Harvard University.

CHAPTER 14

1. Letter dated July 2, 1891, Theodore Roosevelt Collection, Houghton Library, Harvard University.

2. Edmund Morris, *The Rise of Theodore Roosevelt* (New York: Random House, 1979), 430.

3. Letter dated February 15, 1891, T.R. Collection, Harvard.

4. Morris, 437.

5. Letter dated May 10, 1891, T.R. Collection, Harvard.

6. Blanche Wiesen Cook, *Eleanor Roosevelt, Volume 1: 1884–1933* (New York: Penguin, 1993), 60.

7. Letter dated June 14, 1891, T.R. Collection, Harvard.

8. Sylvia Jukes Morris, *Edith Kermit Roosevelt: Portrait of a First Lady* (New York: Coward, McCann and Geoghegan, 1980), 142.

9. Letter dated June 14, 1891, T.R. Collection,

Harvard.

10. Ibid.

11. Morris, 439.

12. Letter dated June 26, 1891, T.R. Collection, Harvard.

13. Ibid.

14. Cook, 60.

15. Peter Collier and David Horowitz, *The Roosevelts: An American Saga* (New York: Simon and Schuster, 1994), 82.

16. Cook, 66.

17. Letter dated July 12, 1891, T.R. Collection, Harvard.

18. Letter undated, marked only "Private," "Sagamore Hill," T.R. Collection, Harvard.

19. Morris, 437.

20. Letter undated, marked only "Private," "Sagamore Hill," T.R. Collection, Harvard.

21. Ibid.

22. Morris, 431.

23. Letter dated March 20, 1891, T. R. Collection. Harvard.

24. Morris, 431.

25. Letter dated May 2, 1890, T.R. Collection, Harvard.

26. Letter dated March 20, 1891, T.R. Collection, Harvard.

27. Letter dated June 7, 1891, T.R. Collection, Harvard.

28. Letter dated June 14, 1891, T.R. Collection, Harvard.

29. Letter dated January 25, 1891, T.R. Collection, Harvard.

30. Cook, 61.

31. Letter dated May 2, 1890, T.R. Collection, Harvard.

32. Cook, 64.

33. Letter dated January 25, 1891, T.R. Collection, Harvard.

34. Letter dated May 29, 1891, T.R. Collection, Harvard.

35. Cook, 61.

36. Anna Eleanor Roosevelt, *This Is My Story* (New York, Harper and Brothers, 1937), 10.

37. Ibid., 11.

38. Cook, 62.

39. Roosevelt, *This Is My Story*, 11–12.

40. Ibid., 12.

41. Ibid.

42. Ibid., 17.

43. Cook, 64.

44. Letter dated July 12, 1891, T.R. Collection,

Harvard.

45. Cook, 63.

46. Letter dated January 25, 1891, T.R. Collection, Harvard.

47. Morris, 438.

48. Cook, 64.

49. Ibid., 62.

50. Letter dated December 24, 1890, T.R. Collection, Harvard.

51. Letter dated June 7, 1891, T.R. Collection, Harvard.

52. Letter dated June 17, 1891, T.R. Collection, Harvard.

53. Ibid.

54. Letter dated July 8, 1891, T.R. Collection, Harvard.

55. Letter dated July 21, 1891, T.R. Collection, Harvard.

56. Letter dated June 14, 1891, T.R. Collection, Harvard.

57. *The New York Sun*, August 17, 1891.

58. Letter dated August 19, 1891, T.R. Collection, Harvard.

59. Cook, 67.

60. Morris, 443.

61. Letter dated June 20, 1891, T.R. Collection, Harvard.

62. Letter dated August 19, 1891, T.R. Collection, Harvard.

63. Cook, 68.

64. Letter dated August 24, 1891, T.R. Collection, Harvard.

65. Letter dated June 20, 1891, T.R. Collection, Harvard.

66. Cook, 67.

67. Ibid.

68. Letter dated August 22, 1891, T.R. Collection, Harvard.

69. Letter dated October 28, 1891, T.R. Collection, Harvard.

70. Letter dated August 22, 1891, T.R. Collection, Harvard.

71. Letter dated August 24, 1891, T.R. Collection, Harvard.

72. Letter dated September 1, 1891, T.R. Collection, Harvard.

73. Letter dated August 19, 1891, T.R. Collection, Harvard.

74. Morris, 445.

75. Ibid.

76. Cook, 73.

77. Letter dated January 21, 1892, T.R. Collec-

tion, Harvard.

78. Undated letter, composed by Theodore Roosevelt at "1820 Jefferson St.", Washington, D.C., T.R. Collection, Harvard.

79. Undated letter, marked only "Private," T.R. Collection, Harvard.

80. Joseph Lash, *Eleanor and Franklin: The Story of Their Relationship* (New York: Norton, 1971), 38.

81. Ibid.

CHAPTER 15

1. Edmund Morris, *The Rise of Theodore Roosevelt* (New York: Random House, 1979).

2. William L. White, *Slaying the Dragon: The History of Addiction Treatment and Recovery in America* (Bloomington, Il.: Chestnut Health Systems/Lighthouse Institute, 1998), 3–8.

3. Blanche Wiesen Cook, *Eleanor Roosevelt, Volume 1: 1884–1933* (New York: Penguin, 1933), 76.

4. White, op. cit.

5. Cook, 75.

6. Betty Boyd Caroli, *The Roosevelt Women* (New York: Basic Books, 1998), 242.

7. Joseph Lash, *Eleanor and Franklin: The Story of Their Relationship* (New York: Norton, 1971), 39.

8. *Richmond Times-Dispatch*, "When a Roosevelt Found Health in Virginia Hills," by Goodridge Wilson, February 24, 1935, Vertical File "Elliott Roosevelt 1850–1894." See also original manuscript "Roosevelts in Virginia," Franklin D. Roosevelt Presidential Library, Roosevelt Family Papers Donated by the Children.

9. J. William T. Youngs, *Eleanor Roosevelt: A Personal and Public Life* (Boston: Little, Brown and Company, 1985), 37.

10. Lash, 40.

11. Ibid.

12. Goodridge Wilson, op.cit.

13. Lash, 39.

14. Cook, 76.

15. Lash, 40.

16. Ibid.

17. Ibid.

18. Youngs, 38.

19. Ibid.

20. Cook, 76.

21. Ibid.

22. Undated letter, FDRL.

23. Youngs, 38.

24. Letter dated March 18, 1892, Theodore Roosevelt Collection, Houghton Library, Harvard University.

25. Youngs, 38.

26. Ibid.

27. Anna Eleanor Roosevelt, *This Is My Story* (New York: Harper and Brothers, 1937),

28. Lash, 52.

29. Lash, 43.

30. Undated letter, Elliott Roosevelt to Mrs. Lloyd, FDRL.

31. Goodridge Wilson, op. cit.

32. Ibid.

33. Cook, 69.

34. Roosevelt, *This Is My Story*, 17.

35. Ibid., 16.

36. Lash, 40.

37. Ibid.

38. Ibid, 41.

39. Roosevelt, *This Is My Story*, 17.

40. Lash, 41.

41. Youngs, 40.

42. Youngs, 41.

43. Ibid, 42.

44. Lash, 42–43.

45. Ibid.

46. Cook, 77.

47. Lash, 44.

48. Cook, 78.

49. Ibid.

50. Lash, 44.

51. Cook, 78.

52. William Turner Levy, *The Extraordinary Mrs. R: A Friend Remembers Eleanor Roosevelt* (Hoboken, N.J.: John Wiley & Sons, 2001), 142.

CHAPTER 16

1. Unidentified newspaper clippings, Vertical File "Elliott Roosevelt 1860–1894," Franklin D. Roosevelt Presidential Library.

2. Blanche Wiesen Cook, *Eleanor Roosevelt, Volume 1: 1884–1933* (New York: Penguin, 1993), 81.

3. Anna Eleanor Roosevelt, *This Is My Story* (New York: Harper and Brothers, 1937).

4. Joseph Lash, *Eleanor and Franklin: The Story of Their Relationship* (New York: Norton, 1971), 44–45.

5. Letter dated March 4, 1893, Eleanor Roosevelt Papers, FDRL.

6. Roosevelt, *This is My Story*, 20–21.

7. Ibid., 22.

8. J. William T. Youngs, *Eleanor Roosevelt: A Personal and Public Life* (Boston: Little, Brown and Company, 1985), 44–45.

9. Letter from Mrs. James D. Bulloch, dated only September 21, estimated between 1902–1904, Box 1, Folder 1, E.R. Papers, FDRL.

10. Undated letter, E.R. Papers, FDRL.

11. Ibid.

12. Ibid., letter dated "Sunday Eve," 1892.

13. Ibid., letter dated March 4, 1893.

14. Ibid., letter dated January 23, 1893.

15. Ibid., letter undated.

16. Ibid., letter dated "Sunday Eve," 1892.

17. Ibid., letter dated April 20, 1893.

18. Ibid., letter dated "Sunday Eve," 1892.

19. Letter dated April 26, 1891, Theodore Roosevelt Collection, Houghton Library, Harvard University.

20. Ibid., letter dated May 15, 1891.

21. Letter dated March 4, 1893, E.R. Papers, FDRL.

22. Letter dated September 21, 1902–04(?), Box 1, Folder 1, E.R. Papers, FDRL.

23. Ibid., undated letter.

CHAPTER 17

1. Letter dated September 22, 1922, Theodore Roosevelt Collection, Houghton Library, Harvard University.

2. Blanche Wiesen Cook, *Eleanor Roosevelt, Volume 1: 1884–1933* (New York: Penguin, 1993), 87.

3. Joseph Lash, *Eleanor and Franklin: The Story of Their Relationship* (New York: Norton, 1971), 46.

4. Ibid.

5. Ibid., 47–48.

6. Ibid.

7. Ibid., 48.

8. Ibid., 42.

9. Ibid., 48–49.

10. Ted Morgan, *FDR: A Biography* (New York: Simon and Schuster, 1985), 94.

11. Lash, 49.

12. Cook, 84.

13. Peter Collier and David Horowitz, *The Roosevelts: An American Saga* (New York: Simon and Schuster, 1994), 468.

14. J. William T. Youngs, *Eleanor Roosevelt: A Personal and Public Life* (Boston: Little, Brown and Company, 1985), 45.

15. Ibid.

16. Letter dated June 2, 1893, Franklin D. Roosevelt Presidential Library.

17. Ibid., letter dated May 26, 1893.

18. Ibid., letter dated June 11, 1893.

19. Ibid., undated letter.

20. Ibid., letter dated June 8, 1893.

21. Ibid., letter dated June 14, 1893.

22. Ibid., letter dated June 5, 1893.

23. Ibid., letter dated May 28, 1893.

24. Ibid., letter dated May 29, 1893.

25. Ibid., letter dated "Friday, Sagamore Hill."

26. Ibid., Western Union telegram, May 24, 1893.

27. Ibid., Western Union telegram, May 27, 1893.

28. Ibid., undated letter.

29. Ibid., letter dated May 27, 1893.

30. Ibid., Letter written at "Gracewood," dated May 28, 1893.

31. Letter dated June 7, 1893, T.R. Collection, Harvard.

32. Ibid., letter dated June 9, 1893.

33. Betty Boyd Caroli, *The Roosevelt Women* (New York: Basic Books, 1998), 243.

34. Lash, 50–51.

35. Undated letter, FDRL.

36. Cook, 512*n*.

37. Ibid., 85.

38. Youngs, 46–48.

39. Cook, 83.

40. Lash, 46.

41. Undated letter, FDRL.

42. Geoffrey Ward, *Before the Trumpet: Young Franklin Roosevelt 1882–1905* (New York: Harper and Row, 1985).

43. Lash, 51.

44. Ibid.

45. Cook, 86.

46. Lash, 52.

47. Alfred Steinberg, *Mrs. R.: The Life of Eleanor Roosevelt* (New York: G. P. Putnam's Sons, 1958), 27.

48. Cook, 86–87.

49. Lorena Hickok, *The Story of Eleanor Roosevelt* (New York: Grosset & Dunlap, 1959), 27–28.

50. Lash, 65.

51. Ibid., 51–52.

52. Ibid., 53.

53. Ibid., 54–55.
54. Ibid., 55.
55. Youngs, 49.
56. Ibid.
57. Cook, 87.
58. Youngs, 48.
59. Collier and Horowitz, 87.
60. Cook, 92.
61. Collier and Horowitz, 87.
62. Cook, 88.
63. Caroli, 243.
64. Cook, 88.
65. Corinne Roosevelt Robinson, *My Brother Theodore Roosevelt* (New York: Charles Scribner's Sons, 1921), 156.
66. Cook, 88.
67. Letter dated August 18, 1894, T.R. Collection, Harvard.
68. Cook, 88.

CHAPTER 18

1. Alfred Steinberg, *Mrs. R.: The Life of Eleanor Roosevelt* (New York: G. P. Putnam's Sons, 1958), 28.
2. Blanche Wiesen Cook, *Eleanor Roosevelt, Volume 1: 1884–1933* (New York: Penguin, 1993), 91–92.
3. Theodore Roosevelt Collection, Houghton Library, Harvard University.
4. Undated letter, Corinne Robinson to Susan Elliott, T.R. Collection, Harvard.
5. Cook, 88.
6. Undated letter, Corinne Robinson to Susan Elliott, T.R. Collection, Harvard.
7. Authorship of letter unclear, T.R. Collection, Harvard.
8. *The New York World*, Aug. 16, 1894.
9. Quoted in Joseph Lash, *Eleanor and Franklin: The Story of Their Relationship* (New York: Norton, 1971), 56.
10. Cook, 89.
11. Ibid.
12. Ibid.
13. Letter dated Aug. 22, 1894, Eleanor Roosevelt Papers, Franklin D. Roosevelt Presidential Library.
14. Cook, 89–90.
15. Letter written from "Henderson Home," September 4, 1894, T.R. Collection, Harvard.
16. Cook, 90.
17. J. William T. Youngs, *Eleanor Roosevelt: A Personal and Public Life* (Boston: Little, Brown and Company, 1985), 49.
18. Cook, 91.
19. Ibid.
20. Letter dated July 7, 1896, FDRL.
21. Ibid.
22. Cook, 91.
23. Ibid., 513*n*.
24. Corinne Robinson to Susan Elliott, undated letter, T.R. Collection, Harvard.
25. Ibid.
26. Lash, 56.
27. Undated letter, T.R. Collection, Harvard.
28. John S. Elliott to Helena Elliott, letter dated August 31, 1894, T.R. Collection, Harvard.
29. John S. Elliott to Helena Elliott, letter dated September 13, 1894, T.R. Collection, Harvard.
30. Cook, 88.
31. Sylvia Jukes Morris, *Edith Kermit Roosevelt: Portrait of a First Lady* (New York: Coward-McCann and Geohegan, 1980), 143, 144.

CONCLUSION

1. Blanche Wiesen Cook, *Eleanor Roosevelt, Volume 1: 1884–1933* (New York: Penguin, 1993), 55.
2. Jerry Patterson, *The First Four Hundred: Mrs. Astor's New York in the Gilded Age* (New York: Rizzoli International Publications, 2000), 147.
3. Ibid., 149.
4. Elyce Wakerman, *Father Loss: Daughters Discuss the Man That Got Away* (New York: Henry Holt and Co., 1987), 270.
5. David Frum, *How We Got Here: The '70s: The Decade That Brought You Modern Life—For Better or Worse* (New York: Basic Books, 2000), 155.
6. George F. Will, "A Choice of Three," *The Washington Post*, March 8, 2007.
7. Edmund Morris, *Theodore Rex* (New York, Random House, 2001), 450.
8. Paul M. Angle and Earl Schenk Miers, *The Living Lincoln: The Man, His Mind, His Times, and the War He Fought* (New Brunswick, N.J.: Rutgers University Press, 1955; reprint, Barnes & Noble Books, 1992), 54.
9. Blanche Wiesen Cook, *Eleanor Roosevelt, Volume II: The Defining Years, 1933–1938* (New York: Penguin Books, 1999), 217.
10. Hazel Rowley, *Franklin and Eleanor: An Extraordinary Marriage* (New York: Farrar, Straus and Giroux, 2010), 13.

11. Anna Eleanor Roosevelt, *This Is My Story* (New York: Harper and Brothers, 1937), 362–363.

12. Charles Dickens, *The Old Curiosity Shop* (Mineola, N.Y: Dover Publications, 2003), 330. Originally published 1841.

AFTERWORD

1. Christian F. Reisner, *Roosevelt's Religion* (New York: The Abingdon Press, 1922), 298.

2. Ibid.

3. Ibid., 299.

4. Ibid., 300.

5. Ibid.

6. Ibid., 301.

7. Ibid., 302.

8. *The New York Times*, Sept. 26, 1941.

9. Ibid.

10. James Roosevelt, *My Parents: A Differing View* (Playboy Press, 1976), 14.

11. "My Day," September 26, 1941.

12. Joseph Lash, *Eleanor and Franklin: The Story of Their Relationship* (New York: Norton, 1971), 60.

13. Alfred Steinberg, *Mrs. R.: The Life of Eleanor Roosevelt* (New York: G.P. Putnam's Sons, 1958), 170.

14. Maureen Hoffman Beasley, Holly Cowan Shulman, and Henry R. Beasley, eds., *The Eleanor Roosevelt Encyclopedia* (Westport, Ct.: Greenwood Press, 2001), 458.

15. March 9, 1908, Franklin D. Roosevelt Presidential Library, Roosevelt Family Papers Donated by the Children, Box 19, Folder 5.

16. Ibid., May 9, 1908.

17. Ibid., April 30, 1908.

18. Ibid., spring 1908.

19. March 3, 1915, Roosevelt Family Papers Donated by the Children, Box 3, Folder 10, FDRL.

20. "My Day," September 26, 1941.

21. Steinberg, 171.

22. *The New York Times*, September 26, 1941.

23. Ibid.

24. Joseph Lash, *Eleanor Roosevelt: A Friend's Memoir* (New York: Doubleday, 1964).

25. Steinberg, 281.

26. Ibid., 105–106.

27. Eleanor Roosevelt, II, *With Love, Aunt Eleanor: Stories from My Life with the First Lady of the World* (Petaluma, Calif.: Scrapbook Press, 2004), 51.

28. *The New York Times*, September 26, 1941.

29. Jan. 5, 1921, FDR Family, Business and Personal Papers, Box 5, FDRL.

30. May 20, 1921, FDR Family, Business and Personal Papers, Box 5, FDRL.

31. Nov. 9, 1932, Eleanor Roosevelt Papers, Box 3, FDRL.

32. Letter dated Aug. 18, 1924, from Thomas Stokes of Philadelphia to Franklin D. Roosevelt, FDR Family, Business and Personal Papers, Box 5, FDRL.

33. Steinberg, 170.

34. Ibid.

35. March 29, 1932, E.R. Papers, Box 3, FDRL.

36. Franklin D. Roosevelt Papers as President, President's Secretaries' File, Box 162, FDRL.

37. January 22, 1934, President's Personal File, Box 285, FDRL.

38. Ibid., June 30, 1933.

39. President's Personal File, Box 285, FDRL.

40. Stephen T. Early Papers, FDRL.

41. Letter from Jesse H. Jones, Chairman of Reconstruction Finance Corporation, to G. Hall Roosevelt, July 19, 1934, President's Personal File, Box 281–289, 1933–1938, FDRL.

42. President's Personal File, Box, 285, FDRL.

43. Mrs. Roosevelt refers here to Kipling's story, "The Cat That Walked by Himself," in which the character Wild Cat, unlike Wild Dog, refuses to befriend humans and be of service to them. Wild Cat "went back through the Wet Wild Woods waving his wild tail, and walking by his wild lone." Rudyard Kipling, *Just So Stories for Little Children* (New York: Doubleday, Page & Company, 1902), 14.

44. Letter dated August 19, 1930, Dorothy Kemp Roosevelt Papers, Box 1, FDRL.

45. Ibid., letter dated May 6, 1932, Box 1, Folder 2, FDRL.

46. Ibid., letter dated March 29, 1931.

47. Ibid., letter dated March 29, 1931.

48. Ibid., letter dated Feb. 12, 1933.

49. Ibid., letter dated Dec. 3, 1931.

50. Letter dated Nov. 25, 1942, Dorothy Kemp Roosevelt Papers, Box 1, Folder 4, FDRL.

51. Steinberg, 281.

52. President's Personal File, Box 285, FDRL.

53. James Roosevelt, *My Parents: A Differing View*, 14–15.

54. Telegram dated Dec. 26, 1939, President's Personal File, Box 285, FDR Papers, FDRL.

55. "My Day," September 26, 1941.

56. James Roosevelt, *My Parents: A Differing View*, 14.

57. Aug. 19, 1938, concerning letter from B. McKenna of Detroit, President's Personal File, Box 285, FDRL.

58. Richard Sanders Allen, unpublished article, "Hall Roosevelt and the 100-Plane Deal," Vertical File, G. Hall Roosevelt, 1891–1941, FDRL.

59. Steinberg, 224.

60. Sept. 1, 1939, President's Personal File, Box 285, FDRL.

61. *Poughkeepsie Evening Star*, March 30, 1940, FDR Papers as President, President's Secretaries' File, Box 62, FDRL.

62. April 11, 1940, President's Personal File, Box 285, FDRL.

63. Eleanor Roosevelt Papers, Box 700, FDRL.

64. Sanders article, Vertical File, G. Hall Roosevelt, 1891–1941, FDRL.

65. Steinberg, 281.

66. Letter dated September 11, 1941, Stephen T. Early Papers, FDRL.

67. Telegram dated September 8, 1941, Stephen T. Early Papers, FDRL.

68. Roosevelt Family Papers Donated by the Children, Box 19, Folder 11, FDRL.

69. Lash, *Eleanor and Franklin*, 643.

70. "My Day," September 26, 1941.

71. David B. Roosevelt and Manuela Dunn Mascetti, *Grandmere: A Personal History of Eleanor Roosevelt* (New York, Warner Books, 2002), 173–174.

72. Western Union telegram, September 25, 1941, Dorothy Kemp Roosevelt Papers, Box 1, Folder 2, FDRL.

73. Eleanor Roosevelt, II, *With Love, Aunt Eleanor*, 53.

74. *The New York Times*, September 28, 1941.

75. Eleanor Roosevelt, II, "Before I Forget," June 29, 1999, Vertical File, FDRL.

76. Ibid.

77. Eleanor Roosevelt, II, *With Love, Aunt Eleanor*, 52.

78. "My Day," September 26, 1941.

79. Beasley, Shulman and Beasley, *The Eleanor Roosevelt Encyclopedia*, 459.

80. Eleanor Roosevelt, II, *With Love, Aunt Eleanor*, 50.

81. Ibid., 53.

82. Eleanor Roosevelt, II, "Before I Forget," July 8, 1999, Vertical File, FDRL.

83. E.R. to Dorothy Kemp Roosevelt, Sept. 12, 1930, Dorothy Kemp Roosevelt Papers, Container 1, FDRL.

84. March 18, 1942, President's Personal File, Box 285, FDRL.

85. Steinberg, 79.

86. Ibid.

87. John Allen Gable, ed., "The Roosevelt Family in America: A Genealogy," *Theodore Roosevelt Association Journal*, Spring 1990, p. 2, p. 62.

88. Blanche Wiesen Cook, *Eleanor Roosevelt, Volume 1: 1884–1933* (New York: Penguin, 1993), 65.

89. Ibid., 65.

90. Ibid., 510n.

91. Letter dated January 12, 1941, FDRL.

92. Undated letter, FDRL.

93. Cook, 249.

94. Steinberg, 36.

95. Ibid., 41.

96. Ibid.

97. Cook, 163.

98. Eleanor Roosevelt, *This Is My Story*, 360.

99. Cook, 263–264.

100. Steinberg, 42.

101. Undated letter from Mrs. Lewis Thomas to Eleanor Roosevelt, quoted in "Before I Forget," June 8, 1999, Vertical File, FDRL.

102. Peter Collier and David Horowitz, *The Roosevelts: An American Saga* (New York: Simon and Schuster, 1994), 104.

103. Ibid.

104. "My Day," January 13, 1941.

105. Collier and Horowitz, 299.

106. Ibid., 274.

107. David McCullough, *Mornings on Horseback* (New York: Simon and Schuster, 1981), 362.

108. Cook, 90–91.

109. Ibid., 513n.

110. Letter dated March 23, 1894, Theodore Roosevelt Collection, Houghton Library, Harvard University.

111. "My Day," January 13, 1941.

112. Blanche Wiesen Cook, *Eleanor Roosevelt: Volume II. The Defining Years, 1933–1938* (New York: Penguin Books, 1999), 20.

113. Betty Boyd Caroli, *The Roosevelt Women* (New York: Basic Books, 1998), 181.

114. Ibid.

115. Cook, *Eleanor Roosevelt, Volume 1: 1882–1933*, 92.

116. Edith C. Roosevelt to Emily T. Carow, undated letter, T.R. Collection, Harvard.

117. Cook, *Eleanor Roosevelt, Volume 1: 1882–*

1933, photo insert.

118. Collier and Horowitz, 299.

119. Cook, *Eleanor Roosevelt: Volume II*, 10.

120. Joseph Lash, *Eleanor and Franklin: The Story of Their Relationship* (New York: Norton, 1971), 57.

121. Ibid., 59.

122. Ibid.

123. Ibid., 59.

124. Ibid., 68.

125. Ibid., 729*n*.

126. Ibid., 729*n*.

127. Ibid., 82.

128. J. William T. Youngs, *Eleanor Roosevelt: A Personal and Public Life* (Boston: Little, Brown and Company, 1985), 52.

129. Ibid., 53.

130. Cook, *Eleanor Roosevelt: Volume II*, 26.

131. Ibid., 23.

132. Ibid., 216.

133. Virginia Bristol, *Herald Courier*, August 12, 1933, Vertical File "Elliott Roosevelt 1860–1894," FDRL.

134. Beasley, Shulman and Beasley, *The Eleanor Roosevelt Encyclopedia*, 422.

135. Ibid.

136. Ibid.

137. Beasley, Shulman and Beasley, 423.

138. Cook, *Eleanor Roosevelt: Volume II*, 25.

139. Elliott Roosevelt and James Brough, *Mother R: Eleanor Roosevelt's Untold Story* (New York: G.P. Putnam's Sons, 1977), 175.

140. "My Day," August 13, 1958.

141. Joseph P. Lash, *Eleanor: The Years Alone* (New York: W.W. Norton & Co., 1972), 201.

142. Anna Eleanor Roosevelt, *India and the Awakening East* (New York: Harper and Brothers, 1953), 171.

143. Ibid., 169–170.

144. "My Day," March 22, 1952.

145. Roosevelt and Brough, *Mother R.*, 192.

⚞ BIBLIOGRAPHY ⚟

146. *Detroit Free Press*, November 8, 1962, Dorothy Kemp Roosevelt Papers, Box 12, Folder 1, FDRL.

147. Ibid.

Alcott, Louisa May. *Little Women*. New York: Grossett and Dunlap, 1947 (originally, Boston: Thomas Niles, 1868).

Anderson, Robert. *I Never Sang for My Father*. New York: Random House, 1968.

Angle, Paul M., and Earl Schenck Miers. *The Living Lincoln: The Man, His Mind, His Times, and the War He Fought*. New Brunswick, N.J.: Rutgers University Press, 1955 (reprinted by Barnes & Noble Books, 1992).

Beasley, Maureen Hoffman, Holly Cowan Shulman, and Henry R. Beasley, editors. *The Eleanor Roosevelt Encyclopedia*. Westport, Conn.: Greenwich Press, 2001.

Bishop, Joseph Bucklin. *Theodore Roosevelt and His Times, Shown in His Own Letters*. New York: Charles Scribner's Sons, 1920.

Brands, H.W. *Traitor to His Class: The Privileged Life and Radical Presidency of Franklin D. Roosevelt*. New York: Doubleday, 2008.

Carnegie, Dale. *How to Develop Self-Confidence and Influence People by Public Speaking*. New York: National Board of Young Men's Christian Associations, 1926.

Caroli, Betty Boyd. *The Roosevelt Women*. New York: Basic Books, 1998.

Collier, Peter, and David Horowitz. *The Roosevelts: An American Saga*. New York: Simon and Schuster, 1994.

Cook, Blanche Wiesen. *Eleanor Roosevelt, Volume 1: 1884–1933*. New York: Penguin Books, 1993.

———. *Eleanor Roosevelt: Volume II, The Defining Years, 1933–1938*. New York: Penguin Books, 1999.

Davis, Kenneth S. *FDR: The Beckoning of Destiny 1882–1928*. New York: G.P. Putnam's Sons, 1972.

Dickens, Charles. *The Old Curiosity Shop*. Mineola, N.Y.: Dover Publications,

2003 (originally published in 1841, serialized in *Master Humphrey's Clock*).

Finney, Jack. *Forgotten News: The Crime of the Century and Other Lost Stories*. New York: Simon and Schuster, 1986.

———. *Time and Again*. New York: Simon and Schuster, 1986.

Frum, David. *How We Got Here: The '70s: The Decade that Brought You Modern Life — for Better or Worse*. New York: Basic Books, 2000.

Glendon, Mary Ann. *A World Made New: Eleanor Roosevelt and the Universal Declaration of Human Rights*. New York: Random House, 2002.

———. *The Forum and the Tower: How Scholars and Politicians Have Imagined the World from Plato to Eleanor Roosevelt*. New York: Oxford University Press, 2011.

Gullan, Harold I. *Faith of Our Mothers: The Story of Presidential Mothers from Mary Washington to Barbara Bush*. Grand Rapids, Mich.: William B. Eerdman's Publishing Company, 2001.

———. *First Fathers: The Men Who Inspired Our Presidents*. Hoboken, N.J.: John Wiley & Sons, 2004.

Hemingway, Ernest. *A Farewell to Arms*. New York: Scribner's, 1929.

Hickok, Lorena A. *The Story of Eleanor Roosevelt*. New York: Grosset & Dunlap, 1959.

Homberger, Eric. *Mrs. Astor's New York: Money and Social Power in a Gilded Age*. New Haven, Conn.: Yale University Press, 2002.

Hughes, Thomas. *Tom Brown's School Days, by an Old Boy*. Boston: Ginn and Company, 1918 (originally published 1857).

Johnson, Vernon E. *Intervention: How to Help Someone Who Doesn't Want Help*. New York: New American Library, 1988.

Kipling, Rudyard. *Just So Stories for Little Children*. New York: Doubleday, Page and Company, 1902.

Lash, Joseph P. *Eleanor and Franklin: The Story of Their Relationship*. New York: W.W. Norton & Co., 1971.

———. *Eleanor Roosevelt: A Friend's Memoir*. Garden City, N.Y.: Doubleday, 1964.

———. *Eleanor: The Years Alone*. New York: W.W. Norton & Co., 1972.

Levy, William Turner. *The Extraordinary Mrs. R.: A Friend Remembers Eleanor Roosevelt*. Hoboken, N.J.: John Wiley & Sons, 2001.

McCullough, David. *Mornings on Horseback*. New York: Simon and Schuster, 1981.

Miller, Nathan. *The Roosevelt Chronicles*. Garden City, N.Y.: Doubleday and Co., 1979.

Morgan, Ted. *FDR: A Biography*. New York: Simon and Schuster, 1985.

Morris, Edmund. *The Rise of Theodore Roosevelt*. New York: Random House, 1979.

———. *Theodore Rex*. New York: Random House, 2001.

Morris, Sylvia Jukes. *Edith Kermit Roosevelt: Portrait of a First Lady*. New York: Coward, McCann, and Geoghegan, 1980.

Patterson, Jerry E. *The First Four Hundred: Mrs. Astor's New York in the Gilded Age*. New York: Rizzoli International Publications, 2000.

Persico, Joseph. *Franklin and Lucy: Mrs. Rutherfurd and the Other Remarkable Women in Roosevelt's Life*. New York: Random House, 2008.

Pottker, Jan. *Sara and Eleanor: The Story of Sara Delano Roosevelt and Her Daughter-in-Law, Eleanor Roosevelt*. New York: St. Martin's Press, 2005.

Putnam, Carlton. *Theodore Roosevelt: The Formative Years 1858–1886*. New York: Charles Scribner's Sons, 1958.

Reid, Captain Mayne. *The Rifle Rangers: A Thrilling Story of Daring Adventure and Hairbreadth Escapes During the Mexican War*. Hurst & Company, 1899 (originally published 1850).

———. *The Young Yagers, a Narrative of Hunting Adventures in Southern Africa*. Boston: Ticknor and Fields, 1857.

Reisner, Christian F. *Roosevelt's Religion*. New York: The Abingdon Press, 1922.

Rixey, Lillian. *Bamie: Theodore Roosevelt's Remarkable Sister*. New York: David McKay Company, 1963.

Robinson, Corinne Roosevelt. *My Brother Theodore Roosevelt*. New York: Charles Scribner's Sons, 1921.

Roosevelt, Anna Eleanor, editor. *Hunting Big Game in the 'Eighties: The Letters of Elliott Roosevelt, Sportsman*. New York: Charles Scribner's Sons, 1933.

———. *India and the Awakening East*. New York: Harper and Brothers, 1953.

———. *This Is My Story*. New York: Harper and Brothers, 1937.

Roosevelt, David B., and Manuela Mascetti. *Grandmere: A Personal History of Eleanor Roosevelt*. New York: Warner Books, 2002.

Roosevelt, Eleanor, and Allida Black, ed. *What I Hope to Leave Behind: The Essential Essays of Eleanor Roosevelt*. Brooklyn, N.Y.: Carlson Publishing, 1995.

Roosevelt, Eleanor II. *With Love, Aunt Eleanor: Stories of My Life with the First Lady of the World.* Petaluma, Calif.: Scrapbook Press, 2004.

Roosevelt, Elliott, and James Brough. *An Untold Story: The Roosevelts of Hyde Park.* New York: G.P. Putnam's Sons, 1973.

———. *Mother R.: Eleanor Roosevelt's Untold Story.* New York: G.P. Putnam's Sons, 1977.

Roosevelt, James, with Bill Libby. *My Parents: A Differing View.* Playboy Press, 1976.

Roosevelt, Theodore. *Theodore Roosevelt's Diaries of Boyhood and Youth.* New York: Charles Scribner's Sons, 1928.

Rowley, Hazel. *Franklin and Eleanor: An Extraordinary Marriage.* New York: Farrar, Strauss and Giroux, 2010.

Smith, Jean Edward. *FDR.* New York: Random House, 2007.

Steinberg, Alfred. *Mrs. R.: The Life of Eleanor Roosevelt.* New York: G.P. Putnam's Sons, 1958.

Teague, Michael. *Mrs. L.: Conversations with Alice Roosevelt Longworth.* Garden City, N.Y.: Doubleday & Company, 1981.

Vaillant, George. *The Natural History of Alcoholism: Causes, Patterns, and Paths to Recovery.* Cambridge, Mass.: Harvard University Press, 1985.

Vanderbilt, Arthur T. *Fortune's Children: The Fall of the House of Vanderbilt.* New York: William Morrow & Company, 1989.

Wakerman, Elyce. *Father Loss: Daughters Discuss the Man that Got Away.* New York: Henry Holt & Company, 1987.

Ward, Geoffrey C. *Before the Trumpet: Young Franklin Roosevelt 1882–1905.* New York: Harper and Row, 1985.

———. *A First-Class Temperament: The Emergence of Franklin Roosevelt 1905–1928.* New York: Harper and Row, 1989.

White, William L. *Slaying the Dragon: The History of Addiction Treatment and Recovery in America.* Bloomington, Ill.: Chestnut Health Systems/Lighthouse Institute, 1998.

Wilson, Walter E. *The Bulloch Belles: Three First Ladies, A Spy, A President's Mother and Other Women of a Nineteenth-Century Georgia Family.* Jefferson, N.C.: McFarland and Company, 2015.

Youngs, J. William T. *Eleanor Roosevelt: A Personal and Public Life.* Boston: Little, Brown and Company, 1985.

❧ INDEX ❧

Y

❧ ABOUT THE AUTHOR ❧

Geraldine Hawkins cannot remember a time when she wasn't in love with U.S. history in general, and the Roosevelt family in particular. She has served as an historical interpreter at the Franklin D. Roosevelt National Historic Site, Eleanor Roosevelt's Val-Kill, and the Vanderbilt Mansion (all in Hyde Park, New York); Theodore Roosevelt Birthplace, the Statue of Liberty, and the African Burial Ground National Monument in New York City; and at John Fitzgerald Kennedy National Historic Site and Louisa May Alcott's Orchard House in Massachusetts.

Geraldine majored in history at Principia College in Illinois, studied journalism at New York University School of Continuing Education, as an intern at the National Journalism Center in Washington, D.C., and as a Public Affairs Officer for the U.S. Navy Reserve. Her byline has appeared in several publications, including *Human Events*, *Classic Images*, and *ALL HANDS: The Magazine of the U.S. Navy*, frequently on historical subjects.

She makes her home in New York City, where she enjoys her many friends, classic films, and the hundreds of books in her ever-growing collection.

Also by
Black Dome Press

The True Story of Fala

*By Margaret (Daisy) Suckley and Alice Dalgliesh
Paper, 6" × 9", 80 pages, 48 drawings & historic
photographs ISBN 9781883789787 $13.95*
This classic children's book about a dog and
his president has been reissued by Wilderstein
Preservation and Black Dome Press with a new
foreword by J. Winthrop Aldrich, founding
board president of Wilderstein Preservation,
and with new photographs and background
information on author Daisy Suckley—but with all the old photographs
and drawings and the style and design of the original that has entertained generations. Written by Margaret (Daisy) Suckley for her close
friend and distant cousin Franklin Delano Roosevelt, *The True Story of
Fala* celebrates the loveable Scotty dog she gave the president—the dog
that became FDR's constant companion at the White House, at press
conferences, during meetings with ambassadors and heads of state, at
home in Hyde Park, on the yacht *Potomac*, and even aboard the *HMS
Prince of Wales* when FDR had his first historic, and highly secret, meeting at sea with Winston Churchill during World War Two. Fala, "The
dog that owned a president," was the most famous dog of his time and
maybe the most famous dog in all of American history.

BLACKDOMEPRESS.COM

WILDERSTEIN AND THE SUCKLEYS

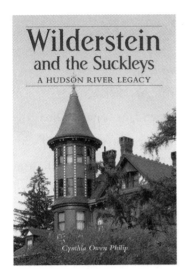

A Hudson River Legacy

By Cynthia Owen Philip. Paper, 6" × 9", 152 pages, 8-page color insert + 95 B&W illustrations, ISBNs 9781883789718 / 1883789710 $17.95

Wilderstein is one of the Hudson Valley's most important examples of Victorian architecture, with interiors designed by Joseph Burr Tiffany and grounds designed by Calvert Vaux, the master landscape architect who designed New York City's Central Park. This is more than just the story of a house, however; it is also the intimate account of three generations of a family that left its mark on the rich social scene of the Hudson River Valley in the Victorian and Edwardian ages, and of its last occupant, Margaret (Daisy) Suckley, whose close relationship with Franklin Delano Roosevelt has been well chronicled and is the subject of much interest.

Masterful in combining a graceful and fluent tone with a brilliant use of the voluminous, revealing archives and photographs at Wilderstein. John Winthrop Aldrich, former NYS Deputy Commissioner for Historic Preservation

BLACKDOMEPRESS.COM

AN AMERICAN ARISTOCRACY

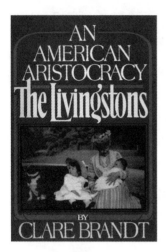

The Livingstons

By Clare Brandt, Paper, 6" × 9", 314 pages,
map & family genealogy
ISBN 9781883789770 $17.95

A Livingston descendant once called the Hudson Valley, "Livingston Valley," and with good reason. At one time forty Livingston mansions lined the east shore. The original 1686 Royal patent of 160,000 acres on the east side of the Hudson River grew within two generations to nearly one million acres and included vast portions of the Catskill Mountains. Intermarriages with other wealthy and influential Hudson Valley families created a dynasty and a landed aristocracy on the banks of the new republic's most important river—an irony embedded at the core of the "American experiment."

A vivid chronicle of a great American family whose members prove to have been every bit as entertaining —and almost as important—as they thought they were. Geoffrey C. Ward, author of *Closest Companion* and former editor of *American Heritage* magazine

BLACKDOMEPRESS.COM

LANDSCAPE GARDENS
ON THE HUDSON, A HISTORY

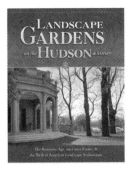

The Romantic Age, the Great Estates, and the Birth of American Landscape Architecture

By Robert M. Toole, Paper, 8½" × 11", 224 pages, 130 maps and illustrations, ISBNs 9781883789688 / 1883789680 $24.95

The Designed Historic Landscapes of the Hudson River Valley: Hyde Park (Vanderbilt) • Sunnyside • Olana • Clermont • Lyndhurst • Montgomery Place • Locust Grove • Wilderstein • Springside • Idlewild • Blithewood • Millbrook • Kenwood • The Point • Philipse Manor • Van Cortlandt Manor • The Pastures (Schuyler Mansion) • and others

The Hudson Valley's role in the mid-1800s as the birthplace of American landscape architecture is explored through the romantically designed grounds of the valley's historic estates and the works of "the father of American landscape design," Hudson Valley native Andrew Jackson Downing. *Landscape Gardens on the Hudson* is the first comprehensive study of the development of these landscapes and the important role they played in the cultural underpinnings of the young United States—a legacy that continues today with the design of America's urban parks and nearly every rural or suburban home.

Upon putting down this volume no reader will be in doubt as to why these gardens are a supreme legacy to our civilization and one of the foundations stones of the environmental movement. This book is a marvel. J. Winthrop Aldrich, Deputy Commissioner for Historic Preservation, New York State Office of Parks, Recreation and Historic Preservation

BLACKDOMEPRESS.COM

IN DEFIANCE

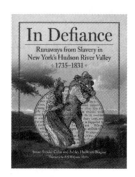

Runaways from Slavery in New York's Hudson River Valley, 1735–1831

By Susan Stessin-Cohn and Ashley Hurlburt-Biagini, Paper, 8" × 10", 352 pages, 36 illustrations, 5 maps, ISBN 9781883789831 $25.95

In Defiance documents 607 fugitives from slavery in the 18th and 19th-century Hudson River Valley region of New York State through the reproduction and transcription of 512 archival newspaper notices for runaway slaves placed by their enslavers or agents. Also included are notices advertising slaves captured, notices advertising slaves for sale, notices offering to purchase slaves, and selected runaway notices from outside the Hudson Valley region. Nine tables analyze the data in the 512 notices for runaways from Hudson Valley enslavers. The book includes a glossary, indexes of names, locations, and subjects.

Based on exhaustive research in dozens of newspapers from across the Hudson Valley, Ashley Hurlburt-Biagini and Susan Stessin-Cohn have compiled hundreds of runaway advertisements from the eighteenth and early nineteenth centuries. An extraordinary achievement. Michael E. Groth, Ph.D., Professor of History, Wells College

It is an interesting, engaging and revealing, though at times gripping, view of humanity as chattel in flight from a diabolical instrument of oppression fashioned at the hands of fellow humans for the expressed purpose of economic gain. This portraiture, pieced together through the array of runaway notices, is a trove of descriptive information. A. J. Williams-Myers, Black Studies Department, SUNY at New Paltz

BLACKDOMEPRESS.COM

FORT CRAILO AND THE VAN RENSSELAERS

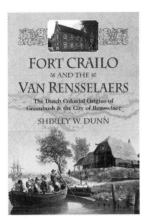

The Dutch Colonial Origins of Greenbush & the City of Rensselaer

By Shirley W. Dunn, Paper, 6" × 9", 208 pages, 40 illustrations, ISBN 9781883789824 $17.95

1663 — As the first farms take root east of the Hudson River across from Fort Orange (Albany), a fortified farmhouse is built by the Van Rensselaers to provide a haven for settlers. Originally surrounded by a tall wooden palisade, Fort Crailo survived King Philip's War, the French and Indian wars, and the Revolution. Armies camped on its grounds as they made their way to the battles, and it was here that a British Army surgeon penned the lyrics to "Yankee Doodle." Generations of Van Rensselaers enlarged the fort into a mansion overlooking their 1,500-acre farm along the east bank, sowing the seeds for the Village of Greenbush and the City of Rensselaer. Today, Crailo State Historic Site is a museum of Dutch colonial life in New York and stands as a rare victory of historic preservation.

I have read the book by Shirley Dunn on Ft. Crailo with anticipation and found that it is well researched, beautifully written and extremely interesting. It gives information in a clear and readable manner. It is a significant addition to our understanding about this important house as well as the history of the City of Rensselaer and our state. The book must be considered a monument in itself. Dr. Charles Semowich, Historian Emeritus for the City of Rensselaer

BLACKDOMEPRESS.COM